THE
NEW TESTAMENT DOCTRINE
OF BAPTISM

THE NEW TESTAMENT DOCTRINE OF BAPTISM

by

W. F. FLEMINGTON, M.A.

Tutor in New Testament Language and Literature, Wesley House, Cambridge

There is one body, and one Spirit, even as also ye were called in one hope of your calling; one Lord, one faith, one baptism, one God and Father of all, who is over all, and through all, and in all. Ephesians 4.4–6.

LONDON
S·P·C·K
1953

First published 1948
Reprinted 1953

TO THE MEMORY OF
MY FATHER AND MY MOTHER

MADE IN GREAT BRITAIN

CONTENTS

The following abbreviations have been used:

E. R. E.	.	.	.	.	*Encyclopædia of Religion and Ethics.*
J. T. S.	.	.	.	.	*The Journal of Theological Studies.*
Theol. Wört. .	.	.	.	*Theologisches Wörterbuch zum Neuen Testament* (ed. by G. Kittel).

ACKNOWLEDGEMENTS

For permission to make certain quotations on the pages indicated thanks are due to the following publishers: Messrs. Macmillan and Company, Limited (p. 7), Messrs. Charles Griffin and Company, Limited (p. 21), the Cambridge University Press (p. 78), Messrs. J. M. Dent and Sons, Limited (p. 81), Messrs. T. and T. Clark (p. 91) and the Independent Press (p. 137).

PREFACE

During recent years in various Christian communions attention has been directed to the pastoral problems which gather round the Sacrament of Baptism. It has become increasingly clear that baptismal practice is confused because baptismal theology is indefinite. There is need for a more thorough study of the biblical, patristic and liturgical evidence which must form the foundation for a more adequate theology of Christian baptism. Without denying the value, and indeed necessity, of the two latter methods of approach, some Christians are pledged by their official standards of belief to acknowledge the divine revelation recorded in Holy Scripture as the supreme rule of faith and practice. There would therefore seem room for a study of Christian baptism which should confine itself almost exclusively to the biblical evidence, and seek above all, by a patient interrogation of the New Testament writers, to discover the earliest Christian belief and practice in relation to baptism and the authority on which this belief and practice rested. It is as a contribution towards such a study that this book is offered.

Since my typescript was completed there has been considerable discussion in some quarters concerning the relation between baptism and confirmation. It has not been possible to include in the body of the work any reference to this discussion but some comments upon it will be found in an Appendix (pp. 148 ff.). In the printing of pronouns referring to the divine names the usage of the English Bible has been followed, except in quotations from authors whose practice is different.

Dr. D. Daube was good enough to read and comment upon the typescript of Chapters 1–3. For certain comments and criticisms I am indebted also to Professor S. A. Cook, Litt.D., F.B.A., to the Rev. W. F. Howard, D.D., Principal of Handsworth College, and to my colleague, the Rev. R. Newton Flew, D.D., Principal of Wesley House. This acknowledgement in no way commits these scholars to any necessary agreement with the argument set forth in the book, the responsibility for which is my own. My gratitude is due to my brother, the Rev. G. H. Flemington, M.A., who has helped in the reading of the proofs. The debt I owe to my wife is only in part expressed by acknowledging the help she has given in proof-reading and the making of the indexes.

W. F. F.

Wesley House,
Cambridge,
July 30th, 1947.

INTRODUCTION

THE use of water for the purpose of religious purification is an obvious and almost universal practice. In all ages man has used water for the cleansing of his body. It is not surprising that from very early times water has been used also for the purpose of religious lustration. The practice is common in all parts of the world and at all stages in the history of religion. A glance at the article entitled " Baptism (Ethnic) " in the *Encyclopædia of Religion and Ethics* will show the variety and abundance of the evidence.[1] Examples are quoted from Africa, Malay, Polynesia, New Zealand, North and South America, Asia and many parts of Europe. Some of these are rites of purification performed regularly by those who have incurred pollution. Others are more closely akin to what we understand by " baptism ", a rite using water and performed at some stage of human life once and for all. Such a rite is, in some widely differing forms of religion, administered soon after the birth of a child. In other religions the rite is performed not in infancy but at some other period of life—e.g. at puberty.[2] A study of the evidence leads to the conclusion that the use of water for purificatory purposes is one of the most common usages of religion, and further that in many religions there is a tendency to concentrate the purification in one important and significant rite.

To realize these facts may help towards the gaining of a proper perspective. Though none of these rites has any historical connexion with Christian baptism, yet the belief and practice implied by them are in some sense common to almost every religion. Thus it is not that Christianity has borrowed its distinctive rites from paganism; the truth is rather that these ethnic practices witness to a fundamental human need for purity of body and soul.

But though in the presence of these ethnic parallels it is necessary to remember constantly that " analogy does not mean genealogy ",[3] the situation is very different when attention is being given to the relations between Christianity and Judaism. There it is to be expected that the student of Christian baptism should be able to trace some of the ante-

---

[1] Cf. *E.R.E.* Vol. II, pp. 367 ff. [2] Op. cit., pp. 373–374.
[3] Cf. J. Moffatt, *The First Five Centuries* (1938), p. 102.

cedents of the rite within the Jewish religion. Jesus was a Jew. The first disciples were Jews. The man whose genius shaped the new religion, when it came into close contact with the Gentile world, had been born " the Hebrew son of Hebrew parents ".[1] Even the anti-Judaic party in the early Church, the so-called Hellenists, had learned almost all their first lessons in religion at the feet of Jewish teachers. Before investigating alleged parallels to Christian baptism, in the mystery religions and else-where, it would seem legitimate to look within Judaism for much that may explain the origin of this characteristic and primitive Christian rite. If the attempt to account for the practice on a Jewish basis should afford a satisfying explanation of the way in which the Christian rite arose, then the parallels adduced from the Græco-Roman world would be relevant rather for the investigation of the later developments of Christian baptism than for the determination of its origin.[2]

---

[1] Phil. 3. 5 (Moffatt).
[2] For a consideration of the alleged relation between Christian baptism and the mystery religions, cf. *infra*, pp. 76–79, 93–95 and 104–105.

PART I

THE ANTECEDENTS OF CHRISTIAN BAPTISM

1

Jewish Washings and Proselyte Baptism

THE Jews made frequent use of water for the purpose of religious purification.[1] It has been pointed out that this is the more noteworthy owing to the relative shortage of water in Palestine.[2] In so far as the object was explicit, this " washing " seems to have aimed at what we should term a *ritual* rather than a *moral* purification. The purpose was " to recover the levitical purity without which a share in worship was forbidden ". Thus, though it might be in fulfilment of a pious duty that a man touched a corpse (cf. Tob. 1. 17), such an act had to be followed by a rite of lustration before the man could take part in worship (cf. Num. 19. 11–13). Though the stress in such passages seems to be laid rather on the ceremonial than on the ethical side, we need to beware of reading into Old Testament documents a distinction which is far sharper and clearer for us than it was for the Jews themselves.[3] Certain other passages, especially in the prophets, suggest that sometimes at least these acts of lustration were interpreted as in some way morally significant:

Wash you, make you clean; put away the evil of your doings from before mine eyes; cease to do evil: learn to do well (Isa. 1. 16).

I will sprinkle clean water upon you, and ye shall be clean: from all your filthiness, and from all your idols, will I cleanse you (Ezek. 36. 25).

In that day there shall be a fountain opened to the house of David and to the inhabitants of Jerusalem, for sin and for uncleanness (Zech. 13. 1).

Purge me with hyssop, and I shall be clean: Wash me, and I shall be whiter than snow (Ps. 51. 7).

Such passages as these are most intelligible when understood against a background in which the act of ritual lustration had come to be seen as possessing some sort of moral significance.[4] That the action of washing with water could so naturally be used to symbolize moral cleansing is a warning against a too narrow restriction of the scope of these lustrations to the purely " ceremonial " in our sense of the word.

At certain stages in later Judaism a far more pronounced emphasis was laid on acts of lustration. Josephus describes how the Essenes bathed daily in cold water before partaking of their common meal.[5]

[1] As typical passages cf. Lev. 15. 5, 8, 13, 16; 16. 4, 26, 28; Exod. 30. 19–20. See also Note A at the end of this chapter (pp. 11–12) on " The Meaning of the Word βαπτίζω ".

[2] Cf. W. Brandt, *Die Jüdischen Baptismen* (1910), p. 34; J. Leipoldt *Die Urchristliche Taufe im Lichte der Religionsgeschichte*, (1928), p. 1; but note also the remarks of I. Abrahams in *J. T. S.* Vol. XII (1911), p. 609.

[3] Cf. also *infra*, pp. 9–11.

[4] Cf. also washing as a sign of " innocency ", Pss. 26. 6, 73. 13; Deut. 21. 6.

[5] Jos., *B. J.*, 2. 8. 5; § 129.

In another passage he writes of the hermit Bannus, who bathed himself frequently in cold water by night and by day.[1] Such an intensified use of religious washings shows how entirely natural it was for a Jew to make use of water for purificatory purposes. It is not in these rites, however, that the antecedents of Christian baptism are to be sought. These ceremonies of lustration were not confined to one particular moment of a man's life; on the contrary, they were repeated as often as the need for purification might arise. An antecedent for Christian baptism may more appropriately be sought in some act of lustration performed once and for all, and, moreover, an act associated with the transition from one state of life to another. Such an act was the Jewish rite known as " proselyte baptism ".

Proselyte baptism, as the name implies, was administered not to Jews but rather to Gentiles who desired to become Jews. It came to be regarded as the acknowledged way whereby one who had not been born a Jew could enter the congregation of Israel. Owing to the absence of any mention of the rite in certain important authorities, some critics have thought that proselyte baptism cannot have been in existence early enough for it to have served in any sense as an antecedent of Christian baptism. The extent of the silence must be recognized, but other considerations make it highly probable that proselyte baptism was practised in the first century A.D., if not earlier, and that it was understood as a recognized method of entering Judaism.

There is no mention of proselyte baptism in the Old Testament or in the Apocrypha; nor do Josephus or Philo make any reference to the practice. Our detailed information comes from Jewish writings which, in their present form, are not earlier than the end of the second century A.D. In view of these facts it has even been argued that, so far from proselyte baptism having been an antecedent of Christian baptism, the Christian rite may itself have suggested the Jewish practice. A closer investigation, however, shows the extreme improbability of such a hypothesis. The use by New Testament writers of βάπτισμα and its cognates of John's baptism, without any attempt to explain their meaning, is most intelligible if some similar rite were already in widespread use. Again, in view of the intense bitterness which existed between Judaism and the early Church, it would seem in the highest degree unlikely that the Jews would have borrowed so distinctive a practice from a Christian source.[2]

There are also more positive grounds for maintaining that proselyte baptism was an established practice in the first century A.D.

(1) Epictetus (*c.* A.D. 94) contrasts the man who has become a full convert to Judaism with the man who hesitates, and describes the former as " one who has been baptized (βεβαμμένου) and has made his

---

[1] Jos., *Vita,* 2., § 11.
[2] Cf. Oepke in *Theol. Wört.,* Vol. I., p. 533.

choice ".[1] The argument of this passage would be invalid if any significant rite were omitted. This implies that by the last decade of the first century the rite had been in existence long enough for it to be regarded as well established and its sufficiency for the reception of a proselyte (apart from circumcision) to be generally appreciated.

(2) Another reference to the rite may be found in the Sibylline Oracles, Book IV, a work which is generally regarded as having been strongly influenced by Jewish conceptions. The heathen are warned to repent in view of the coming world catastrophe, and the warning is followed by the injunction " bathe your whole body in continually-flowing streams; stretch your hands to heaven and ask pardon for your former deeds ". There follows a promise that God will grant repentance and will refrain from destroying them.[2] This document is usually dated about A.D. 80. Here, too, there is the assumption that baptism is the recognized way of entering Judaism, and, again, there is no reference to circumcision. This passage is further noteworthy because it makes a connexion between baptism and repentance and forgiveness.

(3) The Rabbinic evidence, though contained in writings which in their present form cannot be dated earlier than the end of the second century A.D., doubtless reflects the traditions of a much earlier period. The relevant passages have been collected in Strack-Billerbeck, and may be summarized thus: [3]

(a) The earliest rabbinic testimony to proselyte baptism occurs in the record of a dispute between the schools of Shammai and Hillel. The argument concerned a proselyte who came over to Judaism on the eve of Passover (Nisan 14). The school of Shammai said that such a man might take the " bath " immediately after his circumcision and in the evening eat Passover. The school of Hillel, however, claimed that the man who had been circumcised must wait seven days for his full cleansing. The *tebilah* must therefore be taken not less than seven days after circumcision.[4]

Strack-Billerbeck conclude from these passages that for these two rabbinic schools in the first century A.D. proselyte baptism had already become a recognized and generally acknowledged institution. The way in which in these contexts the bath of proselytes is mentioned side by side with the bath taken by Israelites who had become " unclean "

---

[1] Arrian, *Dissert. Epictet.*, 2. 9. 20 (ὅταν τινὰ ἐπαμφοτερίζοντα ἴδωμεν, εἰώθαμεν λέγειν, οὐκ ἔστιν Ἰουδαῖος ἀλλ' ὑποκρίνεται. ὅταν δ' ἀναλάβῃ τὸ πάθος τὸ τοῦ βεβαμμένου καὶ ᾑρημένου, τότε καὶ ἔστι τῷ ὄντι καὶ καλεῖται Ἰουδαῖος.)

[2] *Orac. Sibyll*, 4. 165 ff.

ἐν ποταμοῖς λούσασθε ὅλον δέμας ἀενάοισιν,
χεῖράς τ' ἐκτανύσαντες ἐς αἰθέρα τῶν πάρος ἔργων
συγγνώμην αἰτεῖσθε καὶ εὐλογίαις ἀσέβειαν
πικρὰν ἱλάσκεσθε· θεὸς δώσει μετάνοιαν
οὐδὲ ὀλέσει.

[3] *Kommentar zum Neuen Testament*, Vol. I, pp. 102 ff.

[4] *Pes.* 8. 8, *Eduy.* 5. 2; H. Danby, *The Mishnah* (1933), pp. 148, 431.

shows that the baptism of proselytes was essentially a rite of *purification* whereby a Gentile might become qualified to share the privileges of an Israelite. The argument between the two schools in no way concerned the validity of the rite, but had to do rather with a secondary matter, namely, whether the bath should be taken immediately after circumcision or only after an interval of seven days.[1]

(*b*) Another group of passages concerns a later controversy between Rabbi Eliezer and Rabbi Jehoshua (*c.* A.D. 90). They argued about the relative importance of circumcision and the proselyte's bath. Rabbi Eliezer (belonging to the school of Shammai) declared that a man who has been circumcised counts as a proselyte, even though he might not have taken the bath. Rabbi Jehoshua (a follower of Hillel) regarded a man not yet circumcised as a full proselyte, as soon as he had undergone the bath.[2]

This evidence would suggest that the followers of Hillel laid considerable stress on proselyte baptism, and at times were prepared to regard it as the indispensable rite. For women who became converts to Judaism baptism must always have been the significant ceremony. For male converts the requirements included not only baptism but also circumcision. There may, however, have been a movement, strongly supported by the followers of Hillel, to make the procedure more uniform and regard as the rite *par excellence* the *tebilah* which could be administered to men and women alike. This tendency to regard baptism as the significant rite of entry into Judaism may have been strengthened after the fall of Jerusalem in A.D. 70 and the consequent discontinuance of the Temple-worship. There is evidence that before that date proselytes had not only to be circumcised and baptized but also to offer sacrifice.[3] When such sacrifice became impossible, it would seem natural that an increasing importance should come to be assigned to the one remaining rite, the performance of which could be demanded from men and women alike.

In view of this evidence from Epictetus, the Sibylline Oracles and the Talmud, the conclusion seems well grounded that, despite the silence of other authorities, proselyte baptism was in use at least as early as the first century A.D. as an established rite of entry into Judaism. The position is well summed up by Brandt when he says: [4] [5]

[1] Strack-Billerbeck think it possible that the interval between circumcision and baptism required by the school of Hillel may have been due not to greater strictness but rather to the desire to spare a convert unnecessary pain; cf. Strack-Billerbeck op. cit., Vol. I, p. 104.

[2] *Yeb.* 46 *a*.

[3] *Ker.* 2. 1, Danby, op. cit., pp. 564–565.

[4] *E. R. E.*, Vol. II, p. 408, art. " Baptism (Jewish) ". Strack-Billerbeck (op. cit., p. 103) go farther than Brandt, " man darf . . . deren Anfänge mit Sicherheit in die vorchristliche Zeit verlegen ".

[5] The criticisms of Reitzenstein, *Die Vorgeschichte der Christlichen Taufe* (1929), pp. 231 ff., seem to be sufficiently answered by Oepke in *Theol. Wört.*, Vol. I, p. 533, who points out that the passages in Epictetus and the Sibylline Oracles cannot be satisfactorily explained as references to hermits like Bannus, and further that Reitzenstein has completely overlooked the rabbinic evidence.

Making all the reservations necessary in view of the diffusion, conception and various forms of the rite, we may safely assume that the Jewish baptism of proselytes was not of later origin than Christian baptism.

The manner in which proselyte baptism was administered is described in a passage occurring in one of the treatises of the Babylonian Talmud (*Yebamoth* 47 *ab*),[1] concerning which Montefiore has commented that, since the commandments selected as illustrations are mainly agricultural and precede even the Sabbath, " one is inclined to assign an early date to the material contained in this passage ". This would seem to provide further confirmation for our conclusion concerning the probable date at which proselyte baptism began to be practised. The passage runs:

The Rabbis say: If anyone comes nowadays, and desires to become a proselyte, they say to him: " Why do you want to become a proselyte? Do you not know that the Israelites nowadays are harried, driven about, persecuted and harassed, and that sufferings befall them? " If he says, " I know it, and I am not worthy ", they receive him at once, and they explain to him some of the lighter and some of the heavier commandments, and they tell him the sins connected with the laws of gleaning, the forgotten sheaf, the corner of the field and the tithe for the poor: and they tell him the punishments for the transgressions of the commandments, and they say to him, " Know that up till now you could eat forbidden fat without being liable to the punishment of ' being cut off ' (Lev. 7. 23); you could violate the Sabbath without being liable to the punishment of death by stoning; but from now you will be liable ". And even as they tell him of the punishments, they tell him also of the rewards, and they say to him, " Know that the world to come has been created only for the righteous ". They do not, however, tell him too much, or enter into too many details. If he assents to all, they circumcise him at once, and when he is healed, they baptize him, and two scholars stand by, and tell him of some of the light and of some of the heavy laws. When he has been baptized, he is regarded in all respects as an Israelite.

This passage has been quoted at length mainly to call attention to the way in which proselyte baptism was set in the context of the " commandments ". There is a reiterated emphasis on the obligations of the candidate. He takes upon himself " the yoke of the Law ". It is to be noted further that the rite was administered, apparently, by the candidate himself in the presence of witnesses, and, moreover, it is clear that the moment of entry into Judaism was regarded as coinciding with the moment of emergence from the bath; proselyte baptism is essentially a rite of initiation into the new religion. By it a man signified that he abandoned the old life and entered into a new one.

Other extracts quoted in Strack-Billerbeck give further information about the rite. The *tebilah* could not be administered by night, but only by day.[2] The children of a proselyte shared the benefit of what their father had done and were forthwith circumcised and baptized.[3] They retained the privilege, however, of reconsidering the matter

---

[1] The translation is taken from C. G. Montefiore and H. Loewe, *A Rabbinic Anthology* (Macmillan, 1938), pp. 578–579. Montefiore's note occurs on the latter page.
[2] *Yeb.* 46 *b*.   [3] *Ket.* 11 *a*.

B

when they came of age, and could revert to a Gentile status without
incurring any penalty for apostasy. Anyone under age whose father
was dead and whose mother desired him to enter Judaism could be
baptized on the authority of a court of law. The justification for this
was held to be the principle that one might act for another without his
consent, so long as it was for his advantage.

There has been considerable discussion whether the proselyte who
was being baptized underwent total immersion. C. F. Rogers[1]
considered the rabbinic evidence and came to the conclusion that it
cannot be proved that the Jews in Biblical times, or even during the
first few centuries of the Christian era, baptized by submersion. His
view was that, though in mediæval times submersion was required,
the passages in the Mishnah require only the washing of the entire
body in fresh or running water, or, failing this, in a quantity of water
not less than forty *seahs*. Where immersion is spoken of, it is only
partial, and seems to be required for the sake of decency.

I. Abrahams[2] replied in another article, where he pointed out that
in every act of ritual *tebilah* total submersion was required. A number
of rabbinic references make it clear that there must be no " separation "
(חציצה) between the water and the body. Among the objects which
may thus render a *tebilah* useless are specified several sorts of *headgear*.
Such an argument presupposes that at some point in the ceremony the
whole head must have been submerged. Now, if such a requirement
were specified for a ritual *tebilah* to be carried out by an Israelite, it
must also have been demanded in the *tebilah* of a proselyte. Abrahams
therefore concluded that " there is no adequate ground for doubting
that Jewish baptism in the first century A.D. was by total immersion ".

A far more important question is that concerning the significance of
the rite. Unfortunately it is far from easy to determine at all precisely
the meaning attached to proselyte baptism. At first sight there would
seem much to be said for the view of those who claim that proselyte
baptism possessed no " sacramental " significance. Thus according to
Bousset[3] proselyte baptism was as little " sacramental " as circumcision.
It is to be classed with the rites of lustration and purification performed
by the Pharisees. Such rites had ritual significance but no " inner
value " for the religious life. In the same context Bousset asserted
that there were no sacraments in Judaism, " if by sacrament we mean a
sacred action in which a supernatural grace is imparted to the believer
through material means ".[4] When, with such a definition in mind,
we examine the chief passages about proselyte baptism, there would
seem to be much to bear out Bousset's view. There is no sign that this
rite employing the " material means " of washing with water was

[1] *J. T. S.*, Vol. XII (1911), pp. 437–445.   [2] *J. T. S.*, Vol. XII (1911), pp. 609–612.
[3] W. Bousset, *Die Religion des Judentums im späthellenistischen Zeitalter* (1926), pp. 199–200.
[4] Op. cit., p. 199 (". . . wenn wir unter Sakrament eine heilige Handlung verstehen, in der
dem Gläubigen durch dingliche Mittel eine übernatürliche Gnadengabe zuteil wird ".).

regarded as itself bringing about a supernatural change in the moral and spiritual life of the convert. The significance of proselyte baptism, like that of other Jewish " washings ", would seem, on this view, to lie wholly in the sphere of the ceremonial law. The importance attached by the Jew to ceremonial cleanness is obvious in almost every part of the Old Testament. When a Gentile sought to join the people of God, it was commonly held that his former manner of life demanded the fullest rites of purification before he was qualified to mingle with the true Israelite. The application of this principle demanded the institution of some rite like proselyte baptism, a special example for the Gentile of that rule of ceremonial ablution on which the Jew laid so much emphasis for himself. Again, while it is true that the lines in the Sibylline Oracles definitely connect baptism with repentance and forgiveness, it is by no means implied that the washing of the entire body in flowing water, which is there recommended to the Gentile, will itself become the means whereby the divine pardon is to be secured. Further, it has to be recognized that even if such a causal connexion could be traced in this passage, the association there made of baptism with repentance and forgiveness is unique. The association is not made in the rabbinic passages about proselyte baptism, nor is there any mention of moral renewal.[1] In view of these facts it is hardly surprising that Strack-Billerbeck conclude that these rabbinic passages prove " by the very way in which they mention the proselyte-bath side by side with the baths of Israelites who had become unclean, that both schools (i.e. of Shammai and Hillel) regarded proselyte baptism as essentially the bath of purification by means of which the Gentile coming over to Judaism might obtain a share in all the privileges of an Israelite ".[2] Oepke similarly argues against any sacramental association of proselyte baptism as un-Jewish, when we take into account the meaning attached to other " baths of purification ".[3] Thus he points out that the bath of the High Priest on the Day of Atonement had no expiatory significance. It was essentially a cleansing from ritual impurity.[4] While forgiveness could be *compared with* such a rite, it could not be *mediated through* it, much less could moral purity be achieved by the due performance of such an act of lustration.

There are, however, other considerations to be taken into account before proselyte baptism can be dismissed as nothing but a ceremonial observance. Though in the *tebilah* we cannot find anything sacramental in the sense which Bousset gives to the term, it may be questioned whether such a judgment may not proceed from a wrong assumption.

[1] Cf. Strack-Billerbeck, *Kommentar*, Vol. II, p. 421, " Besonders beachtenswert ist, dass die rabbin. Gelehrten bei der Neuschöpfung des Menschen nirgends seine sittliche Erneuerung im Sinn der neutestamentl. Wiedergeburt im Auge haben. Die sittliche Erneuerung des Menschen gehört nach rabbin. Anschauung erst der Zukunft an, die allein den verheissenen neuen Geist oder das neue Herz bringen kann."

[2] Op. cit., Vol. I, pp. 103–104.   [3] *Theol. Wört.*, Vol.I, p. 533.

[4] Cf. Lev. 16. 4, 24; cf. also 16. 26, 28.

The modern conception of a sacrament presupposes a clear distinction between the *outward and material* and the *inward and spiritual*. There is much to suggest that such a separation would have meant little or nothing to Hebrew thought. F. Gavin [1] from this angle has subjected Bousset's statements to vigorous criticism. His argument is that for the Jew " body " and " soul " are an indissoluble unity. What is done to the one cannot fail to affect the other.[2] He argues further that though there was no explicit sacramental doctrine in Judaism yet the germinal principles of a sacramental outlook lay at the centre of Hebrew religion. It is rooted in the belief of the Old Testament that the world was made by God and that God saw it to be good.[3] G. F. Moore also has laid it down that originally Hebrew thought made no clear distinction between uncleanness, disease and moral wrong. " The physical means efficacious in removing uncleanness are employed to purify a man from moral defilement." [4] Further, there is some evidence that circumcision was sometimes regarded as possessing a moral significance.[5] Again, Dr. Wheeler Robinson has pointed out that " Hebrew psychology has been approached too often under the influence of Greek dualism. . . . The Hebrew idea of human personality is an animated body, not an incarnated soul." [6] A little reflection will show that a people who thought thus would be most unlikely to make any clearly defined distinction between body and soul, and, further, that in the thought of such a people anything done to the body must necessarily have been deemed to have more than what we should term purely " physical " consequences.

Thus it may be that in enquiring whether the concept of the " sacramental " is to be found in Jewish teaching concerning proselyte baptism, we are seeking something the explicit acknowledgment of which really involves the drawing of a distinction which Jewish thought did not make. The absence of definitely sacramental teaching in the rabbinic passages

---

[1] F. Gavin, *Jewish Antecedents of the Christian Sacraments* (1928), pp. 3 ff.

[2] Cf. the parable quoted by Gavin from *Sanhedrin* 91 (op. cit. pp. 10–11) : " Antoninus said to Rabbi : ' The body and soul of a man may free themselves on the Day of Judgement '. How is this so? The body can say : ' It is the soul that transgresses, for since I am sundered from it I am as inert as a stone,' while the soul can say : ' It is the body that transgresses, for separated from it I soar like a bird in the air '." But Rabbi answered : " Let me expound a parable which bears on this. There was once a king who had an excellent garden of fine figs and set two watchmen over it—of whom one was blind and the other lame. The latter said to the former : ' I see some fine figs in the garden. Do you take me on your shoulders and I shall get them for us both to eat '. So it was done and from the back of the blind man the lame man plucked the fruit which both consumed. When later the master returned, he found no figs, and to his questions the blind man made answer : ' Have I eyes wherewith to see, that you suspect me of taking the fruit? ' And after the like manner the lame man : ' Have I feet to go to the fruit? ' The master then placed the lame man on the back of the blind man and had them both punished together. Thus the Holy One (Blessed be He !) puts back the soul into the body and punishes both together."

[3] Gavin op. cit., pp. 22–23.

[4] G. F. Moore, *History of Religions*, Vol. II, (1920), p. 43 (cited Gavin op. cit., 7–8).

[5] Gavin op. cit. p. 17 n. 1 quotes the midrash on Gen. 17. 1, where, after the command about circumcision, it is said, " Thou shalt be perfect ".

[6] H. W. Robinson, *Redemption and Revelation*, (1942), p. 141.

may be due to the fact that the fundamental *unity* of body and soul made the express formulation of the sacramental outlook unnecessary. There was no need to state in explicit terms what could be taken for granted. The idea that an act done to the body could fail to have moral effects would be to a Jew unthinkable. Body and soul are a unity, and what is done to the one must necessarily and inevitably affect the other. What we call the " physical " and the " moral " were to the Jew " parts of one larger and more inclusive whole ".[1] It is reasonable to expect the clear exposition of sacramental teaching only after a people's thought has come to be controlled by a consciously accepted distinction between soul and body.[2]

Rather than ask, therefore, whether proselyte baptism is to be taken as having possessed a sacramental meaning, it would seem more important to observe again what are the outstanding characteristics of the rite. Proselyte baptism was a ceremonial purification whereby a Gentile was enabled to enter the congregation of Israel. Since it was demanded by Jews, it must have been regarded as exercising an effect on the whole personality of the man submitting to it. These effects were undefined, so far as we can judge from the rabbinic evidence, but the fact that proselyte baptism was set in the context of the commandments meant that the way was always open for a more explicitly ethical interpretation of the rite.[3] Such an adaptation and extension of the rite of proselyte baptism seems to have been first made by a Jewish prophet, who, towards the end of the second decade of the first century A.D., aroused notice by preaching on the banks of the River Jordan and by associating prominently with his message an act of baptism.

NOTE A

THE MEANING OF THE WORD βαπτίζω

The verb βαπτίζω is an intensive or iterative form[4] of the verb βάπτω, both meaning " to dip " or " to plunge ".

βάπτω is used transitively with this meaning from Homer onwards.[5] It is also used intransitively of a ship sinking (cf. Eur., *Orest*, 1. 707). The passive of βάπτω is used of one who has " been baptized " (in the religious sense) in the passage from Epictetus, quoted *supra*, pp. 4–5. βάπτω occurs sixteen times in the Septuagint, most of these examples translating the Hebrew טבל, and all of them meaning " to dip " or " to plunge ".

[1] Gavin op. cit., p. 9.

[2] Cf. also H. H. Rowley in *Hebrew Union College Annual* (Cincinnati), Vol. XV (1940), p. 327, proselyte baptism was " not an act of ritual purification alone, but an act of self-dedication to the God of Israel, involving spiritual factors as well as physical, with a fundamentally sacramental character ".

[3] Oepke rightly emphasizes that any *magical* notion in connexion with the *tebilah* is impossible in view of the Jewish conviction about the transcendence of God. (The essence of such magical ideas lies in the belief that a man by doing something himself can *coerce* a god to do his will.) Cf. *Theol. Wört.*, Vol. I, p. 533.

[4] Cf. J. H. Moulton and W. F. Howard, *A Grammar of New Testament Greek* Vol. II, (1929), p. 408.

[5] For examples see Liddell and Scott, *A Greek-English Lexicon, s. v.*

The intensive βαπτίζω is used by classical and post-classical authors both in the literal and in metaphorical senses. Among the latter may be noted βεβαπτισμένοι of those "soaked in wine" (Plato, *Symp.*, 176b), and βαπτιζόμενον of a young man "getting into deep water" (i.e. in argument) (Plato, *Euthyd.*, 277d). Josephus uses the word of the crowd that filled Jerusalem to overflowing at the time of the siege, ἐβάπτισεν τὴν πόλιν (B. J., 4. 3. 3; § 137). βαπτίζω occurs four times in the Septuagint:

(*a*) of Naaman dipping himself in the River Jordan, ἐβαπτίσατο ἐν τῷ Ἰορδάνῃ (4 Regn., 5. 14; βαπτίζω = טבל).

(*b*) of Judith who every night washed herself before prayer, ἐβαπτίζετο ἐν τῇ παρεμβολῇ ἐπὶ τῆς πηγῆς τοῦ ὕδατος (Jud. 12. 7).

(*c*) of one who washes himself after touching a dead body, βαπτιζόμενος ἀπὸ νεκροῦ (Sir. 31. (34.) 30).

(*d*) in the fourth passage, ἡ ἀνομία με βαπτίζει (Isa. 21. 4), the Greek of the Septuagint does not correspond to the Hebrew original (which means "shuddering has affrighted me"). The Septuagint rendering appears to be similar to the metaphorical use of βαπτίζω (= "overwhelm"), which has been noted above as occurring in Plato and other authors. Moulton and Milligan quote an occurrence of the word in an illiterate papyrus *c.* 153 B.C. (P. Par. 47. 13) where it similarly seems to mean "flooded" or "overwhelmed" (with calamities); cf. Moulton and Milligan, *Vocabulary of the Greek Testament* (1930), p. 102.

2

The Baptism of John

THE Jewish prophet who, " in the fifteenth year of the reign of Tiberius Cæsar ", attracted notice by his preaching in Judæa, made baptism so central and used it so characteristically to embody his message that he became popularly known as the " baptizer " or the " baptist ".   The significance of John the Baptist for the student of Christian origins becomes obvious from the New Testament.   The Gospels, both Synoptic and Johannine, all give a prominent place to John's activity as in some sense leading up to the ministry of Jesus. Several references in the Acts of the Apostles testify to the importance of John's baptism as that which marked what may be called the upper limit of apostolic testimony.[1]   This no doubt is why in the Gospels and the Acts such prominence is given to the preaching and baptism of John.   He was valued and remembered as the precursor of Jesus.[2] It should be recognized, however, that though all the New Testament evidence about John comes from those whose estimate of him was based on his significance as the forerunner of the Christian Gospel, yet there are signs that the revivalist movement which he led exercised an influence outside Christian circles, and that here and there his followers survived in small groups whose connexion with Christianity was partial and imperfect.[3]

It seems probable that both Mark and Q contained accounts of the message and activity of John.[4]   Certain features peculiar to the Third Gospel may have come from the special Lucan source which Streeter has called L (cf. Lk. 3. 10–14).   Since, however, in the Matthæan and Lucan narratives, as we have them, various elements from these originally separate accounts have been blended together, it will perhaps prove most useful for us to look at the narratives, as they stand in the three Synoptic Gospels.

Mark (1. 1–8) dates the beginning of the gospel of Jesus Christ from the moment when, in fulfilment of prophecy (Mal. 3. 1 and Isa. 40. 3 attributed to " Isaiah the prophet "), John the baptizer proclaimed in

---

[1] Cf. Acts 1. 22; 10. 37; 13. 24–25.

[2] Cf. R. H. Lightfoot, *History and Interpretation in the Gospels* (1935), pp. 63–64, " the baptism and preaching of John were regarded in the primitive church as the immediate prelude of what we may call the divine message or action of salvation ".   Tertullian identifies the " via Domini " with the " baptismum Johannis " (*De Bapt.*, 12.).

[3] Some evidence for this may be provided by the story of Apollos (cf. " knowing only the baptism of John " Acts 18. 25) and the " disciples " at Ephesus (who had been baptized only " into John's baptism " Acts 19. 3) ;   yet it seems clear that these people were regarded by the editor of Acts as in some sense belonging also to the Christian community, cf. *infra*, p. 25, *n.*1.

[4] J. M. Creed, *The Gospel according to St. Luke* (1930), pp. 46–47.

the wilderness " a baptism of repentance unto remission of sins ". The claim that the whole of Judæa and all the people of Jerusalem were baptized, confessing their sins, is surely not to be taken literally; but Mark's language suggests that John excited considerable notice and made many converts.   The description of John's dress and food sets him in the succession of the Old Testament prophets (cf. 2 Kings 1. 8; Zech. 13. 4).   John's message was of a " Mightier One " who was to follow him, so great that John was not worthy to do him even a slave's menial service.   John baptized with water, but the Mightier One would baptize with " holy spirit ".

Matthew (3. 1–12) adds to the Marcan account a statement about John's message, " Repent, for the kingdom of heaven has drawn near ". Matthew also includes a record of John's words to many Pharisees and Sadducees who came to baptism, " Ye offspring of vipers, who warned you to flee from the coming wrath? "   They were urged to bring forth fruit worthy of repentance.   Let them not rely on their connexion by birth with God's people.   God could raise up from these stones children of Abraham.[1]   The time of judgement was very near.   The axe was ready at the root of the tree to cut down whatever is unfruitful. Matthew includes Mark's statement about the Mightier One to come, but describes the present baptism as " unto repentance " and the future baptism as " with holy spirit *and with fire* ".   This statement about the Mightier One is set in a context where the warning of judgement is emphasized by the images of " burning " and " winnowing ".

Luke (3. 1–17) stresses the importance of John's activity for the Christian Gospel which he is going on to describe by prefacing his account of John with an elaborate six-fold dating in the manner of a Greek historian.[2]   In addition to the Marcan account, he takes over (probably from Q) most of the fresh material found also in Matthew. He further gives some examples of John's practical advice to those who asked questions about conduct.   The man with two coats and with extra food was to share with the man who had none.   Tax-gatherers were to exact no more than their due.   Soldiers were to avoid extortion and the laying of false charges, and were to be content with their wages.   In Luke, John's statement about the Mightier One is prefaced by what is probably an editorial introduction describing how the people were wondering whether perchance he might be the Messiah. As in Matthew, the future baptism is to be " with holy spirit and with fire ", and the warning of judgement is stressed by the use of the same two images of " burning " and " winnowing ".

Apart from Matt. 3. 14–15, in the conversation between John and Jesus at the baptism,[3] there is no indication in the Synoptists that John

---

[1] Possibly there is a play on the words בניא (sons) and אבניא (stones); so Klostermann, *Handbuch zum Neuen Testament*, ad loc.

[2] Cf. Thuc. 2. 2.   On this passage *v. infra*, pp. 26–27.

recognized, so early as this, that his hope concerning the " Mightier One " was to find fulfilment in Jesus. In the Fourth Gospel, however, the picture is very different. There John goes out of his way to " witness " repeatedly concerning Jesus,[1] and expressly to describe him as " the Lamb of God, which taketh away the sin of the world " and as " the Son of God ".[2] Further, the Fourth Evangelist knows nothing about a " baptism of repentance unto remission of sins " nor about a baptism " with fire ". To reconcile this Johannine account with that in the Synoptists seems almost impossible. In a Synoptic story which is probably taken from Q,[3] John is described as sending from prison two of his disciples to ask whether Jesus is the " Coming One ". This hesitating doubt seems quite out of keeping with the confident assertions attributed to the Baptist in the Fourth Gospel. J. H. Bernard has tried to circumvent the difficulty by arguing that " hesitation is not incompatible with a previous outburst of enthusiastic conviction ".[4] But, even so, we should surely expect that, if this recognition of Jesus (? as Messiah) by John were historical, it would have left more trace in the Synoptists than the solitary passage Matt. 3. 14–15.

It seems far more likely that the narrative in the Fourth Gospel has been influenced by the desire to combat the teaching of followers of the Baptist at Ephesus, and to prove to them that their own leader recognized and publicly acknowledged his subordination to Jesus.[5] There is a further point which suggests that the narrative in the Fourth Gospel may be less historical than that in the Synoptic Gospels. We shall see that two of the most prominent and characteristic features of the Baptist's message are the note of apocalyptic judgement and the linking of baptism with a new moral life (cf. repentance and remission of sins). It is significant that both these have disappeared from the record of the preaching of John contained in the Fourth Gospel.

How far John's baptism is to be connected with the Jewish baptism of proselytes is a matter of considerable dispute. Leipoldt believes that the similarities are so significant that the contemporaries of the Baptist must have regarded his rite as a special kind of proselyte baptism.[6] In Strack-Billerbeck, on the other hand, the connexion is vigorously denied.[7] There are some obvious similarities between the two rites. Both use baptism by immersion and both employ flowing water. Again, both rites mark in some sense for those baptized the beginning of a new life and incorporation into a new community. But there are

---

[1] Cf. Jn. 1. 7, 15, 19–27.   [2] Cf. Jn. 1. 29, 34, 36.

[3] Matt. 11. 2–6; Lk. 7. 18–23. W. F. Howard has pointed out that strictly speaking the connexion of this embassy with John's *imprisonment* is made only by Matthew and not by Luke. There is nothing in the latter narrative to exclude the possibility that John's disciples may have been sent by him while he was still free. Cf. *Amicitiae Corolla* edited by H. G. Wood (1933), p. 121.

[4] J. H. Bernard, *St. John I. C. C.* (1928), Vol. I, p. ci.   [5] Cf. *supra*, p. 13, *n.* 3.

[6] Leipoldt, op. cit. p. 27, " Die Taufe des Johannes ist danach eine Art Proselytentaufe ".

[7] Strack-Billerbeck, op. cit., Vol. I, pp. 112 f., " Dagegen haben inhaltlich die beiden Riten nichts miteinander gemein ".

also very striking differences. In proselyte baptism the subject seems (in the presence of witnesses) to have baptized himself. In John's baptism, however, the rite seems to have been administered by John.[1] This is confirmed by the distinctive title associated with his name, ὁ βαπτιστής or ὁ βαπτίζων.[2] That he was the agent administering the rite is also suggested by ἐγὼ . . . ἐβάπτισα (βαπτίζω),[3] (Mk. 1. 8, etc.), and by ὑπ' αὐτοῦ (Mk. 1. 5, etc.). Further, John's baptism differs from the baptism of proselytes in that, while the latter was intended only for Gentiles, the former was administered both to Gentiles and to Jews.[4] To John's contemporaries this must have seemed a startling innovation. That a Gentile needed purification before entering the commonwealth of Israel was an axiom of Jewish thought; that a Jew himself should need no less to be purified was a revolutionary conception. John's appeal was a solemn reminder that the people of God themselves through sin had become " alien ". They could be brought back and incorporated into the new Israel only by an act analogous to that by which a Gentile convert was incorporated into the people of God. A third difference concerns the significance of the two baptisms. It has been argued earlier that proselyte baptism was an outstanding example of " ceremonial purification ". It is true that, since the reciting of moral precepts was prominently linked with the act, and once at least forgiveness of sins was expressly mentioned, and, further, since for the Jew what we distinguish as " body " and " soul " were bound up in an indissoluble unity, we must not so interpret proselyte baptism as to exclude what we should describe as moral and spiritual results of the act. Yet the general impression produced by the rabbinic evidence discussed in the last chapter is that proselyte baptism was primarily a means of ceremonial purification designed to render the Gentile, who wished to become a Jew, levitically clean. Any further consequences of the *tebilah* were implicit, and no attempt was made, so far as we know, to draw them out in detail and give them conscious expression in the minds of those who submitted to the rite. It is just here that one of the marked differences between proselyte baptism and the baptism of John becomes apparent. For John the ceremonial aspect of baptism has receded into the background. There would seem to be no evidence that he laid any stress on ritual purity.[5] It is the moral appeal that he

---

[1] Oepke in *Theol. Wört.* makes much of this point (op. cit., p. 544).

[2] ὁ βαπτιστής, Mk. 6. 25; 8. 28; Matt. 3. 1; Lk. 7. 20 etc. ὁ βαπτίζων, Mk. 1. 4; 6. 14 etc.

[3] A closer approximation to the practice in proselyte baptism is found in the Western Text of Lk. 3. 7, ἐνώπιον αὐτοῦ.

[4] Cf. Mk. 1.5; Matt. 3. 5–6, 7; Lk. 3. 12–14.

[5] Cf. Jn. 3. 25. Was John regarded as " lax " by the strict Jew? It is difficult to discover the evidence on which the view of Otto and Goguel is based that John the Baptist laid stress on ceremonial purification, and that Jesus broke with him on this account; cf. M. Goguel, *Jean-Baptiste* (1928), pp. 86 ff., and R. Otto, *The Kingdom of God and the Son of Man*, E. T. (1938), pp. 76–81. As H. G. Marsh has said (*The Origin and Significance of the New Testament Baptism* (1941), p. 120), much of Goguel's position depends upon the acceptance of the emendation in Jn. 3. 25, by which μετὰ Ἰουδαίου is changed to μετὰ τῶν Ἰησοῦ—an emendation which Bernard (op. cit., Vol. I, p. 130, n. 1) described as " violent and unnecessary ".

puts in the forefront of his preaching with a vigour and a solemnity that recall some of the greatest of the Old Testament prophets. He calls for repentance from his hearers.[1] He bids the Pharisees and Sadducees bring forth fruits worthy of repentance.[2] So, too, John's baptism is directly associated with confession of sins. In Mark it is expressly described as " a baptism of repentance unto remission of sins ".[3] These passages taken together make it impossible to doubt that it was this moral emphasis that came first both in the preaching and in the baptism of John. It would seem probable that herein John the Baptist was drawing out the significance of the fact that the *tebilah* was set in the context of the " commandments ". By putting a greater stress on this ethical aspect of the rite, he adapted the *tebilah*, thus making explicit a hitherto latent and unexpressed part of the meaning of the rite, and so causing baptism to be expressive of a thorough-going moral reformation.

The baptism of John therefore differs from proselyte baptism in that it was administered by John himself, it was intended for Jews as well as for Gentiles, and it was far more explicitly expressive of a profound moral reformation. If these striking differences are clearly recognized, there is no reason why the link between the two should not also be acknowledged. As Professor Manson has written : [4]

The baptism of John can perhaps be most readily understood by reference to the Jewish baptism of proselytes. As the baptism of the proselyte was part of the ceremony of dedication by which a Gentile was incorporated into Israel, so John's baptism is an act of rededication by which Israelites, who through sin have lost their right to the name, may be incorporated afresh into the true Israel.

The most important difference, however, between proselyte baptism and the baptism of John has yet to be stated. The full meaning of John's baptism cannot be understood apart from the realization that the rite was not only thoroughly " moral " in its significance, but also thoroughly " eschatological ". There is the closest connexion between John's baptism and his proclamation of the Kingdom of God.[5] Modern study of the New Testament has shown how essential it is that we should rid our minds of many of the present-day associations of the phrase " Kingdom of God " and look at the conception, so far as we can, through first century eyes. The Old Testament religion rested on the idea of a " Covenant " between God and Israel. When Israel kept the Law, he was righteous and enjoyed " salvation ". At the beginning of the first century A.D. this was clearly not so, for the Romans were in

[1] Cf. Matt. 3. 2.   [2] Cf. Matt. 3. 8; Lk. 3. 8.
[3] Mk. 1. 4, Lk. 3. 3 (βάπτισμα μετανοίας εἰς ἄφεσιν ἁμαρτιῶν).
[4] *The Mission and Message of Jesus* (1937), p. 333.
[5] For a discussion of Otto's view that John did not speak of the " kingdom ", and that Matt. 3. 2 represents an assimilation of John's message to that of Jesus, see Marsh op. cit., pp. 82–94. Dr. Marsh concludes that the most probable view is that John's message did include a proclamation of the coming Kingdom of God.

power.[1] Hence all over Palestine at that time there was an eager expectation of God's intervention, for only by such intervention could the well-being of Israel be secured.   Thus according to the thought of the New Testament the Kingdom of God is not another name for the sum and culmination of human progress.   The Kingdom of God is the divine order, the " rule of God " which is to supervene upon the present world-order.   This governing conviction of the apocalyptic writers rests upon the Old Testament faith concerning the divine omnipotence.[2] The coming of this Kingdom of God cannot be hastened by man.[3]   All that man can do is to " repent ", to " turn back " towards God,[4] so that when the Kingdom dawns, his eyes may be fixed on the things of God and not on the things of the world.   " Only those who had turned to God could escape the wrath to come." [5]   This is the significance of John's call to repentance, a call which in Matthew is directly linked with the thought of the Kingdom:

And in those days cometh John the Baptist . . . saying, Repent ye, for the kingdom of heaven is at hand (Matt. 3. 1-2).

Against this eschatological background must be set the words of the Baptist in which he speaks of the " Mightier One " to come.[6]   All the Synoptists represent John as emphasizing his own inferiority.   In all these records there is also a contrast between John's baptism and the baptism still to come.   It is far from easy, however, to determine the precise nature of this contrast.   According to Mark (1. 8), the baptism " with water " is set over against a future baptism " with holy spirit ". According to Matthew (3. 11) and Luke (3. 16), baptism " with water " will be followed by baptism " with holy spirit and with fire ".   Christian interpreters have found the fulfilment of this promise in the outpouring of the Holy Spirit at Pentecost (cf. Acts 2. 3-4 ". . . . tongues as it were of fire . . ."). Two references in Acts (1. 5, 11. 16) suggest that the earliest disciples saw a contrast between John's baptism with water and the Christian baptism with " holy spirit " and believed that they had the authority of Jesus for this interpretation.

Now, whether or not this contrast was drawn by our Lord, there is a difficulty in the claim that it formed part of the teaching of John the Baptist.   It is not that John *could* not have made this connexion between " baptism " and " holy spirit ".   There are several Old Testament passages which make a similar connexion of ideas or associate with

---

[1] Cf. J. V. Bartlet in *E. R. E.*, Vol. II, p. 375.
[2] Cf. R. N. Flew, *The Idea of Perfection in Christian Theology*, (1934), p. 9, " The central idea o apocalyptic is thus seen to be a development of the faith in the eternal sovereignty of God ".
[3] Cf. V. Taylor, *Jesus and His Sacrifice* (1937), p. 10, " From first to last the *Basileia* is super-natural; man does not strive for it or bring it into being ".
[4] Cf. J. M. Creed, *The Gospel according to St. Luke* (1930), p. 50, where it is shown that the fundamental idea of μετάνοια is that of the Hebrew שׁוּב: " turning away from sin ", 1 Kings 8. 47-48; Ps. 78. 34, etc., and " towards God ", 2 Kings 23. 25; Amos 4. 6, 8, etc.   The etymological meaning of the Greek word " change of mind " should not be pressed.
[5] Creed, op. cit., p. 311.
[6] Cf. Mk. 1. 7-8; Matt. 3. 11-12; Lk. 3. 16-17.

" spirit " verbs appropriate to the use of water. Thus Ezekiel in successive verses speaks of the sprinkling of clean water and the bestowal of a new spirit,[1] and Joel looks forward to a time when God will " pour out " his spirit upon all flesh.[2]   Thus it would but have been carrying this connexion a stage farther if John, who stood in the prophetic succession, had made this link between " baptism " and the " Spirit ". But though John might well have spoken thus, there is good reason for doubting whether he did so speak.

T. W. Manson has argued that these references to the Holy Spirit are not an original part of John's teaching, but rather represent an interpretation of the early Church.[3]   Dr. Manson points out that in Acts 19. 2 the " disciples " at Ephesus who had been baptized " into John's baptism " have not even heard " whether there is a holy Spirit ". " This is very strange if John did in fact teach that his own baptism was only a preliminary to another and richer baptism with the Spirit." Dr. Manson therefore suggests that John originally spoke only of baptism " with fire ", and that this was interpreted as baptism " with the Spirit " by the early Church.   This interpretation was then read back into the record of John's teaching.   According to this hypothesis, the Matthæan and Lucan forms of the saying contain the symbol (" fire ") together with the interpretation (" spirit ").   The Marcan form has the interpretation (" holy spirit ") without the symbol.   The original saying in Q had the symbol alone without any interpretation— i.e. Q read, " he shall baptize you *with fire* ".   This was understood from the context as the fire of judgement.   The chief argument in favour of this view is that in Matthew (who here presumably is following Q closely) both the verse before and the verse after the statement about the two contrasted baptisms use " fire " as a symbol of judgement.[4]

> . . . every tree . . . that bringeth not forth good fruit is hewn down and cast into the *fire* . . . he will gather his wheat into the garner but the chaff he will burn up with unquenchable *fire*.

It would seem natural that the intervening verse also should speak of fire in the same sense of judgement.   If this reconstruction of John's teaching is right, then his words hold out no promise of hope—they contain rather a solemn warning of the coming judgement—" I have baptized you with water . . . he shall baptize you with fire ".   John stood in the line of the Old Testament prophets.   His message was a consistent and solemn warning of judgement to come.   Only by

[margin note: ? perhaps they could only have heard one part of it.]

[1] Ezek. 36. 25–26.   [2] Joel 2. 28; cf. Ezek. 39. 29.
[3] T. W. Manson, *The Mission and Message of Jesus* (1937), p. 333; cf. also M. Dibelius, *Die urchristliche Ueberlieferung von Johannes dem Täufer* (1911), pp. 50, 56 f., Creed, op. cit., p. 54, and Marsh, op. cit., pp. 28–29.   Dr. Marsh points out that this interpretation was put forward by C. A. Briggs in 1894, and thinks that the suggestion may receive some support from the Sinaitic Syriac of Matt. 3. 11, (" . . . with fire and with Holy Spirit . . ."). Alteration in the order of words is sometimes a sign of textual uncertainty.
[4] Matt. 3. 10, 12; cf. Lk. 3. 9, 17.

repentance could his hearers (Jews no less than Gentiles) be prepared to meet this judgement and have a part in the coming Kingdom of God.[1]

It is probable that, beside his insistence on judgement, in another respect also John the Baptist stood in the succession of the Old Testament prophets. A marked characteristic of the prophets on occasion was the tendency to perform symbolic actions, often of a sort that seems strange to us. We are apt to regard such actions as a somewhat emphatic and even grotesque kind of illustrative gesture, designed to call attention to the accompanying prophetic message. Dr. Wheeler Robinson, however, in a paper read some years ago before the Society for Old Testament Study, showed that such symbolic actions need to be interpreted far more realistically and given more than a purely illustrative significance.[2] Dr. Wheeler Robinson himself suggested that prophetic symbolism might have light to throw on Pauline teaching about Christian baptism. It seems worth carrying the hint farther back and enquiring whether the " prophetic " activity of John, and in particular his use of baptism, may not be illuminated by being viewed from this angle. The parallel would seem to be of sufficient importance to make it profitable to summarize somewhat fully those parts of the argument most relevant for our purpose.

Dr. Wheeler Robinson claims that the Jewish love of " signs and symbolic acts " is not due simply to the " concrete and individualizing imagination " of the Semite " which leads him to transpose the thought into the deed as well as into the spoken word ". He quotes a number of examples of significant actions in Semitic records, both biblical and non-biblical, and argues that they are far more than just " Oriental duplication " of the spoken word. Thus during the attack on the town of Ai, Joshua, at the bidding of the Lord, stretches out his javelin towards Ai, and keeps it so stretched out until Ai has been destroyed.[3] Or again, when Zedekiah the son of Chenaanah was seeking to assure Ahab of victory against the Syrians, we read that he " made him horns of iron and said, Thus saith the Lord, With these shalt thou push the Syrians, until they be consumed ".[4] Some of the most striking of these symbolic acts are recorded of the prophets. Thus Jeremiah is bidden by Yahweh to make bands and bars and put them on his neck. This wooden yoke represents the subjugation of the nations to Babylon. Later it is described how Hananiah broke this wooden yoke as a sign that the Babylonian subjugation of the peoples should speedily cease. Jeremiah was then commanded by the Lord to make instead a yoke of iron.[5] Many other symbolic acts are recorded not only of Jeremiah

---

[1] R. Eisler, *The Messiah Jesus and John the Baptist*, E. T. (1931), pp. 275–276, has suggested that in the record of John's saying πνεύματι might be retained without ἁγίῳ in the sense not of " spirit " but of " wind "—the wind that separates the wheat from the chaff. This would equally preserve the note of " judgement ".

[2] Cf. *Old Testament Essays*, ed. by D. C. Simpson (Charles Griffin, 1927), pp. 1–17.

[3] Josh. 8. 18, 26.   [4] 1 Kings 22. 11.   [5] Jer. 27. 1–7; 28. 10–14.

but also of other prophets both before and after his time, including Elijah, Elisha, Isaiah and Ezekiel. Dr. Wheeler Robinson contends that these symbolic acts recorded as having been performed by the Hebrew prophets were actually done with a definite purpose in view, and that for us to appreciate this helps us the better to understand the prophetic consciousness.

These actions, so far as their *form* is concerned, are very similar to the mimetic magic with which the study of anthropology has made us familiar. But Dr. Robinson shows clearly that here, as elsewhere, when elements from the religion of surrounding peoples were taken over into Hebrew religion they were profoundly modified in the very process of being borrowed. Of such acts it can be said, " Their *forms* are an inheritance from the past; their *meaning* is transformed by being taken up into the prophetic religion, with its far higher outlook ".[1] The original elements of magic are overshadowed by moral and spiritual elements, and the predominance of these makes utterly inadequate any attempt to explain prophetic symbolism purely in terms of mimetic magic. There is no idea on the part of the Hebrew prophet that by these actions he can exert compulsion on Yahweh to bring about the desired end; on the contrary, the context always makes clear that the purpose which the symbolic act expresses, and in some way helps to fulfil, is the purpose not primarily of the prophet but rather of Yahweh himself. Yet, though the stage of purely mimetic magic has been transcended, the Hebrew outlook, even in the prophets, is still realistic enough for it to matter profoundly that the symbolic action shall really be wrought out and accomplished.

At a higher level of religion, such as we see in the earlier prophets of Israel, these imitative acts have, not only a much more subordinate place, but have gained a new setting, by which they are ascribed to Yahweh, working through the personality of His prophet, who represents Him. At a still higher level, that of Isaiah and Jeremiah, there is a new emphasis on the inner consciousness of fellowship with Yahweh, which enables the prophet to interpret His ways and thoughts to man, in moral and spiritual terms. But the traditions of earlier usage remain by their natural momentum, and the prophet still on occasion may act as well as speak in Yahweh's name. . . . The symbolic deed, of course, reacts psychologically on the consciousness of the doer, and confirms him in his experience; it also forcibly expresses the divine purpose to others, since actions speak louder than words. But there is something more than this, something brought over from earlier phases of the imitative act. *The prophetic act is itself a part of the will of Yahweh, to whose complete fulfilment it points; it brings that will nearer to its completion, not only as declaring it, but in some small degree as effecting it.* It corresponds with the prophetic perfect of Hebrew syntax, by regarding the will of God as already fulfilled.[2]

Thus, if we would " think Semitically ", we have to see the symbolic action of a Hebrew prophet not only as a vivid means of expressing the will of God but also in some sense as that which helped to bring about

---

[1] Robinson op. cit., p. 5.   [2] Op. cit., pp. 14–15 (italics mine).

its fulfilment. The variety and extent of the evidence cited by Dr. Wheeler Robinson make clear how entirely natural and appropriate it was for a Hebrew prophet who believed himself charged with a divine message and chosen as an instrument of the divine purpose, to embody that " word of the Lord " not only in speech but also in act. Just as the Word of Yahweh uttered through the prophet was, to the Hebrew, itself not just a human utterance but a pregnant divine reality,[1] so the prophetic " action " was no merely illustrative gesture but rather itself the powerful deed of the divine will, made expressive and effective through the outward behaviour of God's chosen representative.

In the light of Wheeler Robinson's treatment of Old Testament " symbolism ", the present writer would claim that the baptism of John may be understood as an extension of the symbolic actions of the prophets. We have seen how John took the *tebilah*—the rite expressive of purification for Gentiles—and so adapted it that it became a rite for Jews also, and moreover one in which all the emphasis was laid upon repentance and moral reformation. This baptism of John becomes yet more significant when we see this adaptation of the *tebilah* as a development of prophetic symbolism. John's baptizing with water went farther than any symbolic action of an Old Testament prophet, in that what for the prophet was an isolated act, done by him alone, becomes for John a corporate act in which he called others to share.[2] But, though there is development, there is none the less an underlying continuity. Just as Isaiah or Jeremiah expressed their prophetic insight into the moral realities present in a particular historical situation, by performing a symbolic act, so John gathered up his conviction about divine judgement, and the need for " turning " to God, in this " baptism of repentance unto remission of sins ". Further, as a Hebrew prophet saw his act not only as expressive, but also as in some way effective, of the divine purpose, so John summoned men to submit to baptism, convinced that thereby they became equipped, as it were, and made bold to face the Day of the Lord. The rite of baptism was realistically understood, so much so that those who had submitted to it could know that their repentance was accepted, their sins would be forgiven, their membership of the future Messianic community was secure.

[1] Cf. for example Isa. 55. 11.

[2] It is possible that certain actions in the Old Testament, such as the public reading of the Law by Ezra (cf. Neh. 8. 1–12), should be viewed in this light as *corporately* symbolic. A still clearer example would be furnished by the High Priest's sending away of the scapegoat " for Azazel " on the Day of Atonement (cf. Lev. 16. 10, 20–22). The instructions concerning this in the Mishnah show that, while the High Priest himself performed the act making public confession of sin, the rest of the priests and the people shared in it, since they made a corporate response as they stood in the Temple Court (cf. *Yoma* 6. 2, H. Danby, *The Mishnah* (1933), p. 169). Further, that this sending away of the scapegoat was regarded as more than a mere gesture, and was itself seen as part of the completion of the divine purpose, seems to be attested by the reference to the crimson wool (which had been tied to the door of the Sanctuary) turning white as soon as the scapegoat reached its destination: this was interpreted as a sign of forgiveness (cf. *Yoma* 6. 8; Danby, op. cit., p. 170). I am indebted to Dr. D. Daube for the substance of this note.

Later an attempt will be made to trace the process whereby this baptism of John was further adapted and transformed, so as to become the Christian baptism we know in the Acts of the Apostles and in the Epistles. Before that task is undertaken, however, and before the evidence for early Christian baptism is passed in review, it is necessary to look carefully at one particular example of the baptism of John. To do this is not to turn aside from the main direction of our journey. We could not pass from John's baptism to Christian baptism if there were not this particular instance of John's baptism to help bridge the gap. This particular example of John's rite is to be found in the baptism of Jesus himself.

NOTE B
JOSEPHUS'S REFERENCE TO JOHN THE BAPTIST

The only other primary source of information concerning John the Baptist is contained in the writings of the Jewish historian Josephus. There is a short section in the *Antiquities* (18. 5. 2 ; § 117).[1] After describing how Herod's army had suffered defeat at the hands of Aretas, king of Arabia, Josephus continues :

But some of the Jews were of the opinion that Herod's army had been destroyed by God, and that quite justly as a punishment for his treatment of John who was surnamed Baptist. For this good man was put to death by Herod. He bade the Jews practise virtue and behave righteously towards one another and piously towards God and come together in baptism (βαπτισμῷ συνιέναι). For thus the immersion (τὴν βάπτισιν) would be acceptable to him, if they employed it not as a means of seeking pardon for particular sins but as a means of purifying the body, providing that the soul had been thoroughly cleansed beforehand by righteousness. When people flocked round him since they took the greatest delight in listening to what he said, Herod, afraid lest the great power John had of persuading men might incite them to a rebellion (for they seemed ready to follow his advice in everything), thought it far better to take the initiative and put him to death before he caused any fresh disturbance, lest, if a riot actually took place, he might himself be involved in trouble and have cause to regret it. Thus John, a prisoner thanks to Herod's suspicion of him, was sent to Machaerus the fortress previously mentioned and there executed. The Jews thought that it was in revenge for him that destruction came upon the army, since God willed that Herod should be punished.

We may reasonably conclude that this passage was written by Josephus himself. As early as Origen it was noticed that no connexion is traced in it between John and Jesus.[2] Israel Abrahams argued that this silence " of itself is almost enough to authenticate the passage ".[3] A Christian interpolator would have produced something far more closely resembling the accounts in the New Testament.

Josephus agrees with the Synoptists that John was killed by Herod,[4] that he

---

[1] The fuller account in the Slavonic version of Josephus, rated so highly by R. Eisler (op. cit., pp. 223 ff.), is by most other authorities regarded as spurious and devoid of historical value. It may represent the work of a Christian interpolator, since certain of the statements contained in it seem to depend on passages in the New Testament; cf. J. W. Jack, *The Historic Christ* (1933), pp. 110–122; and see also the article by J. M. Creed, *Harvard Theological Review*, Vol. XXV (1932), pp. 277 ff.

[2] Orig., *Contra Cels.*, 1. 47.

[3] I. Abrahams, *Studies in Pharisaism and the Gospels*, First Series (1917), p. 31.

[4] But the reason given in each case is different. Josephus says that it was because Herod feared that John might lead a revolt. The Gospels account for the imprisonment and death of John on more personal grounds (Mk. 6. 17–18; Matt. 14. 3–4). For an estimate of the two accounts see A. E. J. Rawlinson, *St. Mark* (1925), p. 82.

C

enjoined baptism, and that he laid stress on moral conduct. He differs, however, from them considerably in the account he gives of John's mission and of the significance of his baptism. According to Josephus, John's emphasis was ascetic. Whereas in the Synoptic Gospels John's rite is described as " a baptism of repentance unto remission of sins ", in Josephus the connexion of John's baptism with pardon for sins is expressly denied; on the contrary, the rite is practised for the sake of bodily purity by those whose souls have first been thoroughly cleansed by righteousness. The curious phrase βαπτισμῷ συνιέναι may mean that baptism was regarded as the rite of entry into a new community.[1] A further difference from the Synoptists is that in Josephus the eschatological aspect of John's mission is altogether lacking. There is no expectation of divine judgement, and no word about the " mightier one " to come.

It seems probable that, in regard to John's use of baptism and the ideas associated with it, the Synoptists give more reliable information than Josephus. Josephus may well have altered the character of John's " eschatological " baptism and presented it in the guise of an ascetic rite in the hope that his account would thereby be rendered more acceptable to Gentile readers. On the other hand, John's portrait of the " mightier one ", as depicted in the Synoptic Gospels, cannot well be put down to the " theologizing " of the later Church.[2] Further, if the movement led by John were simply as Josephus describes it, it is hard to understand why Herod needed to put him to death. If, however, John proclaimed the coming " Rule of God ", and the end of the present world-order, with the apocalyptic intensity implied in the Synoptic accounts, he may well have been regarded by Herod as a dangerous revolutionary.[3] " No government views with a friendly eye those who foretell its end, even by the act of God." [4] Thus it is Josephus himself who, in the reason he gives for John's death, leads us to doubt the completeness of his account of the Baptist's movement. The picture of John's mission and message given by the Synoptists enables us far more readily to understand both the opposition which he aroused, and the fate which he suffered.[5]

---

[1] Cf. R. N. Flew, *Jesus and His Church* (1938), p. 51, and Marsh, op. cit., p. 64.

[2] Cf. Creed, op. cit., p. 312, " The prophecy of the coming one, ' whose fan is in his hand ', is not likely to have been invented in the Christian church, for it contains nothing to suggest the peculiar character and fate of the Christian Messiah ".

[3] Lk. 3. 15 is evidence that John not only foretold the coming of the Messiah, but was, at least by some, tentatively identified with him.

[4] F. Jackson and K. Lake, *The Beginnings of Christianity*, Vol. I (1920), p. 107.

[5] For a somewhat more favourable view of Josephus' account, see Marsh op. cit., pp. 50–51. In reply to Dr. Marsh, the present writer would argue that the complete suppression by Josephus of the eschatological note in John's message, while capable of explanation as a tactful omission or as a failure to understand, does nevertheless seriously distort the picture of John's preaching and baptism, and thereby renders Josephus in this matter a less reliable historical authority than the Synoptists.

3

Jesus and Baptism

BOTH in the Synoptists and in the Fourth Gospel there is a close connexion between John the Baptist and Jesus. It has already been pointed out how John's preaching was regarded as the immediate prelude to the Christian gospel. We may notice further how John enquired about Jesus and how Jesus delivered himself of an estimate concerning the worth of the Baptist and his mission (Matt. 11. 2–19; Lk. 7. 18–35), and how later John's disciples told Jesus about their master's death (Matt. 14. 12). Congruous with the impression derived from the Gospels concerning the connexion between the activity of John and that of Jesus is the tradition preserved in the Fourth Gospel that some of our Lord's followers had previously been followers of John the Baptist (Jn. 1. 35). It is to be noticed how later some followers of John at Ephesus were treated by St. Paul as " disciples " needing further instruction.[1] All these references indicate a close relation between the Baptist and Jesus. It is noticeable also that Jesus laid stress on some of the main ideas prominent in the preaching of John, especially several in which he differed fundamentally from contemporary Judaism : the proclamation of the Kingdom of God in a sense other than the political, the lack of stress on law, tradition and temple-worship, the teaching that physical descent from Abraham is no guarantee of divine favour, and that man can establish no claim on God for reward, but owes everything to his free grace.[2] Again, profound as are the differences in respect of their teaching between John and Jesus, it can hardly be without significance that the words in which Matthew records the Marcan saying containing the first message of Jesus are used by Matthew not only of Jesus but also of John.[3]

The most indisputable link, however, between John and Jesus lies in the fact that Jesus himself accepted baptism at the hands of John. That this tradition was invented by the early Church is rendered in the highest degree improbable by the difficulty which the incident aroused in the minds of some early Christians.[4] The baptism of Jesus is described in each of the Synoptic Gospels.[5] There is some evidence for thinking

[1] The twenty-seven other occurrences of $\mu\alpha\theta\eta\tau\dot{\eta}s$ in Acts all imply membership of the Christian community. It is therefore natural to take the word as meaning *Christian* disciples also in Acts 19. 1; cf. H. J. Cadbury in Jackson and Lake op. cit., Vol. V, pp. 376–378, esp. p. 377, *n.* 2.
[2] Cf. Leipoldt op. cit., pp. 29–30.
[3] " Repent ye; for the kingdom of heaven is at hand ", Matt. 4. 17 (cf. Mk. 1. 15); Matt. 3. 2. See also *supra*, p. 17. *n.* 5.
[4] Cf. Matt. 3. 14–15, and see *infra*, pp. 26–27.
[5] The incident is not narrated in the Fourth Gospel, but is probably implied by Jn. 1. 32–34; cf. Bernard ad loc.

that the story was told not only in Mark but also in Q.[1]   *Mark* (1.9–11) tells how " in those days " Jesus came from Nazareth and was baptized by John in the River Jordan.   As he came up out of the water, he saw the heavens cleaving asunder ($\sigma\chi\iota\zeta o\mu\acute\epsilon\nu o\upsilon s$)[2] and the Spirit coming down like a dove upon him.   A voice came out of heaven saying, " Thou art my Son, the Beloved: in thee I have taken delight ". *Matthew* (3. 13–17) follows closely the Marcan story, but inserts an account of John's reluctance to baptize Jesus.   Jesus persuades John to consent to the baptism by asserting that for them to carry it out will be an act of " righteousness " ($\delta\iota\kappa\alpha\iota o\sigma\acute\upsilon\nu\eta\nu$).   Matthew also defines the Spirit as " the Spirit *of God* ", and records the words of the voice in the third rather than the second person.   *Luke* (3. 21–22) emphasizes the connexion of the baptism of Jesus with the baptism of " all the people ", states that Jesus was praying, inserts " holy " before " Spirit ", adds the words " in bodily form " ($\sigma\omega\mu\alpha\tau\iota\kappa\tilde\omega$ $\epsilon\tilde\iota\delta\epsilon\iota$) to the passage about the dove, and records the voice, according to the text of B$\aleph$, etc., in the Marcan form, and according to the text of D, etc., in the form " Thou art my Son: this day I have begotten thee ".   Thus for Mark the significance of the baptism was for Jesus himself.   He saw the heavens opening and the words of the *Bath-Qol* were addressed to him. Matthew saw this significance as something recognized also by John (and perhaps by others), " lo, the heavens *were opened* ",[3] and the words of the voice are put into the third person.   Luke further stresses the outward " objective " character of the incident by adding the words " in bodily form ".

It is hard to believe that the addition in Matthew (3. 14–15) is a record of historical fact.   Apart from these verses there is no hint in the Synoptists that John the Baptist was as yet conscious that the " Mightier One " was no other than Jesus.   (The narrative of the message brought by John's disciples is, on its most natural interpretation, a strong suggestion to the contrary.[4])   The verses read like an early attempt to meet the objections of those who claimed that our Lord's submission to the " baptism of repentance unto remission of sins "[5] involved a tacit acknowledgement of wrongdoing.   The well-known passage

[1] Points in which Matthew and Luke agree together against Mark, and which may therefore suggest the use of a common non-Marcan source, are: (*a*) participle as against indicative for " baptized "; (*b*) $\dot\alpha\nu o\acute\iota\gamma\omega$ used instead of $\sigma\chi\acute\iota\zeta\omega$; (*c*) $\dot\epsilon\pi$' $\alpha\dot\upsilon\tau\acute o\nu$ instead of $\epsilon\dot\iota s$ $\alpha\dot\upsilon\tau\acute o\nu$.   Further, it has been argued that the words in Q's Temptation story, " if thou art Son of God ", look back to a Baptism narrative which must have stood in Q.   The existence of this independent Q version would be all the more likely if the Western text of Lk. 3. 22 were original, as Harnack and Streeter thought, but see Creed, op. cit., p. 58.

[2] For " rending of the heavens " associated with the " coming down " of Yahweh, cf. Isa. 64. 1; Pss. 18. 9, 144. 5.

[3] " To him " ($\alpha\dot\upsilon\tau\tilde\omega$) is omitted in B$\aleph$*, etc (cf. Westcott and Hort and R. V. mg.).

[4] Matt. 11. 2 ff., Lk. 7. 18 ff.

[5] Is it significant that the latter part of this phrase found in Mk. 1. 4 and Lk. 3. 3 does not occur in Matthew?   The First Evangelist seems to reserve the words " unto remission of sins " for the saying of Jesus about the Cup at the Last Supper (Matt. 26. 28).

quoted by Jerome from the Gospel according to the Hebrews [1] represents another endeavour to meet the same difficulty.

Behold the Lord's mother and brethren said to him, John the Baptist is baptizing unto remission of sins: let us go and be baptized by him. Then he said to them, What sin have I done that I should go and be baptized by him?—unless perchance this very saying of mine is a sin of ignorance.

This was felt as a difficulty in early times, but there need in fact be no contradiction between our Lord's acceptance of John's baptism and the Christian belief about his sinlessness. The preaching of John the Baptist was the occasion of a new awakening, a revival of prophetic religion. Jesus could not exclude himself from this movement. He could not separate himself from the sinners whom he would save. [2] For Jesus this acceptance of John's baptism need imply no consciousness of sin save in a corporate sense, but this identification of himself with the people of God was involved in the conception of Messiahship which we know our Lord found in Deutero-Isaiah.

There is little doubt among the critics, that of the accounts which have come down to us, Mark's is the most primitive. In view, however, of the criticisms of the *Formgeschichte* school, this by no means guarantees its historicity. Some have tried to preserve a degree of historicity by regarding the Gospel narratives as embellishments of a quite natural occurrence. Thus J. H. Bernard thought that the historical nucleus of the story lay in the fact of a dove alighting on Jesus. This was then interpreted as a sign of " Spirit ".[3] It may be questioned whether such an incident of a dove alighting on Jesus is really implied by any of the Gospel records (excepting perhaps in Luke). In all the Gospels (even including Luke) the word for dove is preceded by a word denoting " as " or " as if ".[4] This seems to imply that the word " dove " is meant to be interpreted metaphorically and not literally. But even if it be granted that some such incident may have occurred, or that the narratives imply such an occurrence, the argument would still seem to be open to criticism. We have to suppose that a perfectly common-place phenomenon was misunderstood, and that this misunderstanding gave rise to a profound theological belief. Such a " rationalizing " interpretation seems akin to the criticism which, as someone has said, sees the history of early Christianity as " a series of insignificant events out of which superstition or piety has made a Gospel ". It seems more probable that the " dove " should be interpreted quite differently.

---

[1] Jerome, *Contra Pelag.*, 3. 2, " Ecce mater domini et fratres eius dicebant ei: Iohannes baptista baptizat in remissionem peccatorum; eamus et baptizemur ab eo. Dixit autem eis: Quid peccavi ut vadam et baptizer ab eo? nisi forte hoc ipsum quod dixi ignorantia est ".

[2] Cf. Oepke in *Theol. Wört.*, Vol. I, p. 536.

[3] Cf. Bernard op. cit., Vol. I, p. 49, " all the evangelists . . . agree in recording that a dove alighted upon Jesus when presenting Himself for baptism ". Bernard cites Jewish comments on Cant. 2. 12 and Gen. 1. 2 showing that a " dove " could be regarded as a symbol of the Divine Spirit, op. cit., p. 49.

[4] ὡς, Mk. 1. 10; Lk. 3. 22; Jn. 1. 32; ὡσεί, Matt. 3. 16.

Israel Abrahams has shown that the Dove, the *Bath-Qol* and the Spirit
form a group of associated ideas in rabbinic writings.[1] In comments on
Eccles. 7. 9 and 12. 7 the *Bath-Qol* is connected with " chirping " or
" with the voice of a bird ". In *Berachoth 3a* occurs the sentence " I
heard a *Bath-Qol* moaning as a dove . . .". In the passage cited by
Abrahams about Hillel the *Bath-Qol* and the Spirit are mentioned
together. Other references show that a proselyte entering Judaism
was said to come " under the wings of the Divine Presence ".[2] All
these taken together with Bernard's passages connecting " dove " and
" spirit " suggest that the imagery of this story is thoroughly Jewish,
but that it should be treated as imagery, and not as external fact.

Because parallels of this sort can be drawn between this story and
rabbinic literature, some critics have wondered whether the narrative
of our Lord's baptism should not be regarded as the work of some early
Christian preacher or writer who reflected on the beginning of the
ministry of Jesus and cast into a dramatic form the Church's conviction
about his divine Sonship. Dibelius, for example, regards the story as an
instance of " mythologizing ".[3] H. J. Cadbury has argued that the
story arose because when " Christ " was not yet a surname some
evidence was required that Jesus the Messiah had actually been
" anointed ", and the *Elias redivivus* legend would assign such an act to
John the Baptist.[4] We may grant that such " reflective " activity
on the part of the early Church may have affected the form of the
story, and, as we have seen, this probably accounts for the question and
answer of Matt. 3. 14–15; but the very fact that difficulties were felt
about our Lord's acceptance of John's baptism makes it antecedently
improbable that anyone in the early Church should himself have
constructed the episode. The Church might seek to mend the story:
it would hardly have invented the incident.

A further argument in favour of the substantial historicity of the
narratives concerning the baptism is furnished by the improbability
that Jesus should have stood aloof from a movement like that of the
Baptist. The striking testimony to John given by Jesus (Matt. 11. 7–11,
Lk. 7. 24–28), and the enquiry he made when questioned about his
" authority " (" the baptism of John was it from heaven or from
men? " Mk. 11. 30, Matt. 21. 25, Lk. 20. 4) imply that he fully appreciated the significance of one who, by our Lord's own confession, was
" more than a prophet ". In view of the importance of these passages,
which show the light in which Jesus regarded the Baptist's mission,
Professor Creed has concluded: " It seems unlikely that Jesus had not
himself been baptized by John. And if he was baptized, it is *a priori*
probable that his baptism was a crisis in his life and was connected with

---

[1] I. Abrahams, *Studies in Pharisaism and the Gospels*, First Series (1917), pp. 47 ff.
[2] *Yeb.* 46*b* (cf. Ruth 2. 12), cited by Abrahams, op. cit., p. 36.
[3] Cf. M. Dibelius, *From Tradition to Gospel* (1934), pp. 271–274.
[4] Cf. H. J. Cadbury, in *Quantulacumque* (1937), p. 103.

the call to his mission ".[1] If the historicity of the baptism be accepted in this sense, it is clear that the story of it must have come ultimately from Jesus himself. The attempts which have been made to divide the narrative into separate *pericopæ* seem curiously beside the point.[2] If Jesus was baptized by John, and if he ever spoke of it to the Twelve, it is hard to think that he did not make clear to them something of what the experience meant to himself.[3] We may reverently suppose that in the moment of baptism Jesus became overwhelmingly conscious of the Spirit of God coming upon him and that thus he became convinced more than ever before of his unique Messianic Sonship. It is not to be wondered at that in describing this experience Jesus should have used some of the imagery with which it was natural for a Jew to clothe such conceptions.

If the story of the baptism came originally from Jesus, the fullest weight should be given to just those elements in it which mark off this baptism from other baptisms administered by John. We notice that in this story of the baptism of Jesus a baptism with water is associated in the most intimate way with an experience of " holy Spirit ", and with a unique consciousness of divine Sonship. Thus, what seemed to the onlooker just another instance of John's baptism, completely transcended, in these two respects, the bounds of John's rite for the thought of Jesus himself. It can hardly be accidental that one, or both, of these two—possession by the Spirit and the status of being sons of God— are connected closely with the rite of Christian baptism in several passages in the Acts and in the Epistles.[4] These two features are *not* part of the ordinary meaning of John's rite; we have seen good reason to doubt whether John ever spoke concerning the Spirit.[5] But they appear prominently in one particular instance of John's baptism, namely the baptism of Jesus. This would seem to suggest that in our attempt to describe the antecedents of Christian baptism we do well to give a conspicuous place to the baptism of our Lord. It may be that this event has exercised a more considerable influence than has hitherto been recognized upon the origin of the Christian rite.

Apart from the outstanding fact that Jesus accepted baptism at the hands of John, and that this event was later held to mark the inauguration of his ministry, there is little or nothing about baptism in the rest of the Synoptic record. It will be argued later from the evidence of the Acts and the Pauline Epistles that, from the earliest days of the

[1] Creed, op. cit., p. 55.

[2] Some of the Form-critics point out that Mk. 1. 10–11 can be omitted without breaking the sequence of the narrative.

[3] Some of the closest parallels to the story of the Baptism of Jesus in Jewish writings are the narratives describing the Call of a prophet (cf. Isa. 6. 1 ff.; Jer. 1. 4 ff.), and the stories in which a *Bath-Qol* pronounced a Rabbi worthy (an example is cited by Abrahams op. cit., p. 48).

[4] Cf. Acts 2. 38; 10. 44–48; 1 Cor. 6. 11; 12. 13; Gal. 3. 26–27; Eph. 4. 4–5; (cf. also Jn. 3. 5).

[5] Cf. *supra*, pp. 18–19.

primitive Church, baptism was the acknowledged rite of entry into the
new community. This primitive Christian practice would be most
satisfactorily accounted for on the hypothesis that the Apostles believed
that such a use of baptism depended in some sense upon the authority
of Jesus. Such a belief clearly underlies the famous passage at the end
of the First Gospel (Matt. 28. 19–20).[1] It will be shown later how
difficult it is to accept this passage in its present form as a record of
ipsissima verba of our Lord;[2] but in view of the conviction expressed
therein—viz., that *c.* A.D. 85 it was firmly believed that baptism in
some way had the authority of Jesus behind it—it is worth asking
whether there are any other traces in the Gospels which express or
suggest the attitude of Jesus towards this rite.

A tradition found only in the Fourth Gospel represents Jesus or his
disciples as actually practising the rite of baptism during his ministry.

> After these things came Jesus and his disciples into the land of Judæa; and
> there he tarried with them, and baptized. And John also was baptizing in
> Ænon near to Salim. . . . When therefore the Lord knew how that the Pharisees
> had heard that Jesus was making and baptizing more disciples than John
> (although Jesus himself baptized not, but his disciples), he left Judæa, and
> departed again into Galilee (Jn. 3. 22–23, 4. 1–3).

Here it is asserted, first, that Jesus and his disciples, exercising a
ministry concurrently with that of John, administered water-baptism;
secondly, that when the Pharisees got to know that this " baptizing "
ministry was more successful than that of John, Jesus withdrew from
Judæa to Galilee. The author also corrects his earlier statement that
Jesus baptized, and says that in fact the administration of the rite was
performed not by Jesus but by the disciples.[3] There is no other evidence
in the Gospels that Jesus used the rite during his ministry. In view of
the complete silence of the Synoptists, it is not surprising that some have
doubted the reliability of this piece of Johannine tradition. A closer
examination, however, suggests that it may well be trustworthy. It
has been shown earlier that the connexion between John and Jesus is
acknowledged, and indeed emphasized, by the Synoptists.[4] If Jesus
carried on some of John's main ideas, if, like John, he associated the
thought of the Kingdom of God with repentance, if, above all, he
accepted baptism for himself, it is hardly to be wondered at that he

---

[1] Mk. 16. 16 also contains an implied injunction to baptize, uttered by the risen Lord, but
since this occurs in the spurious ending added some time in the second century A.D. to complete a
gospel which was thought to be unfinished, the passage cannot be held to provide independent
evidence.

[2] See the discussion *infra*, pp. 105–109.

[3] Bernard, op. cit., Vol. I, pp. xxxiii and 133–134, thought it probable that 4. 2 is not from the
hand of John, " but was added at a revision of the text, because of the idea that it would detract
from the dignity of Jesus to perform the ministry of baptism ". The style of the verse is said not
to be Johannine (cf. καίτοιγε, and 'Ιησοῦς without the article); but the insertion of such a
comment in parenthesis is thoroughly in keeping with the style of the Fourth Evangelist.

[4] Cf. *supra*, p. 25.

should have allowed his disciples to associate with the proclamation of the Kingdom of God the rite of water-baptism with which it had been connected in the preaching of John. This is the more intelligible when we recall that in all probability a number of the disciples had themselves been followers of the Baptist. It may be noted further that the Fourth Gospel associates this use of baptism only with an early ministry in Judæa. There is nothing to suggest that the rite was practised by our Lord's disciples in other parts of Palestine. A recognition of this fact makes the Synoptic silence about baptism much more understandable, since the Synoptists describe a Judæan activity of Jesus only in the narrative of the last week. But though in the Synoptists there is no account of an earlier Judæan ministry, several indications make it likely that such a ministry took place.[1] If during such an early activity in Judæa, prior to the Galilean ministry the beginning of which is described in Mk. 1. 14, baptism were practised with the approval of Jesus, it becomes easier to explain why, immediately after Pentecost, baptism took its place as the normal rite of entry into the Christian community. The recollection that during one stage of the ministry Jesus had allowed his disciples to baptize may be one among a number of considerations that help to explain the readiness with which baptism was accepted by the early Church.

There is nothing corresponding to this tradition in the Synoptic record; but there is a Lucan reference to " baptism " which, though commonly regarded as purely metaphorical, perhaps deserves rather more consideration than it has usually received. It may have some light to throw on the way in which Jesus regarded baptism, and help to explain the origin of some of the ideas later associated with the Christian rite as we meet it in the Acts and in the Epistles. In a section of the Third Gospel which J. M. Creed has described as " a group of discourses loosely put together, in a framework which may be ascribed to the evangelist " occurs the saying:

I have a baptism to be baptized with; and how am I straitened till it be accomplished! (Lk. 12. 50).[2]

This saying of Jesus about his death is regarded, by most critics, as indubitably authentic. The very indirectness of its reference to the Passion seems to guarantee its originality.[3] The saying clearly looks on to the approaching death, but the reference to baptism is usually treated as a purely figurative application of the word comparable with the passages in the Old Testament which describe intense suffering by

---

[1] Cf. Mk. 11. 3 and parallels, 14. 14 and parallels; Matt. 23. 37; Lk. 13. 34; and see Bernard, op. cit., Vol. I, pp. civ–cvi.
[2] With this passage may be compared Mk. 10. 38–39 (and Matt. 20. 22 according to some MSS.), the words of Jesus to James and John, "Are ye able . . . to be baptized with the baptism that I am baptized with? "
[3] Cf. V. Taylor, *Jesus and His Sacrifice* (1937), p. 166.

a somewhat similar image.[1] But it seems likely that the word
" baptism " may be employed here in a far more specific sense. E. F.
Scott has shown that, though to be " plunged in the waters " is a quite
common metaphor for affliction and sorrow, yet it is probable that
the word βάπτισμα is used here with reference to the " special meaning
which baptism had possessed for religious minds since the days of
John ". It had come to mean a " spiritual purification . . . a renewal
of the whole nature preparatory to the entrance into the Kingdom of
God ".[2] May not Jesus therefore in this saying be looking on to his
death as that which will inaugurate his fuller activity, unfettered by the
restrictions of the earthly ministry? Such a " religious " use of the
term seems more appropriate in speaking to the Jews of our Lord's own
day than the employment of it purely as a vivid symbol for distress and
suffering. If E. F. Scott's interpretation is right, then it was Jesus
himself who first forged the link between the ideas of " baptism " and
" death "; a fact of considerable importance for those who are trying
to trace the antecedents of Christian baptism as we know it in the New
Testament. We have not yet reached the stage at which we examine
the teaching of St. Paul, but it can hardly be forgotten that more than
once he links baptism with the death of Christ.[3] Our consideration of
this Lucan saying of Jesus at least suggests the possibility that ideas
about baptism which have often been thought peculiarly Pauline may
have an earlier and a more significant origin.

It may be useful to summarize the conclusions of this chapter. The
evidence for determining the attitude of Jesus towards baptism is
scanty and for the most part indirect. The most striking fact is that
Jesus submitted to baptism at the hands of John in a rite which was
understood to be " a baptism of repentance unto remission of sins ";
and that for him the moment of baptism coincided with an experience
of " holy spirit " and a realization of his unique divine Sonship. This
baptism was regarded as the inauguration of his public ministry. There
is a possibility that during an early period of that ministry Jesus allowed
his disciples to continue the practice of water-baptism with which the
association of some of them with John had familiarized them. Later
in the ministry, Jesus, looking on to his approaching death, referred to it
as a " baptism ", and also spoke of the martyrdom of some of his
followers in similar terms. Such a reference becomes full of meaning

[1] Cf. Ps. 42. 7 (" All thy waves and thy billows are gone over me "); 69. 2 (" I am come into
deep waters, where the floods overflow me "), 15 (" let not the waterflood overwhelm me,
neither let the deep swallow me up "); 124. 4–5 (" Then the waters had overwhelmed us, the
stream had gone over our soul: then the proud waters had gone over our soul "); Isa. 43. 2
(" When thou passest through the waters, I will be with thee ; and through the rivers, they shall
not overflow thee "). It may be remarked that in none of these passages according to the
Septuagint, do βαπτίζω or its cognates occur ; but cf. *supra*, p. 12.
[2] E. F. Scott, *The Kingdom and the Messiah* (1911), pp. 228–230. It is interesting to notice that
Tertullian (*De Bapt.* xvi) alludes to Lk. 12. 50 in connexion with the teaching about martyrdom
as a *secundum lavacrum*.
[3] Cf. Rom. 6. 3–4; Col. 2. 11–12; Eph. 5. 25–26.

if we recognize that it is a matter of history that the death of Jesus and the subsequent belief in his resurrection did in fact mark the inauguration of his wider " ministry " in the world at large, as surely as the baptism in the River Jordan inaugurated his ministry in Palestine. The student of the origins of Christian baptism can hardly lay too much stress on the fact that for Jesus himself his mission was ushered in by a baptism,[1] and that similarly by Jesus himself his approaching death was in a striking saying described as a " baptism " that he must " be baptized with ".[2]   To bear these things in mind will illuminate much of the subsequent teaching concerning the Christian rite.

[1] For the influence upon Christian baptism of the baptism of Jesus, cf. also *infra*, pp. 42 (and *n.* 2), 69 *n.* 2, 91, 95, 120–122.
[2] For the death (and resurrection) of Jesus as the supreme " antecedent " of Christian baptism, cf. *infra*, pp. 71–73, 89–92, 122–125.

PART II
NEW TESTAMENT EVIDENCE CONCERNING CHRISTIAN BAPTISM

4

Baptism in the Acts of the Apostles

To begin a review of the New Testament evidence about Christian baptism with a consideration of the book of Acts is a proceeding that, by many people to-day, will be regarded as standing in need of some critical justification. It may properly be urged that since the date of the composition of Acts is certainly later than that of any of the Pauline Epistles, there is much to be said for beginning not with Acts but rather with the evidence furnished by St. Paul. Only after an examination of his first-hand and contemporary statements are we in a position to deal with what is said about baptism in Acts, a book which, when critically regarded, affords no certain evidence for a period much earlier than, say, about A.D. 80 and onwards. So many critics would argue. There is, however, another attitude towards the books of Acts which, while taking full account of critical difficulties, nevertheless passes a more favourable judgement upon the reliability of its author. The present writer would record his agreement with the conclusions of W. F. Howard in his essay on " The Acts of the Apostles Critically Considered ".[1] Dr. Howard quotes with approval the verdict of C. H. Turner: [2] " St. Luke has given us a rational, articulated, and satisfactory account, which has every claim to be regarded as an honest and faithful attempt to picture things as they really happened."

Thus a consideration of the statements about baptism in Acts at this particular stage of our enquiry may be defended on the ground that, though no doubt the book was written well on in the century, nevertheless it does record with a considerable degree of faithfulness many of the beliefs and practices of pre-Pauline Christianity. For anything like a connected picture of the life of that primitive community we must have recourse to Acts. The narrative certainly raises many questions for which it does not provide the answer, particularly when, in reference to historical and chronological points, the attempt is made to correlate the evidence of Acts with other apparently divergent or contradictory statements of St. Paul. It may, however, be emphasized that, so far as baptism is concerned, the divergence between Acts and Paul is in no way comparable with that, for example, concerning St. Paul's visits to Jerusalem or the proceedings at the Apostolic Council. So long as we refrain from that prejudging of the issue which rules out all possibility that baptism can

---

[1] *The Study Bible : The Acts of the Apostles*, by S. Cave and W. F. Howard (1929) pp. 121–147.
[2] Cited by Howard, op. cit., p. 146, from C. H. Turner, *The Study of the New Testament 1883 and 1920*, p. 31.

have been a primitive Christian practice,[1] the references in Acts would seem to reflect an early period of baptismal belief and practice, during which the rite was theologically significant, but far less explicitly so than it later became in the teaching of St. Paul and his successors. The present writer would claim that the Pauline teaching concerning baptism, as indeed that of later New Testament writers, is far more intelligible when read as the product of reflection upon, and explication of, the early ideas about baptism represented in the Acts of the Apostles. To pass directly to St. Paul without first examining what is said in Acts would be to omit an important link in the chain of evidence, and so to obscure the continuity we are seeking to discover.

It may freely be admitted that the evidence about baptism in the book of Acts is curiously complicated. For the most part the passages are tolerably clear when each is considered by itself; the difficulty arises when the attempt is made to gather together the various strands of evidence and to weave them into a connected whole. In the endeavour to review the evidence afresh, it may be valuable to bear in mind a comment made by Dr. Silva New: [2] " Belief in Jesus (or in his Name), baptism, the remission of sins, the laying on of Apostolic hands, and the reception of the Spirit seem to have formed a single complex of associated ideas, any one of which might in any single narrative be either omitted or emphasized."

It is commonly recognized that a number of the baptismal references in Acts fall into certain well-marked groups, according as the " baptism " is or is not a baptism with water, and, further, according to the way in which the rite is related to the laying on of hands and to the gift of the Spirit.[3]

(*a*) One group of passages draws a contrast between John's baptism with water and the Christian baptism with the Holy Spirit. Thus the risen Jesus says to the Apostles:

John indeed baptized with water; but ye shall be baptized with the Holy Ghost not many days hence (1. 5).

And, again, when Peter recounts the episode of Cornelius to the authorities at Jerusalem, he says:

As I began to speak, the Holy Ghost fell on them, even as on us at the beginning. And I remembered the word of the Lord, how that he said, John indeed baptized with water; but ye shall be baptized with the Holy Ghost (11. 15–16).

This point of view coincides with that represented in Mk. 1. 8 (" I baptized you with water; but he shall baptize you with the Holy Ghost "), a

[1] E.g. on the ground that since baptism came to be " sacramentally " regarded, the practice cannot have had other than a Hellenistic origin.

[2] In Jackson and Lake, op. cit., Vol. V, p. 134.

[3] For a similar grouping of passages cf. Jackson and Lake op. cit., Vol. I, p. 337 ff. An examination of this and another recent attempt (by J. Weiss) to classify these passages may be found in Marsh op. cit., pp. 159–162. As Dr. Marsh points out, the theory of some critics that these divergent attitudes in Acts are due to the piecing together of different sources, is too subjective to be satisfactory.

passage which we have seen reason to believe may be a re-editing of the Baptist's original words.[1] | A sharp contrast is drawn between John's baptism with water and the Christian baptism " with Holy Spirit ".[2] In Acts this contrast is actually attributed to Jesus himself, and the author clearly regards the events of Pentecost as the fulfilment of the promised baptism with the Holy Spirit.[3]

In the narratives about Cornelius (10. 44–48, 11. 15–18) the outstanding thing is the reception of the Holy Spirit by a Gentile. In both narratives the only " antecedent " of this experience is the preaching of Peter (10. 44, 11. 14–15). The reception of the Spirit is not preceded either by baptism or by laying on of hands. What is to be remarked, however, is a curious inconsistency in the account of what followed the gift of the Spirit in the two narratives. In the earlier story (in Chapter 10) Peter is described as giving instructions that Cornelius and his household should be baptized " in the name of Jesus Christ ", and justifying his action on the ground that the obvious reception of the Spirit demanded as a corollary the rite of water-baptism. This clearly implies the closest association in the thought of some early Christians between water-baptism and the gift of the Spirit. Further, the attribution of this view to Peter (in Acts 10) suggests a belief that there was good apostolic authority for this association.[4] Yet in the other story in Chapter 11 where Peter recounts the events at Jerusalem there is no reference to any reception by Cornelius and the others of water-baptism. On the contrary, Peter there justifies his action by quoting the " word of the Lord " which definitely sets the water-baptism of John and the (Christian) baptism with the Holy Spirit in contrast with one another. The clear implication of this account in Acts 11 would seem to be that Cornelius and his household were *not* baptized with water. Kirsopp Lake would explain the inconsistency of these two narratives by the hypothesis that the reference to water-baptism in 10. 47–48 is due to a redactor.[5] On this interpretation, then, the Cornelius story, not only in Chapter 11 but also in the original source of Chapter 10, would be closely parallel with Acts 1. 5, and would represent the point of view which drew a sharp contrast between the water-baptism of John and the Christian baptism with the Holy Spirit.[6]

---

[1] Cf. *supra*, p. 19.

[2] The contrast is not quite so precise as the English rendering would suggest. Both in 1. 5 and in 11. 16 ὕδατι (simple dative) is followed by a prepositional phrase (ἐν πνεύματι ἁγίῳ); in Mk. 1. 8, however, the dative is used in both clauses. It is arguable that the difference should not be pressed in Hellenistic Greek; cf. Marsh, op. cit., p. 22, *n.* 1.

[3] There is evidence in Aug., *Ep.* 265, 3, for *baptizabitis* (active) which Ropes thought might possibly go back to a Greek text with no verb in the second clause. He regarded it as more likely, however, that this reading was purely Latin, and represented the attempt to find in Acts a " commission to baptize "; cf. Jackson and Lake, op. cit., Vol. III, pp. 2, 4.

[4] Cf. also Acts 2. 38, where again Peter is the speaker. It will be argued later that this is not " editorial ", but represents substantially what Peter actually said; cf. *infra*, pp. 43–48.

[5] Jackson and Lake, op. cit., Vol. I, pp. 340–341.

[6] Cf. also *infra*, pp. 115–116, where it is argued that whether or not Cornelius was baptized, his case was clearly regarded as exceptional and must not be taken to represent the normal attitude of the primitive community to baptism.

D

(*b*) Another important passage is that which tells of the " disciples "
at Ephesus :

And it came to pass, that, while Apollos was at Corinth, Paul having passed
through the upper country came to Ephesus, and found certain disciples:
and he said unto them, Did ye receive the Holy Ghost when ye believed?   And
they said unto him, Nay, we did not so much as hear whether the Holy Ghost
was given.   And he said, Into what then were ye baptized?   And they said,
Into John's baptism.   And Paul said, John baptized with the baptism of
repentance, saying unto the people, that they should believe on him which
should come after him, that is, on Jesus.   And when they heard this, they were
baptized into the name of the Lord Jesus.   And when Paul had laid his hands
upon them, the Holy Ghost came on them; and they spake with tongues, and
prophesied.   And they were in all about twelve men (19. 1–7).

Thus Paul found at Ephesus twelve disciples [1] who had not received the
Holy Spirit.   They had been baptized " into John's baptism ".   When it
was pointed out to them that the purpose of John's preaching was to
encourage belief in One who should come after, namely Jesus, they
submitted to baptism " in the name of the Lord Jesus ", and had the
Apostle's hands laid upon them.   The consequence was that they
received the Holy Spirit and " spake with tongues and prophesied ".
In this story there is the closest link between baptism in the name of the
Lord Jesus, the laying on of hands and the reception of the Holy Spirit.
With this passage may be compared the narrative of what followed the
conversion of St. Paul :

And Ananias departed, and entered into the house; and laying his hands on
him said, Brother Saul, the Lord, even Jesus, who appeared unto thee in the
way which thou camest, hath sent me, that thou mayest receive thy sight, and
be filled with the Holy Ghost.   And straightway there fell from his eyes as it
were scales, and he received his sight; and he arose and was baptized (9. 17–18).

Here there is a similar association between the laying on of hands, the
reception of the Spirit and baptism.[2]

The story in Acts 19 is clear and straightforward, but it must be confessed that the verses at the end of chapter 18, which it is natural to take
with it, are full of difficulties :

Now a certain Jew named Apollos, an Alexandrian by race, a learned man,
came to Ephesus; and he was mighty in the scriptures.   This man had been
instructed in the way of the Lord; and being fervent in spirit, he spake and
taught carefully the things concerning Jesus, knowing only the baptism of John :
and he began to speak boldly in the synagogue.   But when Priscilla and Aquila
heard him, they took him unto them, and expounded unto him the way of
God more carefully.   And when he was minded to pass over into Achaia, the
brethren encouraged him, and wrote to the disciples to receive him : and when
he was come, he helped them much which had believed through grace : for he
powerfully confuted the Jews, and that publicly, shewing by the scriptures that
Jesus was the Christ (18. 24–28).

---

[1] μαθητής must denote *Christian* disciple; cf. *supra*, p. 25, n. 1.
[2] Baptism and the washing away of sins are spoken of in one of the parallel accounts (22. 16) ;
the shorter account in Chapter 26 makes no mention of baptism.

These verses describe how Apollos, who knew only the baptism of John, was further instructed by Priscilla and Aquila; in view of 19. 1–7 we might have expected that Apollos would have received Christian baptism and the laying on of hands. Nothing, however, is said about either. Apollos is called a "Jew", but in view of the failure to administer any further baptism it must be assumed that he was regarded as at least as much a Christian as those who in Chapter 19 (verses 1–2) are described as "disciples" who "believed", and *did* receive a further baptism. Moreover, we have to take account of the fact that a man who knew only the baptism of John, and whose grasp of Christian truth was clearly defective, could yet be called "fervent in spirit" (ζέων τῷ πνεύματι). This suggests that long after the Day of Pentecost Christians could use the term "spirit" in a quite general sense, parallel to that in Lk. 2. 25, where it is said of Simeon that "the Holy Spirit was upon him".[1]

(*c*) A third point of view is represented by the passage about the people who had been evangelized by Philip in Samaria:

> But when they believed Philip preaching good tidings concerning the kingdom of God and the name of Jesus Christ, they were baptized, both men and women. . . . Now when the apostles which were at Jerusalem heard that Samaria had received the word of God, they sent unto them Peter and John: who, when they were come down, prayed for them, that they might receive the Holy Ghost: for as yet he was fallen upon none of them: only they had been baptized into the name of the Lord Jesus. Then laid they their hands on them, and they received the Holy Ghost (8. 12, 14–17).

Here again the story is quite clear in itself. Baptism, even baptism "into the name of the Lord Jesus", was not necessarily accompanied by the bestowal of the Spirit; that endowment came only after prayer and the laying on of hands by apostles.

Thus at first sight there would seem to be in the passages so far examined at least three views about baptism represented in the book of Acts:

(*a*) Christian baptism is a baptism with the Holy Spirit, in contrast with the water-baptism of John.

(*b*) John's baptism does not bring the gift of the Spirit: that comes only after baptism in the name of the Lord Jesus and the laying on of hands.

(*c*) Baptism even in the name of the Lord Jesus does not by itself confer the gift of the Spirit: the Spirit is given only after prayer and the laying on of (apostolic) hands. It is by no means impossible to reconcile the second and third of these in a single view. Although in Acts 19. 3–5 baptism in the name of the Lord Jesus is contrasted with John's baptism, and so seems itself to comprise the full Christian initiation, yet in verse 6 the laying on of Paul's hands is spoken of before it is said that "the Holy Spirit came upon them". Thus the antecedent condition made so much of in Acts 8 (namely the laying on of hands) is present also (though with

---

[1] St. Paul uses τῷ πνεύματι ζέοντες of Christians, in Rom. 12. 11.

less obvious stress) in Acts 19. Both in (*b*) and in (*c*) baptism in the name of the Lord Jesus must be conjoined with the laying on of hands for the gift of the Holy Spirit to follow.

The real divergence of view in Acts lies between (*b*) and (*c*) on the one hand (where a rite of baptism with water is practised), and (*a*) on the other hand (where baptism with water seems to have been superseded). It must be recognized, however, that the passages to be grouped under (*a*) are few in number, and occur only in reference to the original apostles or to Cornelius, whose case was obviously regarded as somehow exceptional. In these passages " baptism " (in the Christian sense) is an experience of the Spirit, and not an immersion in water. This attitude to Christian baptism may become less irreconcilable with the other point of view when it is remembered that most, if not all, of the original Apostles had probably been disciples of the Baptist. Thus it was likely that they had already received John's baptism in the River Jordan. They had less need to undergo the outward rite again. The necessity rather was that they should receive that gift of the Spirit which had been foretold by the prophets, and was regarded as a distinctive mark of that New Age which the followers of Jesus believed had been inaugurated by him.[1] This gift of the Spirit they received at Pentecost. In view of other metaphorical uses of the term " baptism ", it is by no means surprising that this experience at Pentecost should have been described as a " baptism with the Holy Spirit ". It was the complement of that baptism with water which they had undergone some time before in the River Jordan. When they sought to impart that experience of the Spirit to others, it was natural that they should associate with it the rite of water-baptism, which for them had preceded their endowment with the Spirit. Thus while for the Apostles water-baptism and baptism with the Spirit had been separated by an interval of time, for most other Christians, in the earliest period, the two were simultaneous. It has already been noticed that this had also been so in the experience of Jesus. For him baptism with water coincided with the descent of the Holy Spirit.[2] It may have been a recollection of this fact in the life of the Master that accounted in part for the practice by the early Church from the first of baptism with water.

[1] Cf. the implications of Peter's sermon at the Day of Pentecost, where it is claimed that Joel's prophecy of the Spirit has been fulfilled in what was taking place then and there, and that this in turn had been made possible by the death, resurrection and exaltation of Jesus; cf. also Leipoldt op. cit., p. 35, " die ersten Christen fühlen sich als das Volk der Endzeit, das der Täufer voraussah ".

[2] Cf. *supra*, p. 29. There are some indications that the Baptism of Jesus was regarded as specially significant in certain early Christian writings, cf. Acts 10. 38, where the Baptism of Jesus seems to be viewed as his " Anointing "; cf. C. H. Dodd, *The Apostolic Preaching* (1936), p. 108; Ignatius twice refers to the Baptism; *Ad Eph.* 18. 2 (" who was born, and was baptized that by his submission ($\tau\hat{\omega}$ $\pi\acute{a}\theta\epsilon\iota$ or by his suffering) he might cleanse the water ") and *Ad Smyrn.* 1. 1 (where the words " baptized by John, in order that all righteousness might be fulfilled by him " occur in a statement of Christian belief). Marsh's claim that there is no reference to the Baptism of Jesus in the earliest Christian literature before the time of Irenæus, op. cit., p. 107 seems to neglect these passages. See also the note in W. L. Knox, *St. Paul and the Church of the Gentiles* (1939), p. 157 *n*. 2.

The claim that baptism was practised from the earliest days of the Christian community is by many modern scholars regarded as unjustified. It is necessary, therefore, to examine the well-known reference to baptism in Acts 2 in the light of the criticisms which have been passed upon it.

And Peter said unto them, Repent ye and be baptized every one of you in the name of Jesus Christ unto the remission of your sins; and ye shall receive the gift of the Holy Ghost (2. 38).

The verse follows the account of Peter's preaching at the Day of Pentecost. At first sight the evidence which it offers seems quite indisputable. Peter demands of his hearers repentance and baptism " in the name of Jesus Christ unto remission of sins ", and he promises that they shall receive the gift of the Holy Spirit. This would link the passage in a general way with the groups (*b*) and (*c*) above, and carry back the association of the gift of the Spirit with a rite of water-baptism to the earliest days of the primitive Church. Here, however, it is noticeable that there is no mention of the laying on of hands.

Some scholars would discount the witness of this passage to baptism as a primitive Christian rite. Thus Foakes Jackson and Kirsopp Lake think that this verse is out of harmony with the context.

This sudden introduction of baptism seems quite inconsistent with what was stated: the disciples had received the Spirit without having been baptized for that purpose, and the words of Jesus in Acts 1. 4 [1] imply a baptism in Spirit as a substitute for baptism in water, not as a consequence of it. [2]

They would regard the reference to baptism as the work of a redactor who viewed baptism as the necessary condition for admission to the Christian society, and consequently read this back into his source. They think that the use of " Jesus Christ " as a double proper name may betray the hand of an editor. [3] For those who adopt this hypothesis that the verse represents an editorial addition into a narrative which originally made no mention of Christian water-baptism, that original narrative may be taken to support the view which earlier we have denoted by (*a*), namely that which saw the phenomenon of Pentecost as itself a " baptism with Holy Spirit " in contradistinction with the previous water-baptism of John. In reply it may be pointed out that the attitude of the editor of Acts (which Jackson and Lake think may account for this verse) does *not* regard baptism in the name of the Lord Jesus as sufficient to confer the gift of the Spirit. On the contrary, it is stated in 19. 6, and expressly emphasized in 8. 15–17, that a further condition is requisite, namely the " laying on of hands ". Now, if an editor were reading back his own view and the baptismal practice of his own day into his original source, would he not have been more likely to make the process complete by

[1] This would seem to be a misprint for Acts 1. 5.
[2] Jackson and Lake, op. cit., Vol. I, p. 340.
[3] It is worth noticing that Irenæus read 'Ιησοῦ (without Χριστοῦ), and the Peshitto τοῦ κυρίου Ιησοῦ; cf. Jackson and Lake, op. cit., Vol. III, p. 22. It may be that one or other of these is more original than the traditional text.

inserting not only a reference to water-baptism but also some mention of the laying on of hands? The fact that the former of these occurs in 2. 38 without the latter may well be an indication of a primitive stage of baptismal belief, which connected the gift of the Spirit directly with the baptismal rite without any mention of the laying on of hands. If this be so, the verse would not be editorial, since it would reflect a stage of baptismal doctrine which, by the time Acts was compiled, had given place to another which connected the Spirit more directly with the laying on of hands.[1] Those who defend the verse as part of the original source have still to account for the apparent disharmony with the context on which the editors of *The Beginnings of Christianity* lay such stress. The explanation may be that those immediately addressed were not Jews, and consequently, as Gentiles, needed, if they were to receive the " promise ", some

---

[1] It is difficult to assess the precise relation which existed in the first century A.D. between baptism and the laying on of hands. There can hardly be any doubt that the laying on of hands was taken over from Judaism. The practice is frequently mentioned in various connexions by Old Testament writers. It was used in acts of " blessing " (Gen. 48. 14, 17), or in connexion with sacrifice to dedicate the victim to God (Lev. 1. 4, 3. 2, 16. 21, Num. 8. 12), or in the " presenting " of Levites (Num. 8. 10), or in the solemn designation of a successor, as by Moses to Joshua (Num. 27. 23, Deut. 34. 9). In later times it formed part of the " Semikhah ", the ceremony by which a Rabbi was appointed to his office (cf. *Bab. Sanh.* 13*b*). In the New Testament, Jesus laid hands on the children whom he blessed (Mk. 10. 13, 16 and parallels); again, he laid hands on many of those whom he healed (Mk. 5. 23, 6. 5, 7. 32)—it has been pointed out that the fact that Jesus was *asked* to do this attests the familiarity of the practice. The early disciples similarly used the laying on of hands in their works of healing (Acts 5. 12, 28. 8). Several references in Acts imply that the practice was used as a " symbol " of the giving of the Spirit for a particular purpose, whether with a view to missionary work (Acts 6. 6, 13. 3), or for the everyday Christian life (8. 17, 19. 6). It is in these latter references that the laying on of hands is closely connected with, though apparently distinguishable from, the rite of baptism. It is not clear whether Acts 9. 12, 17 (the passages which describe how Ananias laid hands on Saul at the time of his conversion) are to be included in this group, or whether the laying on of hands is here connected with " healing ", in this case restoration of sight. It is noteworthy that St. Paul, who clearly connected the Spirit with baptism, makes no mention of the laying on of hands (it is unlikely that any of the references in the Pastoral Epistles come from the Apostle himself). This would seem at first sight seriously to discredit the place accorded to the practice by the author of Acts, who in one passage represents St. Paul himself as laying hands on some disciples (19. 6). But it must be observed that St. Paul frequently speaks about " receiving the Spirit ", using exactly the same words which the author of Acts uses to describe the reception of the Spirit which followed the laying on of hands (Acts 8. 17: cf. Rom. 8. 15; 1 Cor. 2. 12; 2 Cor. 11. 4; Gal. 3. 2). Some scholars argue that once St. Paul appears to suggest that the receiving of the Spirit, though closely connected with baptism, may yet be distinguished from it (cf. 2 Cor. 1. 21–22). In view of this, it may be that the argument from silence should not be pressed. The laying on of hands was, for those with a Jewish background, so obvious and familiar a custom that it may well have been connected with the rite of baptism, and commonly practised from the first, without there being any need that St. Paul should specifically refer to it. Perhaps the true explanation of St. Paul's silence about the laying on of hands is to be found in the fact that to him the symbolism of *immersion* was far more expressive of the particular teaching he desired to emphasize. The mention of the laying on of hands in Heb. 6. 2, side by side with " teaching about baptisms ", in a list of Christian " fundamentals ", would seem to confirm the view that in the first century A.D. the laying on of hands was generally understood to be a concomitant of baptism. It may appear that this treatment of St. Paul's silence about the laying on of hands as negligible is hardly consistent with the argument advanced above against Kirsopp Lake, viz. that the silence of Acts 2. 38 about the same practice is significant. To this it may be replied that the two cases are not parallel. There was no particular reason why St. Paul need refer to the laying on of hands, if he did not so desire. But, *on Lake's theory that a redactor has been at work* in Acts 2. 38, there was very good reason that he should have made the process of antedating later Church practice as complete as possible by specifying *both* elements in the Christian initiation. For such a redactor to omit the laying on of hands, while mentioning baptism, would have been to fail to play the very rôle that is being attributed to him. The silence here, therefore, *is* significant: the fact that in Acts 2. 38 we find baptism spoken of, without the mention of the laying on of hands, would seem to free this verse from the suspicion of editorial manipulation .

rite that would put them in the same position as Jews.[1] Or the truth may more probably be that Peter and the other Apostles were consciously carrying on and adapting the practice of John the Baptist. He had baptized not only Gentiles but also Jews. So, too, the Apostles called those who heard their preaching to be baptized without distinction of race, but they went on to define this new baptism as " in the name of Jesus Christ ", thus indicating more precisely than had been possible for John the Baptist the character of the fresh allegiance. In accordance with Old Testament usage, the " name " was a token of ownership.[2] To be baptized " in the name of Jesus Christ " signified that the convert belonged to Jesus Christ and owed an absolute allegiance to him.

Since, therefore, there would seem to be no conclusive reason why the evidence of this passage should be set aside, it is unnecessary to have recourse to the hypothesis which would regard baptism as an innovation introduced by the Hellenistic section of the Church.[3] Jackson and Lake, arguing from the fact that special emphasis seems to have been laid on proselyte baptism in the Diaspora, claim that Christian " Hellenists " like the Seven were most probably responsible for the introduction of baptism as the rite of entry into the Christian community. But surely if such an innovation had been made by the Hellenists, it would have been resented by the Judaistic section in Palestine. It is obvious that St. Paul regarded baptism as the normal method of entry into the Church. If this were quite without the authority of the original Apostles, it is surprising that no attempt was made to discredit Paul's apostleship on this ground. But no trace of such a controversy is to be discovered. Further, it may be objected that the affinities of Christian baptism are far more closely with the baptism of John than directly with Jewish proselyte baptism. The evidence connecting proselyte baptism with repentance and forgiveness is, as we have seen, very slender. It is far easier to explain the Christian association of these with baptism as due to a carrying on of one of the outstanding features of John's baptism. But if the connexion be thus with the baptism of John, there is no cogent reason for making the Hellenists responsible for the introduction of the Christian rite. It is far more probable that John's rite was continued and adapted by the Twelve, a number of whom before their call by Jesus had probably been followers of the Baptist.

[1] Cf. Jackson and Lake op. cit., Vol. V, p. 135.

[2] The parallels adduced by Deissmann from secular Greek are interesting, and may throw light on the way baptism " in the name of Jesus Christ " came to be interpreted by converts entering the Church from Hellenistic circles. But in view of the frequent occurrence of ὄνομα in the Septuagint, the *origin* of the New Testament phrases about the " name " may surely be sought with greater probability within Judaism, and especially in those Old Testament passages where the " name " offers a mark of ownership, a token whereby something or someone is designated as belonging to someone else; cf. 2. Sam. 12. 28; Isa. 4. 1; 63. 19; Jer. 7. 10; 14. 9; 15. 16. See also Moulton and Milligan, *Vocabulary of the Greek Testament* (1930), pp. 451–452; P. G. S. Hopwood, *The Religious Experience of the Primitive Church* (1936), pp. 281–286; R. N. Flew, *Jesus and His Church* (1938), pp. 165–166.

[3] Cf. Jackson and Lake, op. cit., Vol. I, pp. 341–343.

Another criticism of the view that baptism was a practice of the most primitive Christian communities was made by J. Weiss. Weiss disputed the universality of early Christian baptism mainly on two grounds: (1) There is no evidence that the hundred and twenty, the Apostles and brethren of the Lord, and the women were ever baptized.[1] (2) Apollos and the " disciples " at Ephesus were counted as Christians, when they had not received Christian baptism. From this evidence Weiss concluded that " baptism was not from the outset a necessary mark of the disciples of Jesus ", and that therefore in such passages as Acts 2. 38 the author " has followed a very natural inclination to date back the later institutions of the Church into its period of origin ".[2] Obviously the judgement of Johannes Weiss on such a point demands careful consideration, nevertheless it would seem possible to question the validity of his argument. It may freely be granted that the hundred and twenty, the Apostles [3] and brethren of the Lord, and the women may not have received water-baptism into the name of the Lord Jesus, but, as we have suggested, there was probably a special reason for this. Christian baptism was an immersion in water united with an experience of " Holy Spirit ". For most early Christians these two seem to have coincided, but for the Apostles and the other original disciples it may well be that, as was suggested above, they were separated. Most, if not all, of them had probably undergone the water-baptism of John; the experience of the Holy Spirit came to them at Pentecost. Thus they received Christian baptism, as it were, in two stages. It may also be significant that this group of Apostles and original disciples seems more or less identical with the group of those for whom the resurrection of Jesus was not only a part of the *kerygma*, but also in some sense an objective and datable fact of their personal experience. Those who had thus " seen " Jesus had less need to be outwardly baptized " into his name ". Christian baptism may be viewed as the counterpart *for the ordinary disciple* of that " meeting " with the risen Christ which constituted the distinctive mark of the " apostle " and that to which he was " sent " to bear witness.[4] Thus we might say that for the average convert baptism " symbolized " the Gospel of the Resurrection.[5] Such an interpretation of Christian baptism would satisfactorily explain why the rite was practised from the first and yet was not, so far as we know, administered to the " apostles " (taking

---

[1] Cf. Acts 1. 14–15.

[2] J. Weiss, *Das Urchristentum* (1917), pp. 36–37 (E. T. pp. 50–51).

[3] Tertullian discusses this difficulty that the Apostles had not received Christian baptism; cf. *de Bapt.* xii. He rejects the view of those who claimed that the covering of the disciples' boat by the waves (cf. Mk. 4. 37) served instead of baptism, or that Peter was sufficiently immersed when he walked upon the water (cf. Matt. 14. 30). Tertullian's own answer to the difficulty is that the Apostles' first call by Jesus, and their inseparable intimacy with him, provided for them, as it were, a " short cut to baptism " (*compendium baptismi*).

[4] Cf. the article by Rengstorf in *Theol. Wört.*, which stresses the connexion between ἀπόστολος and ἀποστέλλω, and finds the essential meaning of the term to lie in the meeting with the Risen Christ and the receiving of a commission from him (*Theol. Wört.* Vol. I, p. 423).

[5] The word " symbolized " must be interpreted in the light of what is said earlier about Biblical symbolism, cf. *supra*, pp. 20 ff.

this word in the widest sense of those who had " seen the Lord ").[1]
Further, it would make still more intelligible the Pauline teaching about
baptism as a dying and *rising* with Christ.

The other part of Weiss's argument, namely that from the examples of
Apollos and the μαθηταί at Ephesus we must infer that " baptism was not
the universal and therefore original practice ", seems to go rather beyond
the evidence. After all, the effect of the narrative in Acts 19. 1–7 is surely
to stress the singularity of these " disciples " and the degree to which they
stood apart from the typical early Christian experience. In particular,
the question put to them in verse 3, so far from suggesting that baptism
was not " universal ", would seem rather itself to testify to the universality with which baptism was acknowledged as the way into the new
community and associated with the gift of the Spirit. Confronted by
their ignorance about the Holy Spirit, St. Paul asked, " Into what then
were you baptized? ", i.e. " what sort of baptism did you receive? "—
the clear implication of the question being, how could they have failed to
receive the Spirit if they had been baptized in the normal Christian way?
The answer, of course, was, as their reply indicated, that they had *not*
been so baptized. But in this respect the impression left by the whole
conversation is that these disciples stood quite apart from the main stream
of Christian practice, and the obvious thing to do was to put the matter
right at once, as Paul did by having them baptized into the name of the
Lord Jesus, and by laying his hands upon them. Thus while the story
clearly shows that *here and there* in the early Church baptism was imperfectly administered and understood in less than its full Christian meaning,
it would not seem to justify Weiss's inference that the author of Acts " has
antedated the situation when he introduces baptism as early as the first
Pentecost ". Such a conclusion could be drawn from this story in Acts 19
only if it could be shown that the position of these disciples at Ephesus
was normal and typical. The whole tone of the story, however, suggests
that it was not. Further, it may again be argued (as it was earlier in the
criticism of Lake's rejection of Acts 2. 38) that the author of Acts has *not*
succumbed to the " very natural inclination to date back the later
institutions of the church into its period of origin ", just because in 2. 38
he mentions baptism without any reference to the laying on of hands.
If stress be laid on the fact that in the narrative of Acts 18. 24–28 Apollos
(unlike the " disciples " of 19. 1) was not " re-baptized ", it may be
observed that he (again unlike them) could be described as " fervent in
spirit " (ζέων τῷ πνεύματι), and so perhaps was regarded as less in need
of the outward rite usually connected with that endowment of the Spirit.
But it is not quite certain—in spite of the silence of Acts—that Apollos

---

[1] The difficulty on this hypothesis would be the baptism of St. Paul himself. He claimed no
less than the other Apostles to have " seen the Lord ", yet he was admitted to the Church
by baptism. Was this an early instance of the Apostle proving himself " all things to all
men "?

was not baptized.[1]   The claim that from the earliest days of the Primitive
Church baptism was universally acknowledged as the appropriate rite of
entry into the fellowship of believers does not mean that every single
convert without exception underwent the rite in exactly the same way, but
rather that, when we have allowed for certain striking exceptions (of
which the author of Acts faithfully gives examples),[2] it would seem that
baptism with water was acknowledged from the Day of Pentecost onwards
by the great majority of disciples as the rite which summed up and
" symbolized " the apostolic Gospel of the Resurrection and was in the
closest way associated with that endowment of the Holy Spirit which was
the distinctive mark of primitive Christianity. We conclude therefore
that, in spite of the arguments which have contested its trustworthiness,
the reference to baptism at the end of Peter's Pentecost sermon is thoroughly
explicable and that we need have no hesitation in accepting it as historical.[3]

The other references in Acts to baptism contain far less detail. The
baptism of Simon Magus (8. 13), of the Ethiopian eunuch (8. 36–38), of
Lydia (16. 15), of the Philippian jailor (16. 33) and of the Corinthians
(18. 8) are all mentioned quite summarily, often in conjunction with a
statement that the converts " heard " or " believed ". These passages
thus provide no further evidence about the relation between baptism,
the gift of the Spirit and the laying on of hands. Taken together, however, they may fairly be quoted in support of the view that the rite of
water-baptism, probably conjoined with some simple confession of faith,[4]
was the normal way by which a convert entered the early Christian
community.[5] It is true that in Chapter 15, where Peter at the Apostolic
Council is speaking of the salvation of the Gentiles, there is no reference to
baptism. All the stress is here laid on " hearing the word of the gospel ",
" believing " (verse 7), receiving the Spirit (8), and salvation through
the grace of the Lord Jesus (11). This may have been intentional, since
Peter was answering " certain of the sect of the Pharisees " who were
insisting on circumcision and the Law of Moses (15. 5). But in view of
the fact that the " believing " and the "faith ", on which such emphasis

---

[1] Cf. R. J. Knowling, *Expositor's Greek Testament*, Vol. II (1912), p. 398, who thinks it probable
that Apollos was baptized; and (more tentatively) Lake and Cadbury in Jackson and Lake,
op. cit., Vol. IV, p. 232.

[2] It is significant that Weiss admitted that Acts 18. 24 ff. and 19. 1–7 are " isolated narratives "
(op. cit., E. T. p. 50).   Does not his argument really " universalize " what was true only of a
quite exceptional set of people?

[3] Cf. also Leipoldt op. cit., p. 34, " Petrus fordert die Taufe bereits an Pfingstfeste: sie ist
also von Anfang an Sitte "; Oepke, *Theol. Wört.*, Vol. I, p. 536 (baptism undoubtedly practised
from the first in the Christian community); and E. Meyer, *Ursprung und Anfänge des Christentums*
Vol. I (1921), pp. 91–92, " Die Taufe gehört zwar zu den Institutionen der Urgemeinde und
wird, als die Mission beginnt, überall geübt und als notwendig betrachtet ", and cf. also op.
cit., Vol. III (1923), pp. 245–246.

[4] Acts 8. 37 is almost certainly not part of the original text, but in view of Rom. 10. 9 (" if thou
confessest with thy mouth Jesus as Lord ") it is probable that at a quite early date some such
confession formed part of the baptismal rite.

[5] Cf. P. G. S. Hopwood, *The Religious Experience of the Primitive Church* (1936), p. 31, " The rite
marked the admission of the new convert who in the very reception of the baptism was aware of
his surrender made to and accepted by Jesus the Lord whom he confessed and whose name was
pronounced over him ".

is laid here, were elsewhere in Acts (as will be shown in a moment) associated in the closest way with the outward rite of baptism, it would seem precarious to press an argument from silence in this passage as though it were equivalent to a positive statement that baptism was non-essential.

The conceptions most frequently linked with baptism in Acts are those of " hearing the word " and " believing ":

" when they *heard* this " (ἀκούσαντες), i.e. Peter's sermon, followed by the call to baptism in the next verse (2. 37–38);

" they that *received his word* (οἱ . . . ἀποδεξάμενοι τὸν λόγον αὐτοῦ) were baptized " (2. 41);

" when they *believed* (ἐπίστευσαν) Philip *preaching good tidings* (εὐαγγελιζομένῳ) concerning the kingdom of God and the name of Jesus Christ, they were baptized " (8. 12);

" Simon also himself *believed* (ἐπίστευσεν): and being baptized . . ." (8. 13);

" Philip . . . *preached* (εὐηγγελίσατο) unto him Jesus "; in the following verse the eunuch asks to be baptized (8. 35–36);

" Lydia *heard* (ἤκουεν) us: whose heart the Lord opened to give heed to the things which were spoken by Paul. And when she was baptized . . ." (16. 14–15);

" And they *spake the word of the Lord* unto him (ἐλάλησαν αὐτῷ τὸν λόγον τοῦ κυρίου) . . . and (he) was baptized . . ." (16. 32–33);

" many of the Corinthians *hearing believed* (ἀκούοντες ἐπίστευον) and were baptized " (18. 8);

" and when they *heard* this (ἀκούσαντες), they were baptized into the name of the Lord Jesus " (19. 5).

(It is noticeable also that in the exceptional case of Cornelius both versions of the story emphasize that the reception of the Spirit was immediately consequent upon the preaching of the word by Peter; cf. " while Peter yet *spake these words*, the Holy Spirit fell on all them which *heard the word* (ἐπὶ πάντας τοὺς ἀκούοντας τὸν λόγον) and " Peter, who shall *speak* unto thee words whereby thou shalt be saved. . . . And *as I began to speak*, the Holy Spirit fell on them . . ."; (10. 44, 11. 14–15). The earlier of these two accounts, as we have seen, records the baptism of Cornelius.)

These passages have been set out at length to call attention to the frequency with which baptism immediately follows upon the mention of " hearing " or " receiving the word " and " believing ". It is clear that for the earliest disciples baptism in some vivid way connoted and " symbolized " the Gospel message. It was what might be called an embodiment of the *kerygma*.

To summarize the evidence about baptism in the Acts of the Apostles: it seems most probable that from the earliest days of the Church a rite of baptism with water was the recognized mode of entry into the Christian community. Sometimes this is simply mentioned (8. 13, 36, 38, 16. 15, 33, 18. 8); at other times it is more fully described as baptism " in the name of Jesus Christ " (2. 38, 10. 48), or " into the name of the Lord Jesus " (8. 16, 19. 5). This baptism is associated with " repentance " (2. 38) and " remission of sins " (2. 38, cf. 22. 16). It is also connected

with the gift of the Holy Spirit (2. 38, cf. also 10. 44–48, though here
baptism follows upon the descent of the Spirit instead of accompanying
it). In other passages where the Spirit is thus referred to the implication
seems to be that, for the Spirit to be given, not only baptism but also the
laying on of hands is necessary (8. 16–17, cf. 19; 9. 17–18; 19. 5–6).
But the most important truth about baptism in the Acts (as the passages
cited in the preceding paragraph suggest) would seem to be that it was
regarded as a practical expression of the meaning of the Gospel, a concrete
embodiment of the apostolic preaching. It connoted remission of sins,
membership of the new community, the endowment of the Holy Spirit;
all those blessings of the New Age the offer of which had been made in the
preaching of the Word. For a man to submit to baptism was the
recognized way of giving expression to the fact that he had " heard "
or " received the word "—that he " believed ". To recognize the
emphasis with which this aspect of baptism is brought out in the Acts is
by no means to attribute a merely subjective significance to the rite.
Submission to baptism was an expression of the convert's faith, but it was
not the convert who gave the rite its significance. To repeat what was
said earlier, baptism " symbolized " the Gospel of the Resurrection. The
rite was there already given, a sacrament of " realized eschatology " that
outwardly embodied the meaning and essence of the Gospel.[1] The
convert could appropriate that meaning for himself by undergoing
baptism. Sometimes that meaning was so profound that the baptismal
rite could actually serve as the occasion for the convert's reception of that
distinctive Christian endowment which the early Church called the gift
of the Spirit. At other times, and it would seem increasingly as time went
on, that gift of the Spirit became associated not directly with the original
rite of baptism but with a second rite, that of the laying on of hands,
often united with the first, but sometimes separated from it. For the
overwhelming majority of early disciples this outward embodiment of the
Gospel was normal and necessary. With modern examples from the
mission field to help us to understand what baptism may mean to a
convert to-day, we need not doubt that for countless first-century
Christians, as for their Master, at the moment of baptism the " heavens
were opened ".[2] Here and there, however, there were those who entered
into the fullest Christian experience without the aid of any mediating
" sign ". Such examples need provide a cause of wonder only to those

---

[1] Cf. Oepke, *Theol. Wört.*, Vol. I, p. 538, who emphasizes that in the New Testament baptism is a
" real dealing of the Holy Spirit with sinful men "; this excludes equally both a superstitious
understanding of the rite and also one that is merely symbolical (in the modern sense of that
word).

[2] Cf. Hopwood op. cit., pp. 280–281, " The act of being baptized often coincided with a very
sacred religious experience for the convert, whereby he had broken with his sinful past and
submitted to Christ. . . . As with their Master, the believers discovered that the very intensity
of their baptismal experience led them to feel as if the heavens were opening and the Spirit of
God descending upon them. The baptized convert passed into the Spirit-controlled community, and shared in the new life inspired by the Spirit."

who fail to allow for the working of the principle, *Deus non alligatur sacramentis suis.*[1]

To view Christian baptism in this light as the outward embodiment of what the Gospel means, the " symbol " of the resurrection faith, enables us both to do justice to the various baptismal references in Acts, and also the better to understand the development of baptismal teaching in the Pauline Epistles, and in subsequent New Testament writings. But why the Christian rite of initiation from the earliest days involved a continuance of water-baptism, despite the Baptist's teaching which would more naturally have suggested its abandonment, that is a problem for which the book of Acts offers no direct solution. Certain influences which may have worked powerfully for the continuance of water-baptism have already been indicated, notably the striking example of the baptism of Jesus. But more than this is needed to explain why the early Christian embodiment of the *kerygma* took the form of an immersion in water. Here, as elsewhere, the narrative of Acts raises a question to which it does not provide the answer. To a further consideration of this problem we shall revert later in our enquiry.[2]

[1] Cf. Acts 10. 45 " they of the circumcision which believed were amazed . . . because that on the Gentiles also was poured out the gift of the Holy Ghost ".
[2] Cf. *infra*, pp. 117 ff.

5

Baptism in the Pauline Epistles

THE explicit references to baptism in the Pauline Epistles, though full of significance, are comparatively few in number. This is not surprising if due attention be paid to the purpose of these letters. It has been suggested that the relative importance of a doctrine for St. Paul may often stand in inverse proportion to the number of times it is referred to in the Epistles. This may be an exaggeration, but it is certainly true to say that in none of the extant letters, not even in Romans or Ephesians, is there anything that may be regarded as, in the strict sense, a systematic treatment of Christian theology. It follows as a consequence of this that the importance of a doctrine for St. Paul is never to be measured exactly by the amount of space accorded to it in the Epistles. Each of these Epistles was written to answer particular questions and to meet the needs of a particular group of early Christians. If, for example, none of the Corinthians had felt difficulties about belief in the resurrection, we might never have known the precise grounds on which the Apostle based his own conviction about the life after death.[1] If all the Corinthians had partaken of the Lord's Supper as they should have done, with due decorum and with consideration for their neighbour, we might forever have gone without St. Paul's narrative concerning the institution of the Eucharist.[2] It would seem at times as though some of the passages most vital for our knowledge of Pauline theology are available for us to-day, humanly speaking, because of the failures and shortcomings and imperfect beliefs of certain first-century Christians. Thus it is quite illegitimate to argue that because a particular doctrine is sparingly mentioned in the extant Epistles it therefore had little significance for the author of them. The importance of repentance, for example, as an initial stage of the Christian life is abundantly evident from the frequent use of μετάνοια and μετανοέω in the Synoptic Gospels and the Acts of the Apostles. But, if we were to judge from the number of references to repentance in the Pauline Epistles, we might imagine that the conception meant hardly anything to St. Paul, for he uses the noun only three times and the verb but once.[3] If it be remembered, however, that all the Epistles were addressed to believers already converted, who had " repented " at the outset of their Christian life, the infrequent use of the words by St. Paul is fully explained.

This particular illustration is not without a bearing on the subject of St. Paul's references to baptism. " Baptism " and " repentance " are

---

[1] Cf. I Cor. 15. 1 ff.   [2] Cf. I Cor. 11. 20 ff.
[3] Noun: Rom. 2. 4; 2 Cor. 7. 9, 10; verb: 2 Cor. 12. 21.

closely linked in the Synoptic Gospels and in the Acts. St. Paul's readers had *repented* at the beginning of their Christian life; they had also been *baptized*. By all probability we might have expected no more frequent reference to the latter than to the former. To approach the subject from this angle is to realize how thoroughly significant St. Paul's references to baptism actually are. On the analogy of his use of μετάνοια and μετανοέω he need not have used βάπτισμα and βαπτίζω more than three or four times. A glance at the Concordance reveals that he used the noun on three occasions and the verb no fewer than thirteen times. There is also one occurrence of the verb ἀπολούομαι and one of the noun λουτρόν, besides three uses of the verb σφραγίζομαι which are most probably to be taken as allusions to baptism. For St. Paul a Christian's baptism was something to be remembered. At certain stages in the argument of the Epistles he cannot draw out the inner meaning of some elements of Christian faith and experience more effectively than by recalling his readers to the moment of their baptism and by emphasizing certain implications of the act by which they were incorporated into the Body of Christ.

It will be convenient to arrange the Pauline references to baptism in three groups:

(*a*) Three of the passages about baptism which occur in 1 Corinthians.

(*b*) Five passages taken from various Epistles, in which the meaning of the rite is more fully expressed.

(*c*) Two references in Ephesians (an Epistle which some scholars would regard as not written by St. Paul himself), together with three other passages employing the verb σφραγίζομαι and therefore probably to be taken as allusions to baptism.

We go on to examine these in order.

(*a*) *Three passages in 1 Corinthians* (1. 13–17, 10. 2, 15.29).

Is Christ divided? was Paul crucified for you? or were ye baptized into the name of Paul? I thank God that I baptized none of you, save Crispus and Gaius; lest any man should say that ye were baptized into my name. And I baptized also the household of Stephanas: besides, I know not whether I baptized any other. For Christ sent me not to baptize, but to preach the gospel: not in wisdom of words, lest the cross of Christ should be made void (1 Cor. 1. 13–17).

St. Paul while he was at Ephesus had received news through " those of Chloe " about the prevalence of party strife in the church at Corinth. The various sections rallied themselves under the name of some Christian leader, Paul or Apollos or Cephas. St. Paul devotes the first section of this letter to an appeal that the Corinthians should abandon this quarrelsome spirit. In particular he asks, " Was it Paul who was crucified for you? Was it in Paul's name that you were baptized? " St. Paul implies that the using of his name as a watchword seems almost to suggest the absurdity that *he* had died on the cross for them, that *his* name had been pronounced over them in the solemn moment of baptism. He goes on to record how thankful he is that, in fact, very few at Corinth had been baptized *by him* (much less baptized *into his name*). Only Crispus and Gaius (yes, and the household of Stephanas) had this personal link with him—just as well, in view of the way in which the Corinthians had misunderstood things![1] The horror with which St. Paul contemplates such a complete misconception of the nature and meaning of Christian baptism causes him to give a characteristically emphatic expression to his conviction, " Christ did not send me to baptize, but to preach the gospel ". Far better, St. Paul implies, that he should confine himself to his special work of preaching the Gospel, for which Christ " sent " him (as an " apostle "), and that baptism should be administered by other less prominently placed Church leaders. There would then perhaps be less danger of the Corinthians so failing to grasp what baptism meant as to think that they could be baptized into any other name but that of Christ. Interpreted thus, the passage lends no support to the view that St. Paul is here making light of baptism and depreciating its value. On the contrary, it was just because he had so high a sense of what baptism meant that he regarded with such abhorrence its debasement by Corinthian partizanship. It is worth remarking that *twice* in this Epistle the Apostle complains of the presence of " cliques " (σχίσματα) at Corinth, as that which prevented the proper understanding of a Christian rite.[2] Baptism was misunderstood because the names of Paul, Apollos and Cephas became watchwords of party strife. The Eucharist was misunderstood because the social barriers separating rich and poor were maintained even at the Lord's Supper. In each context the language used by St. Paul marks his sense of how serious was the denial of Christian κοινωνία. But it would be a grave error of exegesis to let Paul's outspokenness in this first chapter of I Corinthians lessen our appreciation of the profound meaning which he discovers in baptism elsewhere in his Epistles.

For I would not, brethren, have you ignorant, how that our fathers were all under the cloud, and all passed through the sea; and were all baptized unto Moses in the cloud and in the sea; and did all eat the same spiritual meat; and did all drink the same spiritual drink: for they drank of a spiritual rock that followed them: and the rock was Christ (I Cor. 10. 1–4).

In this passage St. Paul is warning the Corinthians by means of an example drawn from Hebrew history. Since the Christian community is the new " People of God ", there must be a correspondence between the experience of Christians and that of Israel. Thus it was, argues St. Paul, that " our fathers " had their sacred rites. Just as Christians are baptized *into Christ*, so the patriarchs were baptized *into Moses*. Just as

[1] Cf. J. Moffatt, *I Corinthians, Moffatt New Testament Commentary* (1938), p. 11 ; Dr. Moffatt points out that in some of the mystery cults " the initiated person honoured the priest or mystagogue who introduced him into the mysteries, as his ' father ' ".

[2] Cf. I Cor. I. 10; 11. 18.

Christians partake of food and drink at the Lord's Supper, so those of old ate the same spiritual food and drank the same spiritual drink. Yet the result of it all was that most of them displeased God and perished in the desert. Let Israel's experience be a warning to the new Israel. Their sacred rites could not save them. " Sacraments are no safeguard for a careless life which takes liberties with itself." [1] In this passage St. Paul utters a solemn warning against any merely superstitious attitude towards a Christian sacrament. Only if the Spirit of God is able to work through the outward act can the inward grace be received.

> Else what shall they do which are baptized for the dead? If the dead are not raised at all, why then are they baptized for them? (1 Cor. 15. 29).

In the chapter about the resurrection there occurs this verse in which St. Paul seems to be using an *argumentum ad hominem*.[2] He finds confirmation for his teaching about the life after death by referring to a particular belief and practice of the Corinthians themselves. The exact nature of the practice is far from clear, but the most probable view is that it was a custom at Corinth for certain Christians to undergo baptism by proxy, as it were, for the benefit of departed relatives or friends who themselves had not been baptized. St. Paul seizes upon this usage and argues from it : if there is no such thing as the resurrection, then what can be the meaning of this current practice of getting baptized on behalf of the dead? He is not to be understood then as pronouncing any judgement upon the validity of this practice, rather he seizes upon it in passing to confirm a conclusion already established by other arguments. If those other arguments have not already convinced the Corinthians, then let them ponder the fact that a particular practice of their own implies the very belief they are trying to question. How illogical to doubt the resurrection !—baptism for the dead is meaningless if there is no future life.

(*b*) *Five passages from various Epistles* (1 Cor. 6. 11, 12. 13; Gal. 3. 27; Rom. 6. 3–4; Col. 2. 12)

This group contains the most important Pauline statements concerning baptism. To appreciate their full significance we need to pay attention to some of the other things spoken of in the neighbourhood of these references. It will be observed that in these " baptismal contexts ", as we may call them, a number of associated ideas tend to recur.

> Or know ye not that the unrighteous shall not inherit the kingdom of God? . . . And such were some of you : but ye were washed, but ye were sanctified, but ye were justified in the name of the Lord Jesus Christ, and in the Spirit of our God (1 Cor. 6. 9, 11).

This is one of a number of places where St. Paul emphasizes how absolute

[1] Moffatt, op. cit., p. 129.
[2] Cf. H. A. A. Kennedy, *St. Paul and the Mystery Religions* (1913), p. 253, " It is wholly illegitimate to suppose that because Paul pronounces no condemnation on a custom to which he refers, he must have given it his approval. This is surely a misapprehension of the very nature of an *argumentum ad hominem* ".

E

and decisive for the Christian is the contrast, in respect of moral conduct, between the old life and the new. Here, as elsewhere, he reinforces a moral appeal by solemnly reminding his readers that a Christian is a man who once was *baptized*. Earlier in the chapter he has been telling the Corinthians that Christians ought not to go to law with one another in pagan courts, and, further, that no immoral person can inherit the Kingdom of God. He goes on to give examples of the flagrant immoralities for which Corinth was notorious even in pagan eyes. Once some of them practised these things. But now that is all over and done with! Something happened to them when they became Christians. They were washed in the water of baptism: [1] that meant cleansing from sin, consecration to God's service, being " put right " in God's sight. In other words, a Christian who lives an immoral life is utterly belying the meaning of his own baptism. This passage is important not only because it uses the phrase " in the name of the Lord Jesus Christ " and speaks of the Spirit of our God (both of which recall similar language used about baptism in Acts), but also because it links baptism with the great Pauline conceptions of justification and sanctification. We notice in the immediate context the idea of " inheriting the kingdom " (verses 9–10), the new moral life (implied by the contrast in verses 9–11), and the reference to the action of God in the resurrection of the Lord with its counterpart for the believer (verse 14).

For as the body is one, and hath many members, and all the members of the body, being many, are one body; so also is Christ. For in one Spirit were we all baptized into one body, whether Jews or Greeks, whether bond or free; and were all made to drink of one Spirit (1 Cor. 12. 12–13).

A further manifestation of disunion at Corinth lay in the proneness of some to lay an undue emphasis upon certain " spiritual gifts ". Various members of the Church prided themselves on their particular endowment, for example, the power to speak with a tongue or to prophesy or the gift of healing. St. Paul replies by making a special application of the familiar illustration about the " body " and its " members ", and by connecting it with baptism and the Spirit. The Christian community is a Body. When the Corinthians were baptized into Christ they became corporately members of that Body. That was what their baptism meant. It was the work of God's Spirit, and it was of that Spirit that they were made to " drink " in the moment of their baptism, when they were plunged beneath the water.[2] As Dr. Moffatt has said, St. Paul " never contemplates any

---

[1] That ἀπελούσασθε could be intended purely as a metaphor with no reference to baptism seems impossible in view of the occurrence in the same verse of the mention of the " name of Jesus Christ " and of the Spirit of God, which we have already seen to be conceptions intimately associated with Christian baptism; cf. also Acts 22. 16, βάπτισαι καὶ ἀπόλουσαι in a narrative of St. Paul's conversion.

[2] I. Abrahams, *Studies in Pharisaism and the Gospels*, First Series (1917), p. 43, has shown how natural it was in the Old Testament to use in connexion with the " Spirit " verbs appropriate in relation to water; e.g. שָׁפַךְ cf. Joel 2. 28 (LXX ἐκχεῶ). Also שָׁאַב " to draw " (water) is used in a rabbinic passage of " drawing " the holy Spirit. The use of ποτίζω is probably to be explained as a natural extension of such a usage.

baptism of the Spirit as a higher experience of Christians "; when they first were received into the Church, incorporated into the Body of Christ by baptism, that initial act was done through the agency of the Spirit.[1] We notice in this context (besides the reiterated emphasis on the Spirit) that Christians are baptized " into one body ", a phrase which, in view of what is said in verse 12, represents what Paul elsewhere expresses by the phrase " into Christ ".[2] There is also a stress on baptism as the sacrament of unity, the " effective symbol " whereby all Christians are made one in Christ and racial and social distinctions transcended (". . . whether Jews or Greeks, whether bond or free . . ."). Further, we note that among the " spiritual gifts " spoken of in the earlier verses is " faith " (verse 9).

For ye are all sons of God, through faith, in Christ Jesus. For as many of you as were baptized into Christ did put on Christ. There can be neither Jew nor Greek, there can be neither bond nor free, there can be no male and female : for ye all are one man in Christ Jesus. And if ye are Christ's, then are ye Abraham's seed, heirs according to promise (Gal. 3. 26–29).

St. Paul is contrasting the former condition of his Galatian readers with their new state after their conversion. Formerly they had been " wards in discipline " [3] under Law (verses 23–24) ; now, the Faith has come, and the old tutelage is at an end (verse 25). Then follows the passage quoted above. Again, St. Paul is reminding a group of Christians about the meaning of their baptism. There was a moment in the life of all of them when they stripped off their garments and went down into the water. They were baptized " into Christ ", so as to belong to Christ. They came up out of the water and put on their garments. As they robed themselves again, it meant that in that very moment they " put on Christ ". Leipoldt has argued that this passage can rightly be understood only in the light of the mystery religions.[4] It may be granted that the parallels quoted by Leipoldt show that it was customary for the initiate to be clothed in fresh garments. But does this necessitate a direct reference in St. Paul's language to a contemporary cult? It seems probable that the link, if it existed at all, was far more indirect. Canon Knox has shown that the Judaism of the Dispersion, like the rest of the Græco-Roman world, was considerably influenced by the language of the mysteries. But, as he says, " the whole use of metaphors of clothing was so familiar in the conventional language of Judaism that it could be adapted without any thought of its origin ".[5] The application of such language to baptism was all the more natural since immersion necessarily involved the putting off and putting on of garments.[6] Thus any explicit and direct reference of

[1] Moffatt, op. cit., p. 186.   [2] Gal. 3. 27 ; Rom. 6. 3.
[3] Cf. Moffatt's rendering of verse 24.
[4] Leipoldt, op. cit., p. 60, " Es gibt nur einen Weg, den Tatbestand zu klären. Er führt nicht ins Judentum, sondern in die Mysterien, und ihre Vorgeschichte ".
[5] W. L. Knox, *St. Paul and the Church of the Gentiles* (1939), p. 138.
[6] It would appear that the use of a special baptismal robe cannot be dated with any certainty before the fourth century A.D., cf. Knox, op. cit., p. 138 *n.* 1.

St. Paul's language in this passage to the practice of the mystery religions seems quite unnecessary. If there was any link, it was probably indirect and was mediated through Jewish channels. It may further be questioned, however, whether even an indirect influence is needed to account for St. Paul's thought here, in view of such Old Testament phrases as " the garments of salvation " and " the robe of righteousness " (Isa. 61. 10); or again, the " putting on " of " righteousness as a breastplate " (Isa. 59. 17). Again, in one of Zechariah's visions Joshua the High Priest has his " filthy garments " removed and instead is clothed in " rich apparel " (Zech. 3. 4). The imagery which likens a new status and a new kind of life to a fresh garment belongs no less to Hebraic than to Hellenistic thought.

In the context of this passage in Galatians we notice that St. Paul records some further associations of baptism. In the verses immediately preceding (23-25) we observe, besides a fourfold mention of " faith ", the thought of " justification ", already found in an earlier " baptismal context ".[1] Again, in the succeeding verses there is an emphasis on the abrogation of all distinctions (not only of race and status, as in 1 Cor. 12. 13, but here also of sex) in a new unity realized " in Christ Jesus " (verse 28). A further consequence of baptism is that, as belonging to Christ, believers can claim the privileges formerly peculiar to the Chosen People, Christians are now " Abraham's seed, heirs according to promise " (verse 29). But the " associated idea " which St. Paul develops most fully in this baptismal context is that of Divine Sonship, both the unique Sonship of Jesus and the derived sonship of the believer. That the link between " sonship " and " baptism " is close becomes clear when we notice how the verse affirming the " sonship " of Christians (verse 26) is followed immediately by the verse recalling, and expounding the meaning of, their baptism (verse 27). This association is no surprise to those who remember that " Sonship " is a prominent feature in the story of our Lord's baptism. This thought of Divine Sonship is drawn out and made more explicit in the opening verses of Chapter 4 (treated as part of the same paragraph with the concluding verses of Chapter 3 by Westcott and Hort). The new life in Christ is one of " freedom ", the freedom of a son contrasted with the " slavery " of one who is " under age ". This new dispensation began when God " sent forth his Son " ($\dot{\epsilon}\xi\alpha\pi\acute{\epsilon}\sigma\tau\epsilon\iota\lambda\epsilon\nu$ . . . $\tau\grave{o}\nu$ $\upsilon\acute{\iota}\grave{o}\nu$ $\alpha\grave{\upsilon}\tau\upsilon\hat{\upsilon}$) to deliver those under the Law, that they might receive the status of sonship. The counterpart of this is seen whenever a Christian convert can look back to the moment when into his heart God " sent forth the Spirit of his Son ($\dot{\epsilon}\xi\alpha\pi\acute{\epsilon}\sigma\tau\epsilon\iota\lambda\epsilon\nu$ . . . $\tau\grave{o}$ $\pi\nu\epsilon\hat{\upsilon}\mu\alpha$ $\tau\upsilon\hat{\upsilon}$ $\upsilon\acute{\iota}\upsilon\hat{\upsilon}$ $\alpha\grave{\upsilon}\tau\upsilon\hat{\upsilon}$), crying Abba Father ". We note the repetition of the same verb in the same *aorist* tense, which marks the re-enactment, at a particular moment in the life of the believer, of that divine deed that was achieved once for all in the coming of Jesus Christ. In the second of these two occurrences of

[1] Cf. 1 Cor. 6. 11.

the verb ἐξαπέστειλεν, the aorist tense, as so often in the New Testament, looks back to something that, for each first-century convert, was done once for all at the moment of Christian baptism.

Thus at the heart of one of his most characteristic Epistles St. Paul gives expression to the vivid significance of baptism. Once again we can scarcely state the truth better than by saying that for St. Paul, as for those who were before him in the Gospel, baptism is a sacrament of realized eschatology. St. Paul looks back to baptism as that which marked for each Christian the inauguration of the New Age, the transition from the old life to the new. Everything began for the convert when he came up out of the water and robed himself afresh in his garments. It was really nothing less than a putting on of Christ. By that act he came to share in all the privileges of the new life; he was an heir, he was free, he was a son. He received the Spirit, and heard in his own heart the echo of the very cry which Jesus uttered in his moment of closest communion with God (cf. Mk. 14. 36 " Abba, Father . . ."). Thus the essence of the Christian initiation was that thereby through the agency of the Spirit the Christian entered upon the life of " sonship ". As he " put on Christ ", he was endowed with all the benefits of his new freedom. The gateway through which he entered upon this " inheritance " was the rite of baptism.

What shall we say then? Shall we continue in sin, that grace may abound? God forbid. We who died to sin, how shall we any longer live therein? Or are ye ignorant that all we who were baptized into Christ Jesus were baptized into his death? We were buried therefore with him through baptism into death: that like as Christ was raised from the dead through the glory of the Father, so we also might walk in newness of life (Rom. 6. 1–4).

Here there is essentially the same stress on the " newness " of the Christian life, though the angle of approach is slightly different. St. Paul still reverts to the moment of baptism as that which sums up everything that Christianity means, but the point of comparison which he seizes upon now is not the putting on of the garment after baptism, but rather the actual immersion in and emergence from the water. He is answering a false deduction that might be drawn from his argument about divine grace in Chapter 5. If grace is so essential and all-important (someone might say), then why not go on sinning so as to give grace the greater scope and opportunity? For St. Paul such a conclusion has only to be thought of to be instantly rejected. The man who suggests it must have completely forgotten the meaning of his own baptism! A Christian is a man who at a particular moment once for all *died* to sin (we notice the aorist again ἀπεθάνομεν): how, then, can he do anything which would mean *living* in sin? This is what being baptized " into Christ Jesus " means, a re-enact-ment for the believer of what once happened to our Lord. The convert is plunged into the water: that means *dying* with Christ; he remains there for a moment under the surface: that means being *buried* with him; he emerges from the water: that means *being raised up* with him. Thus the

physical actions involved in baptism have no meaning unless they signify
that the man who has submitted to the rite has thereby died to sin and
must henceforth walk " in newness of life ", that is what makes any
thought of " continuing in sin " absurd! [1] In the latter part of the
chapter (verses 12–23) St. Paul shows that the practical implication of all
this is that we must " become what we are ". The Christian life means
" freedom "—not freedom *to* sin but freedom *from* sin. His love for contrasting terms leads him also to describe this new life as still a life of
slavery; but a new sort of servitude, slavery to righteousness (verse 18)
or to God (verse 22).

It is worth noticing that in another Epistle St. Paul expresses this same
thought of the " death to sin " by saying that " those who belong to Christ
Jesus crucified the flesh with its passions and lusts " (Gal. 5. 24). This
passage in Galatians is not a " baptismal context ", but the aorist tense
($\dot{\epsilon}\sigma\tau\alpha\acute{\upsilon}\rho\omega\sigma\alpha\nu$), taken in conjunction with what is said in Rom. 6 about the
connexion of baptism with " dying " and " rising ", suggests that in
Gal. 5. 24 St. Paul was thinking of that particular moment in the life of
the believer when, at baptism, there had taken place a dramatic re-enact-
ment of Christ's death to sin.[2] Further, when we bear in mind that
" those who belong to Christ Jesus " ($o\dot{\iota} \ldots \tau o\hat{\upsilon} \ X\rho\iota\sigma\tau o\hat{\upsilon} \ '\mathrm{I}\eta\sigma o\hat{\upsilon}$) is a natural
way of describing those who elsewhere are said to have been baptized
" into Christ Jesus " (Rom. 6. 3) or " into Christ " (Gal. 3. 27), and also
that Gal. 5 is the chapter in which the Apostle enumerates " the fruit
of the Spirit ", there seems good reason for the view that baptism was
probably in St. Paul's mind when he wrote Gal. 5. 24, though he does not
explicitly mention it.

Similarly it is noteworthy that in Rom. 8 the thought of " dying " (to
sin) and " rising again " (in a new moral life) is closely linked with the
conception of the " Spirit " (verses 9–11), while the Spirit is connected
with " sonship " (verses 14–15, cf. 23).[3] In this context we also find
" slavery " contrasted with " freedom " (verses 15, 21), the mention of
Christians as " heirs " (verse 17), and three references to the idea of
" glory " (verses 17, 18, 21). Thus several of the phrases Paul uses here to
describe the " life of the Spirit " are conceptions that elsewhere are
expressly associated with baptism.[4] That Rom. 8 lacks any explicit
mention of the rite is probably as accidental as the fact that it equally

---

[1] The implication of $\mathring{\eta}$ $\dot{\alpha}\gamma\nuο\epsilon\hat{\iota}\tau\epsilon$; (verse 3), in a letter to a church in which Paul himself had
not yet preached, would seem to be that baptism and the death of Christ were already connected
in the common tradition.

[2] Cf. G. S. Duncan, *Galatians, Moffatt New Testament Commentary*, (1934), p. 176, " The tense
of the Greek verb makes it plain that he is . . . referring, not to a process of spiritual ' crucifixion ' continued throughout life, but to an act consummated at a definite moment in time. In
short, he is referring to what took place at baptism."

[3] Note that the " cry " of the Spirit is again " Abba Father ", as in Gal. 4. 6.

[4] Cf. Sanday and Headlam, *Romans I. C. C.* (1902), p. 201, where it is significant that in the
paraphrase the meaning of the aorist $\dot{\epsilon}\lambda\acute{\alpha}\beta\epsilon\tau\epsilon$ (verse 15) is drawn out by the words " *when you
were first baptized*, and the communication of the Holy Spirit sealed your admission into the
Christian fold. . . .'' (italics mine).

lacks any explicit mention of *faith*. The one no less than the other must have been in the background of the Apostle's thought.

To return to the "baptismal context" of Rom. 6: besides the primary emphasis on baptism being "into Christ Jesus" and connoting "death to sin" and "rising again" to a new moral life (the thought is carried on throughout verses 5–11), we observe also as associated conceptions, the stress on the action of (God) the Father (verse 4), the strongly eschato-logical word "glory" (verse 4), and a reference to "justification" (verse 7). Thus yet again we mark the recurrence of what we are coming to recognize as "baptismal ideas".

For in him dwelleth all the fulness of the Godhead bodily, and in him ye are made full, who is the head of all principality and power: in whom ye were also circumcised with a circumcision not made with hands, in the putting off of the body of the flesh, in the circumcision of Christ; having been buried with him in baptism, wherein ye were also raised with him through faith in the working of God, who raised him from the dead. And you, being dead through your trespasses and the uncircumcision of your flesh, you, I say, did he quicken together with him, having forgiven us all our trespasses (Col. 2. 9–13).

Again, in this Epistle the same connexion is traced between baptism and the "new life" of the Christian. In the earlier part of Colossians St. Paul has been restating the essential truth of Christian faith in the endeavour to answer the "false teachers". Over against this partly Jewish, partly Oriental theosophy, with its hierarchy of spiritual orders and its insistence on "knowledge", asceticism and the observance of ceremonies, the Apostle maintains the complete sufficiency of Christ. From him all things come; in him all things consist; to him all things lead up. He himself is the "mystery" of God. He, in whom all the treasures of wisdom and knowledge are hidden, alone can supply all that the Colossians are seeking in vain elsewhere, "for in him dwells all the *pleroma* [1] of Deity as a complete and organic whole".[2] He who is the head of all rule and authority alone can satisfy every need of the Colossians —"in him is all the fulness . . . and in him you have been made full ($\pi\epsilon\pi\lambda\eta\rho\omega\mu\acute{\epsilon}\nu o\iota$)". All this follows from the fact (continues St. Paul) that it is in him that you received the spiritual counterpart of bodily circumcision. The "putting off of the body of the flesh" and the "circumcision of Christ" are particular ways of describing what Paul called the "death to sin". All this was realized for the Christian in that rite which re-enacted Christ's renunciation of evil, namely baptism.[3]

[1] Dibelius, (in *Handbuch zum Neuen Testament*, ad loc., suggests that $\pi\lambda\acute{\eta}\rho\omega\mu a$ was a technical term of the Colossian "syncretists"; they applied it, no doubt, to the $\sigma\tauo\iota\chi\epsilon\hat{\iota}a$: St. Paul boldly appropriates their own term and applies it to Christ.
[2] For this interpretation of the difficult word $\sigma\omega\mu a\tau\iota\kappa\hat{\omega}s$ (only here in the New Testament) cf. A. S. Peake in *Expositor's Greek Testament*, ad loc.
[3] This "death to sin" is implied by $\sigma\upsilon\nu\tau a\phi\acute{\epsilon}\nu\tau\epsilon s$ in verse 12; thus we may say that this passage in Colossians combines the thought of Gal. 3. 27 (baptism as a change of moral garments, as it were) with the thought of Rom. 6. 3–4 (baptism as a dying to sin and a rising again to a new moral life). The only difference is that while in the Galatians passage the stress is laid on the "putting *on*" of Christ, here the comparison with circumcision makes more natural an

Nor is that all: it is in baptism that the Colossians were also *raised* together with Christ through their faith in the activity of God who raised him from the dead.   Canon Knox thinks that the Colossian teachers allowed that baptism was " a suitable form of lustration for the laying aside of the sins of the past ", but claimed that for further knowledge and progress other rites were needed.[1]   St. Paul's aim is to show that *everything* needful for salvation is given in baptism, which was not only a " death " (to past sin) but also a " rising again " (to a new life).   Thus the Colossian asceticism was mistaken: no rite other than baptism was necessary.

The thought of the whole passage is closely parallel to that of the section in Romans, which we have just examined, where St. Paul saw Christian baptism as the dramatic re-enactment of the death, burial and resurrection of Jesus.   As in that passage, so here, the practical conclusion is that God who raised Jesus can, with him, " raise " also the man, who has been baptized into Christ and give him the power to live a new sort of moral life.   This new moral life of the believer is as it were an extension of the risen life of the Redeemer.   To this conception already set forth in Romans, St. Paul adds here the striking thought that baptism is the Christian counterpart of Jewish circumcision.   What circumcision meant under the Old Dispensation, that, and no less, is the meaning of baptism for those living in the New Age.   The precise exposition of the verses that follow is confused in part owing to the extreme flexibility with which St. Paul uses the image of " death ".   Thus the death implied by $\sigma υ ν τ α φ \acute{\epsilon} ν τ ε ς$ in verse 12 and expressed by $\acute{\epsilon} κ \ ν ε κ ρ \hat{ω} ν$ is clearly the " death to sin "[2] of Rom. 6. 2–4.   In verse 13, however, death is the condition of the man still in the grip of sin and the " uncircumcision of the flesh ".[3]   Thus in successive verses the same metaphor of " death " is used first of the *new* Christian life, and secondly of the *old* pre-conversion state.   Fortunately, the swiftness of the transition from the one use of the illustration to the other, and the extreme difficulty of interpreting all the details of the clauses in verses 14–15, do not obscure the main trend of the argument.   St. Paul's claim is that the Colossians need no further lustration to make them " bear fruit and increase "; if they will but accept and appropriate all that was offered to them in the moment of their baptism,

---

emphasis on the " putting *off* " of that " body of the flesh " in which sin has entrenched itself.

There is a variant reading for " baptism " in verse 12; B $\aleph^c$ D* Pap. 46 read $\beta α π τ ι σ μ \hat{ω}$, while $\aleph$* A C D^c read $\beta α π τ \acute{ι} σ μ α τ ι$.   There is a good deal to be said for the former, as the less usual word for Christian baptism.   Whichever be preferred, the sense is the same.

[1] Knox, op. cit., p. 149.

[2] Note how this thought is taken up again in Col. 3. 3 ($\acute{α} π ε θ \acute{α} ν ε τ ε \ γ \acute{α} ρ$ . . .) and applied practically in 3. 5 ($ν ε κ ρ \acute{ω} σ α τ ε \ ο \mathring{υ} ν \ τ \grave{α} \ μ \acute{ε} λ η$ . . .).   The baptismal symbolism of putting off and putting on a garment is evidently not far from Paul's mind, cf. 3. 8 ($\acute{α} π \acute{ο} θ ε σ θ ε$) and 3. 12 ($\acute{\epsilon} ν δ \acute{υ} σ α σ θ ε$).   The way in which the Apostle frequently employs language like this suggests the determinative place which baptism occupied in his thought.

[3] The phrase seems to be applied to the Colossians with a double reference, first in the literal sense as belonging to a community largely Gentile in origin (cf. also 1. 21, 27; 3. 7), but also in the profounder sense as those who have not yet received the " circumcision not made with hands ".

they are free to live a new life in the power of Christ, who has overcome by the victory of the Cross every force that might oppose them, whether it be of Jewish Law or of " gnostic " hierarchy.

Among the associated ideas in this baptismal context, besides the governing thought of the death, burial and resurrection of Christ with their counterpart in the life of the believer, and the comparison of baptism with " spiritual circumcision ", we observe also that the Christian " death to sin " is compared to the putting off (of a garment) (verse 11), and, further, that another implication of the phrase " the circumcision of Christ " is that Christians are the " New Israel ". Here, too, there is an emphasis on " faith ", and also on the " activity " of God, as the power which can be seen at work both in the resurrection of Jesus from the dead and in the " quickening " of the believer to a new moral life (verses 12–13). In verse 13 there is a reference to " forgiveness of trespasses ".[1] The " blotting out " of the " bond written in ordinances " (verse 14) is but another way of describing the " justification " which we have noted previously in several other baptismal contexts. In verses 14 and 15 there is a swift succession of metaphors—the annulment of an indictment or note-of-hand, the " nailing " of it to the Cross, the " despoiling "[2] of the principalities and powers, and the public " exhibition " of them in a triumphal procession; all these varied and vivid images serve to bring out yet more clearly the decisive completeness and sufficiency of that victory over the powers of evil which Christ won upon the Cross; the victory which makes possible for the Christian that " death to sin " which here, as in Rom. 6, is an essential part of the meaning of baptism. Our examination of this passage confirms the impression left on our mind by other Pauline teaching, namely that when the Apostle was expounding some of his profoundest doctrine about the death of Christ it was natural for him to link it all up with that rite of baptism through which the benefits of Christ's death and resurrection were mediated to the believer.[3]

(c) *Two passages in Ephesians* (4. 5, 5. 26) *and three passages containing the verb* σφραγίζομαι (2 *Cor.* 1. 22; *Eph.* 1. 13, 4. 30)

There is one body, and one Spirit, even as also ye were called in one hope of your calling; one Lord, one faith, one baptism, one God and Father of all, who is over all, and through all, and in all (Eph. 4. 4–6).

[1] Contrary to what might have been expected from the associations of baptism in the Synoptic Gospels and the Acts of the Apostles, St. Paul rarely links baptism with forgiveness. For a full treatment of the subject of New Testament teaching about forgiveness and " the deliberate preference of St. Paul for the idea of justification, which he rightly believed to be a much richer conception than forgiveness as he knew it and understood it ", see the important article by Vincent Taylor in the *Expository Times* Vol. LI, pp. 16–21, and the same writer's *Forgiveness and Reconciliation* (1941), pp. 1–33.

[2] For this rendering of ἀπεκδυσάμενος, which, though Zahn termed it " an inexcusable caprice ", nevertheless seems preferable, cf. Peake in the *Expositor's Greek Testament*, ad loc.

[3] Oepke in *Theol. Wört.*, Vol. I, p. 540 points out how significant for the understanding of St. Paul's conception of baptism is the close link in Col. 2. 12 ff. between baptism, rising again with Christ, and the " unmystical forensic idea of Justification ". " Jede Darstellung der paulinischen Taufauffassung ist daher verfehlt, welche von subjektiv-naturhaften ' Tauferlebnis ', und nicht in erster Linie von der objektiven heilsgeschichtlichen Situation ausgeht ".

The main theme of Ephesians is something that to one brought up under the Old Covenant could never fail to be a profound paradox. By a miracle of divine grace Jew and Gentile had been made one in Christ.[1] In this chapter St. Paul [2] enumerates some of the marks of this unity; among these he names baptism. The inclusion of baptism in such a sequence is a striking indication of the place taken by the rite in the thought of St. Paul, or, if the Epistle be not by him, in the thought of one who owed so much to his influence. It has frequently been noted with surprise by commentators that in this context about " unity in Christ " there is no reference to the Lord's Supper. In view of 1 Cor. 10. 17 (" we, who are many, are one bread, one body: for we all partake of the one bread "), we might certainly have expected its inclusion here. That it is not so included makes the reference to baptism the more impressive. When we take full account of each member of this significant sequence, there will seem perhaps no other passage in the whole New Testament that speaks more eloquently of all that baptism meant to a first-century Christian. Here again in the immediate context are to be found several of the conceptions associated with baptism elsewhere: the Spirit (verses 3, 4), the " Body " (verse 4), God the Father of all (verse 6) which implies " sonship ", and the new moral life to which Christians are " called " (verses 1–2). The link between baptism and " unity " in this passage is thoroughly Pauline, cf. 1 Cor. 12. 12–13 and Gal. 3. 27–28.

Husbands, love your wives, even as Christ also loved the church, and gave himself up for it; that he might sanctify it, having cleansed it by the washing of water with the word, that he might present the church to himself a glorious church, not having spot or wrinkle or any such thing; but that it should be holy and without blemish (Eph. 5. 25–27).

In a context dealing with the love of husband and wife, St. Paul quotes as the pattern for all such love the love of Christ for the Church. He uses the same two verbs (ἀγαπάω and παραδίδωμι [3]) which previously he used in Gal. 2. 20 (". . . who loved me, and gave himself up for me "); but there the object of Christ's love revealed in his sacrificial death was Paul himself, the individual believer; here in Ephesians it is the whole Church (verse 25). The background of this passage is the sacrificial thought of the Old Testament, but with this difference, that here the Priest is himself

[1] Cf. J. A. Robinson, *Ephesians* (1904), *passim*.
[2] On the vexed question of the authorship of Ephesians the reasoning of C. H. Dodd seems persuasive that if the author were not St. Paul, we have to posit some nameless genius, capable of the sustained thought of this Epistle, who yet could express himself for the most part only by an almost slavish copying of St. Paul's language in Colossians!; cf. C. H. Dodd in *Abingdon Commentary* (1929), pp. 1224 f.; for the other view, which sees the author as the " Ephesian continuator " cf. W. L. Knox, op. cit., pp. 182 ff. Though Ephesians is included here by the present writer as a Pauline Epistle, it may be noted that in the summary of St. Paul's baptismal teaching which will follow, references from Ephesians are used only to confirm conclusions reached on the basis of passages in other undoubtedly Pauline letters.
[3] The meaning of this word in the New Testament is governed by its double occurrence in the LXX of Isa. 53. 12. L. S. Thornton, *The Common Life in the Body of Christ* (1941), p. 229 n. 2 comments " This word (παραδίδωμι) is repeated through the New Testament with the repetitive persistence of a tolling bell ".

the Victim and the purpose of his perfect sacrifice is that the object of his love, the Church, shall ultimately be enabled by virtue of his sacrifice to make a sacrificial offering of itself (verse 27). To this end, Christ (by his own death) " consecrated " the Church, and the means of this consecration is the cleansing that results from the " washing of water with the word " (verse 26). The words καθαρίσας τῷ λουτρῷ τοῦ ὕδατος ἐν ῥήματι must on any natural interpretation refer to baptism. The rite which was actually administered to the individual believer is here regarded as a means whereby the whole Church is purified.[1] The phrase ἐν ῥήματι clearly contains a reference to some " word " pronounced in the solemn moment of baptism. It may denote the baptismal formula " in the name of Jesus ", or perhaps the profession of faith " Jesus is Lord ",[2] which was probably made by the baptized person.

The importance of this passage is twofold: first, it asserts that it is Christ's offering of himself that gives baptism its efficacy; thus explicit expression is given to the conviction that behind every Christian baptism is the death of Jesus. This conception that it is Christ's giving of himself that makes baptism a true sacrament lends added point to the other passages already considered, where St. Paul regards Christians as " baptized into Christ's death ".[3] The Christian repeats in his own experience the act of self-dedication which Christ made when he went to the Cross. But baptism can mean that for the believer only because behind every Christian baptism is the love and self-offering of Jesus himself. Secondly, this passage is important because by its close association of baptism with the " word " it rules out any view of baptism as merely an external rite. " The ceremony itself meant nothing apart from the ' word ' or confession which gave expression to a vital faith." [4] We notice, further, how this passage, besides laying so pronounced a stress upon the death of Christ, also links baptism (as in some other passages which we have examined) with the eschatological conception of " glory " by means of the epithet " glorious " (ἔνδοξον) applied to the Church in verse 27. The other epithets in this verse, " holy " and " without blemish " (ἁγία and ἄμωμος),[5] have markedly sacrificial associations from their use in the Septuagint. In the Old Testament itself,

---

[1] There may possibly be a reference to the lustration of a bride before marriage; cf. Kennedy, op. cit., pp. 251–252; but see also Armitage Robinson, op. cit., p. 207. The word λουτρόν occurs in the New Testament only here and Tit. 3. 5.

[2] Cf. Rom. 10. 9 (. . . ἐὰν ὁμολογήσῃς ἐν τῷ στόματί σου Κύριον Ἰησοῦν . . .).

[3] Rom. 6. 3, cf. Col. 2. 12. Dibelius in *Handbuch zum Neuen Testament*, ad loc. alludes to these passages from Romans and Colossians, and comments, " Die Vorbedingung dieser ' Reinigung ' ist die Selbsthingabe Christi; also steht der Gedanke an die Todestaufe . . . auch hier im Hintergrund ".

[4] E. F. Scott, *Colossians Philemon and Ephesians*, Moffatt New Testament Commentary (1930), p. 240; cf. also Armitage Robinson, op. cit., p. 206.

[5] Armitage Robinson, op. cit., p. 143 observes that ἄμωμος is used in the LXX " almost exclusively . . . as a rendering of תמים, which occurs very frequently of sacrificial animals, in the sense of ' without blemish ' ". But since תמים is also used often of ethical uprightness the idea of moral purity also belongs to ἄμωμος; cf. the use of ἁγίους and ἀμώμους in Eph. 1. 4 and Col. 1. 22.

however, it came to be seen that the only perfect sacrifice was the human will offered to God (cf. Ps. 40. 6–8). Thus, when sacrificial epithets are used by New Testament writers, they necessarily bear an ethical connotation. Here therefore, as so often in baptismal contexts, we find an emphasis on the new moral life. The form in which the conception of moral purity here finds expression is somewhat different from that in other passages, since what St. Paul elsewhere described by the image of a fresh garment,[1] or of " newness of life " [2] consequent upon the sharing by the believer of Christ's risen life, is here described under the figure of an unblemished sacrificial offering. But the idea at the root of the passage, that the death of Christ makes possible a new kind of life and that this is mediated in Christian baptism, is entirely Pauline. What makes this passage so peculiarly impressive is the emphasis upon the Church, the whole community of the redeemed, as the object of Christ's sacrificial love, so much so that the Church can be regarded as itself corporately receiving all that is given in baptism. This does not mean that St. Paul has forgotten his earlier personal expression of adoring gratitude, " He loved me and gave himself up for me ". The truth is rather as Dr. Vincent Taylor has said : " The personal element is not forgotten ; on the contrary it is greatly enriched, because it is seen within the life of a corporate fellowship. . . . *Extra Ecclesiam nulla salus* is the law of sanctification as well as of reconciliation." [3]

Now he that stablisheth us with you in Christ, and anointed us, is God ; who also sealed us, and gave us the earnest of the Spirit in our hearts (2 Cor. 1. 21–22).

In whom ye also, having heard the word of the truth, the gospel of your salvation,—in whom, having also believed, ye were sealed with the Holy Spirit of promise, which is an earnest of our inheritance, unto the redemption of God's own possession, unto the praise of his glory (Eph. 1. 13–14).

And grieve not the Holy Spirit of God, in whom ye were sealed unto the day of redemption (Eph. 4. 30).

In these three passages the verb " to seal " ($\sigma\phi\rho\alpha\gamma\acute{\iota}\zeta\omega\mu\alpha\iota$) is used. It seems almost certain that the word is to be understood as a reference to baptism.[4] St. Paul uses the word " seal " ($\sigma\phi\rho\alpha\gamma\acute{\iota}s$) of circumcision in Rom. 4. 11, speaking of Abraham, " he received the sign of circumcision, a seal of the righteousness of the faith which he had while he was in uncircumcision ". Sanday and Headlam in their note on the passage quote from the prayer used at the circumcising of a child, " Blessed be He who . . . sealed His offspring with the sign of a holy covenant ".[5] From the way in which the word $\sigma\phi\rho\alpha\gamma\acute{\iota}s$ is used by Christian writers in the second century A.D.[6] it is clear that by that time it had become a recognized synonym for baptism. The implication is that at some date previously

---

[1] Cf. Gal. 3. 27.   [2] Cf. Rom. 6. 4.
[3] V. Taylor, *Forgiveness and Reconciliation* (1941), p. 218.
[4] Cf. H. Lietzmann in *Handbuch zum Neuen Testament, I und II Korinther* (1923), p. 103 ; E. F. Scott, op. cit., pp. 148, 223–224 ; Knox, op. cit., p. 186 n. 2.
[5] Sanday and Headlam, *Romans, I.C.C.* (1902), p. 107.
[6] Cf. Hermas *Sim.*, IX, xvi, 3–5 ; 2 Clem. 7. 6 ; 8. 6.

the term σφραγίς, originally used of circumcision, had been transferred to the Christian counterpart of the Jewish rite.[1] It may be that this extension of meaning was first given to the word by St. Paul himself. This would have been the more easy since, as we have seen, he regarded baptism as a sort of Christian circumcision.[2] That baptism was in mind when these three passages were written is rendered still more likely when we note the occurrence in each context of some of the conceptions elsewhere associated with the rite.

In 2 Cor. 1. we observe the phrase " into Christ " (εἰς Χριστόν) and the reference to the Spirit, both characteristic of Christian baptism. Dr. R. H. Strachan has pointed out that three of the words used in verses 21–22 are " popular semi-legal terms, which would be familiar in the commercial life of Corinth ".[3] This no doubt would help to make Paul's meaning more intelligible to his Corinthian readers, but the presence in these two verses of " into Christ " and the " Spirit " suggests strongly that for St. Paul himself the religious significance of " sealing " was uppermost, rather than the commercial application of the term. We notice also in verse 21 the word " anointed "; a word which, as Lietzmann indicates, is used elsewhere in the New Testament only of the " anointing " of Christ.[4] Its use in this context seems to imply that just as Jesus the Messiah was " anointed " at his baptism (cf. Acts 10. 37–38, ". . . after the baptism which John preached; even Jesus of Nazareth, how that God anointed Him with the Holy Spirit and with power "), so those who become incorporated " into Christ " similarly receive an anointing.[5] This would seem to make it more certain that the word " sealed " refers to Christian baptism.

In Ephes. 1. we have to notice (in determining the limits of the " baptismal context ") that verses 3–14 form a single grammatical sentence, the theme of which is " divine sonship ". We observe that this paragraph opens with one of the ideas frequently found in the passages which we have been examining, the activity of God the Father (verse 3 and throughout the paragraph). It includes also the new moral life (verse 4), divine sonship (verse 5), redemption through the death of Christ (verse 7), forgiveness (verse 7), " glory " (verses 6, 12, 14), the Holy Spirit (verse 13) and " inheritance " (verse 14, cf. also verse 11). We further notice that the reference in verse 13 to the readers having been

---

[1] It was customary in some of the mystery cults for the worshipper to be marked with the emblem of his cult—this seal marked him as owned by the god. But in view of the use of σφραγίς in connexion with circumcision, it seems probable that the Christian use of the word was Jewish rather than Hellenistic in origin—the *later* Christian use may have been influenced by the language of the mystery religions.

[2] Cf. Col. 2. 12.

[3] The word βεβαιόω is used of the giving of a guarantee by a vendor; it was customary to " seal " goods, so that they could not be tampered with; the " pledge " or " earnest " is a first instalment " received in advance and guaranteeing that more is due ". Cf. R. H. Strachan, 2 *Corinthians, Moffatt New Testament Commentary* (1935), p. 59.

[4] Cf. Lk. 4. 18; Acts 4. 27; 10. 38; Heb. 1.9.

[5] Cf. for this thought 1 Jn. 2. 20, " ye have an anointing from the Holy One "; here the noun χρῖσμα is used in reference to Christians being anointed.

" sealed with the Holy Spirit of promise " follows immediately upon the statement that they " heard the word of truth, the gospel of . . . salvation ". This recalls vividly the connexion so frequently made in the Acts of the Apostles between " hearing the word " and " being baptized ".[1] The " sealing " which in Ephesians follows the reception of the gospel of salvation is surely the same as the baptism which in Acts takes up and embodies the *kerygma*. This provides yet another confirmation that our interpretation of σφραγίζομαι is justified.

In considering the context of the baptismal reference in Eph. 4. 30 we may examine the section 4. 25–5. 2, which is a single sub-division of a paragraph in Westcott and Hort's text. We observe the word " putting off " (4. 25), which, as elsewhere, seems to belong to the vocabulary of baptism. Also in the same verse the phrase " members one of another " recalls the teaching about the Body and the members in 1 Cor. 12. 12–13.[2] In 4. 30 there is the " Holy Spirit ", and the " day of redemption " (an eschatological idea). There follows in 4. 32 the familiar conception of the new moral life, itself motivated by the " forgiveness " of God " in Christ ". In the opening verse of Chapter 5, the reference to " children " contains the teaching about divine sonship, so often found in baptismal contexts. Finally, in 5. 2 the moral appeal of the whole paragraph is summed up in a solemn reminder of the love and self-offering of Christ, again expressed in strongly sacrificial language and again using the two verbs ἀγαπάω and παραδίδωμι which we noted as so significant in our consideration of Eph. 5. 25.

From this consideration of the context of these passages about " sealing " it would appear that we are fully entitled to treat them as evidence for Pauline teaching concerning baptism.

[1] Cf. *supra*, p. 49.
[2] This, it will be remembered, is one of the passages about baptism which we examined earlier; cf. *supra*, pp. 56–57.

6

Baptism in the Pauline Epistles (continued)

IN the previous chapter the various Pauline statements about baptism were examined in relation to their context. This chapter will endeavour to summarize the teaching to be derived from these passages, and will also be concerned with a consideration of the question, how far St. Paul's baptismal teaching may be described as " sacramental ".

St. Paul saw baptism as the solemn rite whereby converts were incorporated into the Church, the Body of Christ (1 Cor. 12. 13), or " into Christ Jesus " (Rom. 6. 3), or " into Christ " (Gal. 3. 27; cf. 2 Cor. 1. 21). It was an act done through the agency of the Spirit, and through it the Spirit was received (1 Cor. 6. 11, 12, 13; Eph. 1. 13; cf. also the *aorist* tenses in Gal. 3. 2 and Rom. 8. 15). It was a sign of the " oneness " of all Christians in Christ; Jew and Greek, slave and free shared in it alike (1 Cor. 12. 13; Gal. 3. 28; cf. Eph. 4. 5). The Spirit which was received could also be described as " the Spirit of his Son " (Gal. 4. 6 [1]) imparting to Christians a sense of the divine Fatherhood (" Abba Father "—Gal. 4. 6; cf. also Rom. 8. 15). This gift imparted in baptism was received through faith (Gal. 3. 26, cf. 23–25; Col. 2. 12; Eph. 1. 13; 4. 5; cf. also Rom. 6. 8; 1 Cor. 12. 9). Sometimes St. Paul expressly mentions the activity of God the Father (Rom. 6. 4; 2 Cor. 1. 21–22; Col. 2. 12; Eph. 4. 6; cf. also Gal. 4. 6; Eph. 1. 3). The double connexion, Baptism–Spirit, and Spirit–Sonship, helps to explain other passages where St. Paul makes the link between baptism and " sonship " (Gal. 3. 26–27; here the " Spirit " is spoken of a few verses further on in 4. 6). The three conceptions are also to be found together in Eph. 1; though " sonship " (verse 5) is separated by several verses from baptism and the Spirit (verse 13), yet the whole passage is grammatically a single sentence.[2] One passage explicitly connects baptism with sanctification and justification " in the name of the Lord Jesus Christ and the Spirit of our God " (1 Cor. 6. 11); for the link of baptism with justification cf. also Gal. 3. 24 and Rom. 6. 7. Sometimes St. Paul speaks of forgiveness in a baptismal context (Col. 2. 13; Eph. 4. 32; cf. also Eph. 1. 7).

The actions involved in baptism were to St. Paul intensely significant of the meaning of the rite. The convert who had removed his garments to enter the water robed himself afresh when he emerged from baptism. St. Paul saw this as a " putting on " of Christ (Gal. 3. 27). In Col. 2. 11 he makes use of the same imagery (cf. also Col. 3. 8, 12, without express

---

[1] In the same paragraph with the baptismal reference in 3. 27.

[2] It will be remembered that the Spirit and " Sonship " both appear prominently in the story of the Baptism of Jesus.

mention of baptism). In other places St. Paul employs the symbolism of total immersion to express the truth that baptism marks a complete break with the old life and a fresh beginning for the new life. In baptism the Christian " dies " with Christ (Rom. 6. 3; cf. Col. 3. 3 and Gal. 5. 24); he is " buried " with him (Rom. 6. 4; Col. 2. 12); he is " raised again " with him (Rom. 6. 4; Col. 2. 12; cf. 3. 1) through faith in the power of God who raised Christ from the dead (Col. 2. 12; cf. 1 Cor. 6. 14, baptism in verse 11). All this means a moral life of an entirely new quality (Rom. 6. 4, cf. 13, 19; Col. 2. 6, cf. 3. 1 ff., 12 ff.; Eph. 1. 4; 4. 1–2; 4. 32; cf. also the implication of 1 Cor. 6. 9–11). For the same conceptions, without express mention of baptism, cf. " dying and rising again " (Rom. 8. 10–11), and " new life " in the Spirit (Rom. 8 *passim*). Not only does St. Paul thus relate baptism to the death and resurrection of Jesus, but in Ephesians it is expressly stated that it is the love and the self-offering of Christ that give baptism its power to cleanse and sanctify the Church (Eph. 5. 25–27; cf. also 5. 2 following on 4. 30). Several passages show that St. Paul saw a close link between Christian baptism and his teaching about the Church as the " New Israel ". Baptism is for the Christian what circumcision was for the Jew (Col. 2. 11; this may be implied also by the use of the word σφραγίζομαι 2 Cor. 1. 22, Eph. 1. 13, 4. 30). Thus through baptism " into Christ " (Gal. 3. 27) the convert becomes part of the true " seed of Abraham " (Gal. 3. 29), or again, through baptism he is " an heir according to promise " (Gal. 3. 29; cf. 1 Cor. 6. 9–10; Eph. 1. 14; Gal. 4. 7; and also Rom. 8. 17). In several of these baptismal passages the characteristic Pauline phrase " in Christ (Jesus) " is found. It would seem that St. Paul would date the beginning of what to him was the heart of Christian experience from the moment of baptism (Gal. 3. 26; Col. 2. 10 ἐν αὐτῷ; cf. also Rom. 6. 11; Eph. 1. 3; and 1 Cor. 6. 17, part of the ethical application of the principle asserted about baptism in 6. 11).

The connexion of many of the ideas which St. Paul associated with baptism becomes clearer when we view the rite against that eschatological background, with which in the Synoptic Gospels and in the Acts we have already seen it to be so intimately related. St. Paul's teaching about baptism cannot be understood save in an eschatological framework. About the Lord's Supper the Apostle wrote " as often as ye eat this bread and drink the cup, ye proclaim the Lord's death, till he come ". There is no statement quite so explicit about baptism,[1] but the eschatological reference is no less certain. This becomes clear from the nature of the ideas with which baptism is associated. Thus St. Paul connects baptism with the gift of the Spirit; we remember that according to Jewish teaching the full outpouring of the Spirit was to be a mark of the Age to Come.[2]

---

[1] Perhaps Eph. 4. 30 is the nearest approach to a parallel, " Ye were sealed unto the day of redemption ".

[2] Cf. e.g. Joel 2. 28, quoted in Acts 2. 17.

Again, he associates baptism with moral renewal, which as we have seen was regarded by the Rabbis as something that belonged to the future.[1] Further, in several of the baptismal contexts there is the mention of " glory " (δόξα). This was another mark of the Messianic Kingdom.[2]

It is further noticeable that the symbolism of putting off and putting on garments, of which Paul makes much in connexion with baptism (cf. Gal. 3. 27; Col. 2. 11) is used in 2 Cor. 5 of the future life.[3] The words in 2 Cor. 5. 5 " He who wrought us for this very thing is God, who gave unto us the earnest [4] of the Spirit " suggest that for St. Paul the gift of the Spirit here and now (imparted in baptism, cf. 2 Cor. 1. 22) was a guarantee of the fuller gift still to come. Thus the " Spirit " and the " moral renewal " which he associated with the " putting on " of Christ in baptism could be regarded as a foretaste of the full blessedness to be received only in the life to come, when the believer would be " clothed upon " with the " heavenly habitation ".[5]

That baptism in St. Paul must be understood eschatologically becomes yet more clear when we penetrate farther into the significance of the connexion he traces between baptism and the death of Jesus, and the frequency with which he sees the new moral life of the Christian as a sharing of our Lord's resurrection. It is widely recognized to-day that the death and resurrection of Jesus are intimately bound up with the eschatological background of the New Testament. The earlier " thorough-going eschatology " of Schweitzer and Johannes Weiss, which so profoundly affected New Testament study even where it provoked most emphatic disagreement, has in recent years been succeeded by the " realized eschatology ", which has thrown a flood of light on many a passage both in the Gospels and in the Epistles. We have learnt from Rudolph Otto and from Professor Dodd that the apocalyptic hopes of Judaism were " realized " in the coming of Jesus.[6] The powers of this " New Age " broke in upon the world in part during our Lord's ministry, but supremely as a result of his death and resurrection. Thus for St. Paul it was then that Jesus stripped of their power the forces of evil and made an open show of them, triumphing over them by means of the cross.[7] Again, it was at the resurrection that Jesus was " declared the Son of God

---

[1] Cf. *supra*, p. 9 *n*. 1.

[2] Cf. Rom. 6. 4; Eph. 1. 14. For " glory " in O.T. cf. Isa. 35. 2; 66. 18.

[3] There is evidence for the belief that the righteous would be clothed with a " robe of glory ", cf. Enoch 62. 15.

[4] The word ἀρραβών, as Moulton and Milligan show, denotes a first instalment, " a part given in advance of what will be bestowed fully afterwards ". It is interesting to notice that the equivalent in modern Greek (ἡ ἀρραβῶνα) means " the engagement-ring ".

[5] The thought in these verses (2 Cor. 5. 1–5) varies between the two images of a " garment " and a " house ".

[6] Cf. especially " Blessed are your eyes, for they see; and your ears, for they hear. For verily I say unto you, that many prophets and righteous men desired to see the things that you see, and saw them not; and to hear the things that you hear, and heard them not ", Matt. 13. 16–17 (= Lk. 10. 23–24); and Matt. 12. 28 (= Lk. 11. 20), ". . . then is the kingdom of God come upon you ".

[7] Col. 2. 15.

F

with power ".[1] Through the power of God the Father active therein
the way was opened for men to enter into their " inheritance ". Henceforth those who " believed " in Christ could receive the Spirit of " sonship "
and become " sons " or " children " of God.[2] For those who lived " in
Christ " there was " a new creation ",[3] and their character exhibited all
the fruit of a new moral life, what Paul called " the harvest of the Spirit ".[4]
The blessings of the New Age, thus made available for the believer by the
death and resurrection of Jesus, were all expressed for St. Paul in baptism.

In this connexion it is illuminating to remember the saying of Jesus
which has been examined earlier in Chapter 3,[5] " I have a baptism to be
baptized with; and how am I straitened till it be accomplished! "
(Lk. 12. 50). We saw reason to interpret this reference to baptism as
more than a figurative description of intense suffering; it is probable
that Jesus was using the term " baptism " with the meaning of spiritual
purification. The saying becomes far more significant if the " baptism "
for the " accomplishment " of which Jesus waits, is not simply a vivid
metaphor for the sorrow and pain of the crucifixion, but actually represents his death as the inauguration of that wider " ministry " to which he
looked forward, as surely as his baptism in the Jordan was the prelude to
his ministry in Palestine. If Jesus thought of his death *in this sense* as a
" baptism " and spoke thus of it to his followers, we can understand the
better why the moment which marked for the believer his appropriation
of the salvation won for him by Christ's death should have been from the
earliest days of the Church signalized by an act of baptism (the baptism
which, as we saw in Acts, " embodied " the *kerygma*), and, further, how
St. Paul, in seeing the one as representative of the other, was but developing a conception which derived originally from Jesus himself. Behind
every Christian baptism was the death of Jesus—that " baptism " which
when " accomplished " marked the wider inauguration of the Kingdom.
Tu devicto mortis aculeo aperuisti credentibus regna caelorum. Thus it would
seem that the Pauline conception of baptism as " into Christ's death ",
or as a recapitulation for the believer of his death, burial and resurrection,
is far more than a casual metaphor. It has sometimes been suggested
that in such teaching St. Paul was using a passing illustration and invoking
this connexion as an apt means of enforcing a particular moral appeal.
But the assumption seems to have been that the connexion had never
hitherto been traced, and that for the Apostle himself it was little more
than a literary or homiletic device. Several considerations, it may now be
seen, make this assumption questionable. There is the fact that the most
striking expression of this connexion between baptism and the death of
Christ is to be found in Romans and Colossians—letters sent to churches
where (at the time of writing) Paul had not himself preached. The
implication surely is that he is appealing not to any distinctive and private

---

[1] Rom. 1. 4.   [2] Gal. 3. 26; Rom. 8. 14, 16, 21.   [3] 2 Cor. 5. 17.
[4] Gal. 5. 22.   [5] Cf. *supra*, pp. 31–32.

teaching of his own but rather to the common Christian tradition. Further, if Christian baptism was in some sense an outward embodiment of the apostolic preaching, then, since the central thing in that preaching was the death and resurrection of Christ, the discovery of likeness between baptism and these events, so far from being a literary or homiletic device, is rather the recognition of something necessarily inherent in the meaning of baptism itself. If Christian baptism is the outward expression of the Gospel, it must be the death and resurrection of Christ that give the rite all its distinctive meaning. Seen in this light, then, once more, what St. Paul has to say about baptism represents no innovation, but rather the filling out of ideas already implicit in primitive Christian teaching. Moreover, when full weight is given to the saying of Jesus likening his death to a " baptism ", the conclusion becomes highly probable that the ultimate responsibility for the link between Christian baptism and the death of Christ rests neither upon St. Paul nor upon those before him in the Gospel, but upon our Lord himself. St. Paul did not forge the link connecting baptism with the death of Christ: what he did rather was to draw out more clearly the relation between the two, to show how baptism is, as it were, the *kerygma* in action. The rite gathers up into a significant deed the central Fact of the apostolic message. Behind every baptism was the death and resurrection of Jesus, that Act of God which opened the way into the New Age. Christian baptism in the first century marked for the believer the moment when for him, because of what Christ had done, the New Age dawned, and thus he personally became an " heir of the Kingdom ".

But full justice is not done to St. Paul's thought if we speak as though for him all the eschatology were " realized ". A writer in the *Expository Times* [1] has suggested that in order to be faithful to the New Testament as a whole, it is better to speak not of " realized " but rather of " proleptic " eschatology. There is a real sense in which the Kingdom of God " came ", when Jesus lived and died and rose again and gave his Spirit to the Church. But that coming of the Kingdom of God was *proleptic*—it " anticipated " a consummation not yet fulfilled. The false suggestion sometimes roused by the doctrine of " realized eschatology " (especially in the hands of some of its less cautious exponents), namely that the Kingdom of God was completely fulfilled in the life of Jesus and in the events of Good Friday, Easter and Pentecost, is obviously untrue to that element in New Testament teaching which still looked forward with the most intense eagerness to something *not yet* realized. So it is with St. Paul. He believed that in a real sense the New Age dawned with Jesus, and that in baptism the blessings of this New Age are mediated to the believer. The inexhaustible wealth of this inheritance which already belonged to him and his fellow-Christians seems to have become increasingly a present possession, so

---

[1] H. V. Martin in *Expos. Times,* Vol. LI (1939), pp. 88–90.

far as we can trace the development of his thought in the extant epistles.[1] But, with it all, St. Paul never quite ceased to look forward to a consummation in the future. It is noteworthy that in what are probably two of the last letters which St. Paul ever wrote [2] there are unmistakable assertions of a future consummation, side by side with the claim that the present life of the Christian has already, here and now, an other-worldly, " heavenly " quality. Thus in Philippians (3. 20) St. Paul can write, " Our citizenship is in heaven ", and continue without a break " from which also we wait for a Saviour, even the Lord Jesus Christ. . . ." Again in Colossians (3. 3–4) he writes of the " death to sin " (which took place at baptism, cf. the aorist tense) and of its abiding result in the present life of the Christian, " ye died, and your life remains hidden with Christ in God "; similarly he continues, again without any break, " whenever Christ, who is our life, shall be manifested, then you also shall be manifested with him in glory ".[3] Such passages are too striking to be dismissed merely as " survivals of an older point of view ". They belong to the substance of the Apostle's thinking, which throughout the period represented by the extant Epistles never ceased to be conditioned by the expectation of the Parousia.[4]

This aspect of eschatology also affects Pauline teaching concerning baptism. Thus in one passage which we have examined part of the meaning of baptism is that it points forward to something yet to come, " ye were sealed unto a day of redemption ".[5] Just as John's baptism looked on to the future, so Christian baptism itself, above and beyond the reality of the present gifts which it bestowed on the believer, looked forward to a future consummation. Again, while in Rom. 6. 3 ff. part of the meaning of baptism is the " death to sin ", and this in turn issues

---

[1] It will have been noticed in the previous chapter how much of St. Paul's baptismal language involves the assertion that the Christian enjoys *here and now* the blessings which, in the Old Testament and in rabbinic teaching, were reserved for the Age to Come.

[2] Dr. G. S. Duncan in his book, *St. Paul's Ephesian Ministry* (1929), has set forth very fully the arguments for the hypothesis that the Captivity Epistles were written not from Rome but from Ephesus. In spite of the attractiveness of the theory and the skill with which the case has been presented, it would appear that the criticisms of Professor C. H. Dodd make the hypothesis untenable; cf. *Bulletin of the John Rylands Library* (Jan. 1934), pp. 75–92.

[3] If the present writer may venture to differ from one to whom his profound debt for so much in this essay is obvious, and from whom he has learnt so much, it may be observed that Professor Dodd quotes part of this Colossians passage, without the compensating clause, when in the concluding words of his article in *The Kingdom of God and History* (1938), p. 36, he writes: " The future, which can bring with it nothing to supersede that revelation of the Kingdom of God," (i.e. in Christ) " is not our concern, nor is it in the future that we must seek the perfection of which the temporal order is not capable, but in that other world in which the ultimate meaning of history resides, where ' our life is hid with Christ in God '." But surely St. Paul intended the second clause to balance the first. The *hidden* life *now* will be fulfilled in the *manifested* life *hereafter*. Thus though it is true that the future can bring with it nothing to *supersede* the revelation in Christ, yet, according to St. Paul, the future assuredly will bring with it something to *consummate* that revelation. St. Paul's thought is impoverished if this idea of a future " manifestation " of Christ be excluded.

[4] Cf. J. M. Creed in *Theology* (July 1939), pp. 70–71, (". . . Did St. Paul ever cease to think apocalyptically?"), and an article by the Dean of Christ Church in *J. T. S.* Vol. XLII (1941), pp. 129–142 entitled " An Examination of Attempts to Detect Developments in St. Paul's Theology ".

[5] Eph. 4. 30.

in a rising with Christ to " newness of life ", in Col. 3. 3 f. this " death to
sin " is the prelude not only to a life here and now " hid with Christ in
God ", but also to a future manifestation of Christ in glory which is to be
shared by the Colossians themselves.   Further, in yet another passage
those who " believed " were at their baptism " sealed with the Holy
Spirit of promise ", and this Spirit was a " first instalment (ἀρραβών) of
the inheritance " to be fully appropriated in the future.[1]   Thus it may
be said that in St. Paul's thought about baptism there is a double eschatological reference—the hope is partly " realized " now in present experience,
but, none the less, the full consummation of that hope is reserved for the
future.[2]   St. Paul's teaching about baptism and the death of Christ in
this twofold aspect is well expressed by L. S. Thornton : " The whole
work of our salvation was accomplished in Christ's death and resurrection.
By baptism we were made partakers in the fulness of this salvation.   The
full fruits of this saving work, for us and in us, still lie in the future." [3]

Nothing in our examination of the Pauline evidence suggests that St.
Paul himself was primarily responsible for the place assigned to baptism in
the early Church.   It would seem rather that baptism was part of the
primitive Christian tradition which he took over from " those who were
apostles before him ".   He himself had been baptized,[4] and there is no
reason to suppose that he ever thought of any other mode of entry into the
Christian Church.   The record of Acts shows that, for those who
" received the word ", submission to baptism was the normal and typical
response to the proclamation of the *kerygma*.   St. Paul could take this fact
for granted and argue on the basis of it.   It was his task to develop this
connexion and draw out far more richly the implications that made the
rite itself an embodiment of the apostolic preaching.   Canon Knox has
shown that in much of his teaching about baptism St. Paul was adapting
for Christian purposes a well-known method of Jewish *kerygma*.[5]   The
story of the Exodus became a regular " form " under which the message
of Judaism was preached to the Gentile world.   So it was taught that
through circumcision and the *tebilah* the proselyte came out of " Egypt "
and passed through the " Red Sea " into the " Promised Land ".   (The
Passover also was regularly interpreted in the light of the Exodus
narrative.)   In Romans 6 St. Paul transfers this Jewish interpretation to

[1] Eph. 1. 13–14; the same teaching lies behind 2 Cor. 1. 22.
[2] Cf. Edwyn Bevan, *Symbolism and Belief* (1938), p. 117. Dr. Bevan commenting on Dr.
Inge's approval of Bosanquet's saying " to throw our ideals into the future is the death of all
sane idealism ", writes : " The dictum of Bosanquet which Dr. Inge likes is profoundly anti-
Christian.   It is perfectly true, of course, that a right relation to God in this world implies,
according to the Christian view, the present possession of a great deal of ultimate good . . .
but the Christian view also insists that all present realization of good is imperfect, and that for
the complete realization the Christian must look to *the future*. ' Beloved, *now* are we the sons of
God, and it doth *not yet* appear what we shall be '.   It is the combination of the ' *now* ' and the
' *not yet* ' which characterizes the Christian *Weltanschauung*. Dr Inge would be quite right in
condemning a view which eliminated the ' *now* ' and made the realization of ideals merely
future; but it is no less a mistake to eliminate the ' *not yet* '."   If what Dr. Bevan says is true of
the Johannine presentation, it is not less true of St. Paul's outlook.
[3] Thornton, op. cit., p. 61.   [4] Cf. Acts 9. 18; 22. 16.   [5] Knox, op. cit., p. 97.

the death and resurrection of Jesus. " Those who share in it through faith and pass through the waters of baptism are delivered from the old Egyptian bondage to sin and pass instead into a new slavery to righteousness which results in sanctification." [1] Or, as Professor Dodd puts it, when he describes the way in which St. Paul restated more thoroughly the new unity between the Messiah and the Messianic community: " The personality of Christ receives, so to speak, an extension in the life of His Body on earth. Those ' saving facts ', the death and resurrection of Christ, are not merely particular facts of past history, however decisive in their effect; they are re-enacted in the experience of the Church." [2] Thus, whereas others might identify the gift of the Spirit with the power to " speak with tongues ",[3] St. Paul desired earnestly the " greater gifts ", and the " more excellent way ". It will be remembered that 1 Cor. 13 follows upon and sums up a discussion concerning " spiritual gifts " (in the heart of which one of the Pauline references to baptism is embedded). In giving the primacy to " love " it is not that he is laying any less stress upon the miraculous (the new moral life was to St. Paul the supreme miracle), but the point now is rather that the miracle, the " mighty work " of the Spirit, that follows upon baptism, is that of *agape* instead of *glossolalia*. He sought continually to remind his converts that the possession of these " greater gifts " was implicit in their very reception into the Church. They had been baptized " into Christ ", " into his death "; let them realise their " sonship ", and live their life in the Spirit in fellowship with him who had been " declared to be the Son of God with power . . . as a result of the resurrection of the dead ".[4]

In recent years the attempt has been made to explain much of the sacramental teaching of St. Paul as a borrowing from the contemporary mystery religions. It is clear that certain rites of lustration were practised in connexion with these cults. The phrase characteristic of the Eleusinian mysteries, ἅλαδε μύσται, and the account given by Apuleius of the initiation of Lucius into the mysteries of Isis [5] show a certain general similarity in so far as washing with water is employed with a religious significance. This likeness was recognized later by Tertullian, who argued, if baptism was used in these heathen religions, how much more powerful would be its efficacy when used in the worship of the " living God ".[6] But when we make a closer comparison between these pagan rites and Christian

---

[1] Knox, op. cit., p. 97.
[2] C. H. Dodd, *The Apostolic Preaching and its Developments* (1936), pp. 147–148
[3] It is noticeable, however, that even the author of Acts, in spite of his love of the " miraculous ", stresses the new quality of corporate life which characterized the primitive church. As Professor Dodd points out, each of the descriptions of the early Christian " communism " (Acts 2. 44–47; 4. 32–37) follows immediately upon a passage describing the descent of the Spirit; cf. Dodd, op. cit., p. 137 *n.* 1.
[4] Rom. 1. 4.
[5] Apul., *Metamorph.*, xi, 23, " iamque tempore, ut aiebat sacerdos, id postulante stipatum me religiosa cohorte deducit ad proximas balneas et prius sueto lavacro traditum, praefatus deum veniam, purissime circumrorans abluit ".
[6] Tert., *De Bapt.*, v.

baptism as it appears in the New Testament, the differences become far more noticeable than the similarities.[1] We find, for example, that the phrase " in the name of . . ."—so characteristic of Christian baptism—does not occur in any of the extant evidence concerning these rites of lustration in the mysteries. Nor, again, is there any reference to a belief that the baptized person came under the influence of a divine πνεῦμα. Again, as Oepke points out, whereas Christian baptism shares with the death of Christ the characteristic of being done " once for all " (cf. ἐφάπαξ Rom. 6. 10 in a baptismal context), the mystery rites, on the other hand, were repeated.[2] Further, J. M. Creed called attention to the subordinate place which these lustrations occupied in the mystery religions: " The mystery washings were preparatory ablutions, in no case, as it seems, identified with the actual initiation, and far less prominent in the whole economy of the mystery than was baptism in the early Church." [3] It may further be noticed that the extant evidence concerning the practice which has been most generally quoted as affording the most striking parallel to some of the Christian language about baptism, namely the *taurobolium*,[4] is far later than the period during which the New Testament significance of baptism was determined. The celebrated inscription containing the words *taurobolio criobolioque in æternum renatus* is dated no earlier than A.D. 376.[5] No doubt the practice may have been current considerably earlier, but no available evidence entitles us to assign it to a period early enough for it to have fixed the significance, far less for it to have provided the origin, of the New Testament rite of baptism.

It may still be argued that even though Christian baptism did not have its origin in the mysteries, yet some of the language used, for example, by St. Paul about its meaning can be adequately accounted for only on the hypothesis of connexion with the mystery rites. This argument has been partially answered already. Thus, as we have seen, the passage about the " putting on " of Christ (Gal. 3. 27), which Leipoldt claims must have some direct connexion with the mysteries, can be sufficiently accounted for if it is remembered that the idea was already a commonplace in the thought of contemporary Judaism, and belongs indeed to the language of Old Testament prophecy.[6] Again, if the attempt is made to connect the passages about " dying " and " rising " with the mysteries, we have to recognize that even if the evidence about " rebirth " in the mysteries were earlier in date than it actually is, there is the further difficulty that the Pauline conception is not one of " rebirth " but of " resurrection ". " That St. Paul does not use the idea of rebirth, though thinking of

---

[1] Cf. H. A. A. Kennedy, *St. Paul and the Mystery Religions* (1913), pp. 229 ff.
[2] Oepke in *Theol. Wört.*, Vol. I, p. 540.   [3] J. M. Creed, *St. Luke* (1930), p. 310.
[4] Cf. F. Cumont, *Les Religions Orientales dans le Paganisme Romain*, Fourth Edition (Paris 1929), pp. 63–64; also cf. E. T. of Second Edition (Chicago 1911), pp. 66–68; where Cumont gives a description of the *taurobolium*, based upon an account in the writings of Prudentius (*Peristeph.* x, 1011 ff.).
[5] Cf. *Corpus Inscriptionum Latinarum*, vi. 510.
[6] Cf. *supra* p. 58 with the Old Testament passages there cited.

baptism as a death, is a striking illustration of his unfamiliarity with the mysteries." [1]   But the most far-reaching difference between the Pauline teaching and that of Hellenistic religious thought (whether of the mystery cults or of the Hermetic philosophy) is to be found in the ethical sphere. Dr. Moffatt has suggested that this lack of moral emphasis in the Hellenistic religions may have been part of the cause of St. Paul's failure to use the language of " regeneration " and of his preference for " baptism into Christ " (with its associated conception of a " resurrection "); " one definite reason for preferring this to the notion of regeneration may have been that in the Hermetic theosophy the regenerate who rose to an upper level of being was relieved by ecstatic vision from the need for moral endeavour, whereas Paul's ethical passion required a conception which was devoid of such associations ".[2]   Similarly, the attempt to account for the Pauline language on the basis of the mysteries leaves quite unexplained that linking of " dying " and " rising " with moral renewal, which is so much to the fore in St. Paul and so lacking in the teaching of the mystery religions. So far as we can judge, the mystery cults made no ethical demands upon those who took part in them.   F. M. Cornford, after speaking of the " unfailing popularity of the mysteries ", continues: [3]

" The initiate was offered a blank draft upon the unknown future, which he might complete in the terms of any belief that he brought with him, with the assurance that it would be honoured.   Nothing, moreover, was demanded of him in return, save that he should submit to purification and witness the rites. So far as we know, it was at no time enjoined, that, in a moral sense, he should thenceforth walk in newness of life.   It cannot, indeed, be doubted that a ceremonial so impressive must often have produced a more or less enduring moral effect; but the nature of that effect was left to the predisposition of the initiate; it was not prescribed by the religion itself."

Thus there is nothing in the mysteries to account for one of the conceptions which St. Paul most emphatically associates with Christian baptism.   The swift transition by which he at once interprets in a moral sense the idea of dying and rising, so that it denotes the forsaking of sin and the entering upon a new way of life, is left unexplained by those who regard Pauline Christianity as the most successful among a number of competing mystery cults.   If justice is to be done to this moral emphasis in the Pauline teaching about baptism, its roots must be sought in the soil of Judaism, and not in that of the Greek mysteries.[4]   Moreover, if the suggestion made earlier be sound, that this Pauline association of baptism with the death of Jesus goes back ultimately, through the preaching of the primitive

---

[1] A. D. Nock in *Essays on the Trinity and the Incarnation* (1928), p. 116.   H. G. Marsh, op. cit., p. 133 thinks that St. Paul's failure to speak of regeneration may have been deliberate; " every-thing implied in regeneration is found in the teaching of Paul, but the significance is in the absence of the term ".

[2] J. Moffatt, *Grace in the New Testament* (1931), p. 53.

[3] *Cambridge Ancient History* (C.U.P.), Vol. IV, pp. 531 f.

[4] On this whole question the remark of H. L. Goudge is pertinent, " St. Paul was a Hebrew and quite without that sympathy with ethnic faiths which study of comparative religion has given to ourselves (cf. 1. Cor. 10. 20) ", in *Gore's Commentary* (New Testament), p. 420.

Church, to a striking saying of Jesus himself, comparing his death to a
" baptism ",[1] then the connexion of baptism with moral renewal is
entirely appropriate. The death of Jesus marked the wider inauguration
of that " New Age ", one characteristic association of which was with this
very idea of moral renewal.

Thus it would appear that the hypothesis which seeks to derive Pauline
teaching about baptism from the mystery cults will not survive an examination of the content of that teaching. The Pauline statements about
baptism witness to a world of thought far different from that of the
mysteries. That some influences from the side of the mysteries affected
later developments of Christian baptismal doctrine is very probable.
That the beginnings of this process may even be discerned in one or two
post-Pauline passages of the New Testament itself is a less certain though
quite arguable hypothesis.[2] But that the formative influences determining the origin and meaning of baptism, as reflected in the Pauline
Epistles, could have been exerted from the Hellenistic side becomes only the
more dubious, the more closely Christian baptism is studied in the context
of the ideas most prominently and consistently associated with it by St. Paul.

The determination of the source from which St. Paul derived his
baptismal teaching is of the utmost importance for those who would give a
true account of Pauline sacramentalism. No part of the Apostle's teaching
has, during recent years, been more strenuously debated or more one-
sidedly expressed. To some critics St. Paul has seemed the ultra-Pro-
testant, the exponent of a purely " spiritual " religion, for whom all signs
and symbols were superfluous. Others have claimed him as the father of
" Catholicism ", the man who more than any other turned the simple
gospel of Jesus into a sacramental cult, in which the main stress lay in the
due performance of religious rites. It needs to be recognized that extreme
views in either direction are equally unwarranted and mistaken, not least
because they read back into Pauline thought distinctions which were not
present to the mind of the Apostle, and, in fact, became relevant only for
a later age. To credit St. Paul with the belief that salvation comes *ex
opere operato* (in the commonly accepted sense of that phrase) [3] seems

---

[1] Cf. *supra*, pp. 31-32. Heitmüller, *Taufe und Abendmahl im Urchristentum* (1911), pp. 22-23,
denies that there is anything in the teaching of Jesus corresponding to the Pauline idea of
" dying " (or " being crucified ") and " being raised " with Christ. Such a denial seems to
neglect the demand, reiterated in the gospels, that the disciple should take up his cross and
follow Jesus (Mk. 8. 34; cf. Matt. 16. 24 and Lk. 9. 23; Matt. 10. 38; cf. Lk. 14. 27). That
St. Paul should include the idea of " resurrection " was a natural extension of the thought for
one who could make the claim of 1 Cor. 15. 8.

[2] On this question cf. also *infra*, pp. 93-94, 104-105.

[3] The phrase is often used to denote a view of the sacraments which approximates to the
" magical ". It is important to remember that the original meaning of the words is thereby
misunderstood; cf. *An Introduction to Pastoral Theology*, by H. Balmforth and others (1937), p.
46, where it is pointed out in reference to the scholastic formula that " in its full form it is *ex
opere operato non opponentibus obicem*, and that the second half of the formula is of equal validity
with the first. It is possible by interposing an obstacle to render the external act ineffective and
deprive it of its spiritual value. All sacramental acts require for their efficacy the right disposi-
tions in the recipient."

possible only for those who forget both his reiterated insistence upon
" faith " and the impatience with which he thrusts on one side any
reliance on the merely external act of circumcision.[1]   But to believe that
for St. Paul baptism was a bare symbol, expressive of faith and nothing
more, is no less untenable, since it fails to account for the realistic intensity
of the language about baptism in Gal. 3. 27 and other passages, the
implication of which is that in Christian baptism something is not merely
expressed but actually accomplished.

Thus N. P. Williams quotes with approval Kirsopp Lake's statement:
" Baptism is, for St. Paul and his readers, universally and unquestioningly
accepted as a mystery or sacrament which works *ex opere operato ;* and from
the unhesitating manner in which St. Paul uses this fact as a basis for
argument, as if it were a point on which Christian opinion did not vary, it
would seem as though this sacramental teaching is central in the primitive
Christianity to which the Roman Empire began to be converted ".
Professor Williams goes on to argue that " this hypothesis illuminates the
relevant passages of the Pauline writings as no other does or can do, and
. . . can only be refuted on the basis of *a priori* assumptions as to what the
Apostle ought to have believed ".[2]   It is noteworthy, however, that
Professor Williams himself seems clearly to recognize that something more
needs to be said.   A few lines farther on in his summary of Pauline
teaching he sets " faith " prominently by the side of " baptism ", and
defines this faith as " unreserved mental, moral, and emotional self-
surrender to Jesus as risen, Messiah, and Lord ".   This gives proper
emphasis to an element in the Pauline teaching which cannot be omitted
without causing serious distortion.   It is precisely the lack of any stress
upon faith that makes the passage quoted from Kirsopp Lake seem less
than adequate as a description of what St. Paul taught about baptism.[3]
Professor Williams himself provides the necessary corrective, and in what
he says about faith calls attention to something which no interpreter of
the baptismal teaching of St. Paul can afford to forget.   If it be objected
that the important baptismal context in Rom. 6 (in comment upon which
the judgement quoted from Kirsopp Lake was expressly formulated) has
little or nothing about " faith " in it in comparison with other baptismal
passages in St. Paul, it may be replied that this whole context in Rom. 6
must be read in the light of verses 8–9 : " if we died with Christ, we believe
that we shall also live with him ; knowing that Christ being raised from
the dead dieth no more ;   death no more hath dominion over him ".

---

[1] Cf. Gal. 6. 15 " neither is circumcision anything, nor uncircumcision, but a new creation ";
and the argument of 1 Cor. 10. 1 ff.

[2] Cf N. P. Williams, *The Ideas of the Fall and of Original Sin* (1927), p. 135.   The earlier
quotation is taken from K. Lake, *The Earlier Epistles of St. Paul* (second edition, 1919),
p. 385.

[3] It is true that several pages later in the book from which the quotation is taken Kirsopp Lake
writes: " ' Faith ' was, no doubt, the necessary preliminary to Baptism, and was the condition
of salvation "; but such a reference does far less than justice to the distinctive Pauline conception
of faith and the importance which St. Paul attaches to it almost everywhere in his writings.

The emphasis upon faith in this context seems less obvious only because St. Paul chose to express the idea by the verb rather than by the noun. The faith which St. Paul expresses in this baptismal context by means of the verb πιστεύω is essentially that same faith in the activity of God revealed in the " resurrection " which elsewhere also is linked with baptism.[1] What the first-century Christian " believed " was that those who shared in Christ's " death to sin " could also share in his resurrection, and by the same activity of God which was at work therein be " raised " to " newness of life ". This Pauline linking of baptism with faith in the activity of God displayed both in the resurrection of Jesus and in the " raising " of believers would seem to confirm our earlier suggestion (based on a consideration of passages in Acts) that, for the average early Christian, baptism " symbolized " the Gospel of the Resurrection.[2] The interpretation, therefore, of the passage about baptism in Rom. 6—which does not lack a reference to " faith " if πιστεύομεν in verse 8 is rightly understood—must be made in the light of other baptismal contexts in the Pauline writings where the place of faith is even more expressly emphasized.[3] The prominence given to faith in these passages taken as a whole is sufficient to condemn any exegesis of the baptismal teaching in Rom. 6 which does less than justice to the centrality of faith in Pauline theology.

But equal injustice is done to another element in the Apostle's thought when, partly through fear lest his teaching should appear to border on the " magical ", and partly through unwillingness to credit St. Paul with any conception that seems to fall below the purely " spiritual ", an unreal separation is made between faith and the means whereby that faith is awakened and sustained. To persist in this separation, and to see, for example, in baptism nothing more than a symbol expressive of faith, may come perilously near to denying the very principle of the Incarnation. Material things, by the grace of God, may mediate a spiritual process.[4]

---

[1] Cf. Col. 2. 12.   [2] Cf. *supra*, pp. 46–47.

[3] Cf. Gal. 3. 23–27; Col. 2. 11–12; (and Eph. 1. 13; 4. 5).

[4] No one has argued more persuasively in recent times for this particular truth of the Christian religion than the late Baron von Hügel. For a typical passage, see: *Essays and Addresses on the Philosophy of Religion* (J. M. Dent, 1921), p. 251: " That the act and life of faith have nothing to do, in their generation, with the senses, although once faith is awakened, there is no harm in expressing this pure spirituality in symbols of sense, is, objectively, a doctrinaire one-sidedness. I kiss my child not only because I love it; I kiss it also in order to love it. A religious picture not only expresses my awakened faith; it is a help to my faith's awakening. And the whole doctrine of the Incarnation, of any and every condescension of God toward man—man so essentially body as well as mind—is against any such ' pure ' spirituality. Great as doubtless has been the Synagogue, yet the Temple services were not for nothing; and great as Judaism with the Synagogue has been, Judaism with both Synagogue and Temple would have been more complete. And it is not magic, but a sheer fact traceable throughout our many-sided life, that we often grow, mentally and spiritually, almost solely by the stimulation of our senses or almost solely by the activity of other minds. Magic begins only when and where things physical are taken to effect spiritual results apart altogether from minds transmitting or receiving. It is doubtless the fear of priestly power and its intrusion into politics which has determined (from say Wycliff, until now) this quite unphilosophical ' magic ' scare among so many Protestants." Cf. also *Essays and Addresses on the Philosophy of Religion*, Second Series (1926), p. 79, " As to St. Paul . . . nothing can be more certain than that Baptism and the Holy Eucharist are for him sensible-spiritual, and not purely spiritual, and that these sensible-spiritual acts form, for him, the very basis and centre of the Christian religious life and worship."

Thus, when once the Pauline stress on faith has been recognized, the
fullest meaning must also be given to the language in which St. Paul
comes back again and again to the rite of baptism itself. No true interpretation of this is possible unless it is continually read and understood
against the background of the evangelizing and missionary activity of the
early Church. It cannot be too strongly emphasized that many of
the difficulties about the doctrine of baptism arise because statements of
St. Paul and others in the New Testament about *adult* baptism as they
knew it in the first century A.D. are applied, without modification, to
infant baptism as most Christian communions know it to-day. Professor
Dodd has written (in comment upon St. Paul's baptismal teaching in
Rom. 6): " As he is addressing people who were baptized upon conversion, in adult years, the question of the validity of baptism apart
from the conscious assent of the baptized person does not arise ".[1] Baptism
was the recognized way of entering the Christian Church. As in some
parts of the mission-field to-day, so then, to accept baptism was so decisive
a step that the very act possessed a significance which at other periods of
Christian history (e.g. when infant baptism is normal) must necessarily be
separable from it. St. Paul did not have to justify or defend the practice
of baptism. It never seems to have occurred to him, so far as this rite
was concerned, to separate the act from its implication: the two were one.
The rite and its meaning were, for the thought of the Apostle, an indissoluble unity.[2] Baptism was there already as an established part of
Christian belief and practice—an eschatological " symbol " embodying
the most profound realities of the Gospel. St. Paul could thus take the
rite for granted and argue from it. In St. Paul's hands the familiar
symbolism provided a yet more clearly articulated presentation of the
Gospel. Here it may be granted that the Apostle probably went farther
than some of his contemporaries in drawing out the full implications of
baptism, yet, if we accept the evidence of the book of Acts, it would seem
that in this he was but making more explicit truths already acknowledged
in part by those who preached the Gospel before him.

But this is not all. For St. Paul baptism was far more than a highly
dramatic means of preaching the Gospel. In baptism itself something
happened. The symbolism was not only expressive but also effective.
St. Paul was a Jew of the Dispersion, and, as Canon Knox has shown, for
the Judaism of the Dispersion " a past event of history . . . embodied in

[1] C. H. Dodd, *The Epistle to the Romans, Moffatt New Testament Commentary* (1932), p. 86.
[2] It is perhaps going too far to say with Goguel, " L'idée d'une opposition entre action rituelle
ou sacramentaire et action spirituelle est une idée toute moderne "; cf. M. Goguel, *Au Seuil
de l'Evangile : Jean-Baptiste* (1928), p. 93. St. Paul's treatment of circumcision (cf. Gal. 6. 15)
shows that, where he deemed it necessary he could distinguish the " ritual " from the " spiritual "
act. But this makes all the more significant the absence of any such distinction in respect of
baptism; cf. the words of J. M. Creed in *J. T. S.* Vol. XXIX, (1928), p. 57, " Controversy
with Judaism impelled St. Paul to disengage from its outward signs the faith which lay behind
the ordinances of the Jewish Church. But in the case of Baptism in Christ's name such dis-
crimination was not felt to be necessary. In a young and expanding society the outward and the
inward, symbol and reality, are united in natural accord. The problems of sacramental theory
belong to a later stage in the Church's life."

a ritual action, became an ' effective symbol ' for producing a change in the character of the believer ".[1]   This may the better be understood (as we have seen) [2] if we regard it as an extension and a *corporate* application of those " symbolic " actions which formed so striking a feature of the mission of some of the greatest of the Old Testament prophets.   Further (as we have also seen), an example of this corporate application of " symbolism " is provided by the ritual of the Day of Atonement, in which the goat " for Azazel " was sent into the wilderness, bearing the sins of the people.   For St. Paul salvation was essentially the result of a divine act wrought in the death and resurrection of Jesus.   We know that St. Paul saw the Lord's Supper as the means appointed by Jesus himself, an " effective symbol " whereby that Act was solemnly recalled and, as it were, *re-presented* in the worship and experience of the believing community.[3]   When we remember the vividness with which he draws out the meaning of Christian baptism and links it with the death and resurrection of Jesus, it is congruous to surmise that in something of the same way he saw baptism also as a means whereby the dying and rising again of Jesus, and the gift of his Spirit, were repeated in the experience of one who *in that very act* became part of the " Body of Christ ", a " son of God ", an " heir of the Kingdom ".[4]   As a verse in Ephesians puts it (the verse occurs in a context the phraseology of which is in many respects closely parallel to that of the great baptismal passage in Colossians) : [5]   " By grace have ye been saved through faith ".[6]   In St. Paul's thought there was both an objective and a subjective side.   The whole process of salvation was grounded in the death and resurrection of Jesus.   That was an act of God's " grace ".   The benefits of that act had to be appropriated by " faith ".   That was the response of man—a response that was, itself, a divine gift, ". . . and that not of yourselves : it is the gift of God ".[7]

---

[1] Knox, op. cit., p. 98.   [2] Cf. *supra*, pp. 20–22.

[3] Cf. 1 Cor. 11. 26, " As often as ye eat this bread, and drink the cup, ye proclaim the Lord's death till he come ".

[4] Cf. E. C. Hoskyns, *The Fourth Gospel*, ed. by F. N. Davey (1940), Vol. 1, p. 229, " an action, which can, by the grace of God, become what it signifies "; A. Oepke in *Theol. Wört.*, Vol. 1, p. 538, " . . . zieht die Taufe ihre Kraft aus dem versöhnenden Handeln Gottes in Christus, genauer aus dem Sühnetode Christi. . . . Sie versetzt objektiv in Christus, den zweiten Adam, und damit aus der Todesregion des ersten in die δικαίωσις ζωῆς und die Gotteskindschaft hinein "; cf. also the words quoted by Oepke, op. cit., p. 539, from von Soden, " Der Tod Christi ist das Sakrament, die Taufe das sakramentale Bekenntnis zu ihm, in dem die Teilhabe an ihm gewonnen wird : die Einverleibung in den Leib Christi ".

[5] Cf. especially Eph. 2. 5, " . . . when we were dead in trespasses he quickened us together with Christ ", and Col. 2. 13, " and you when you were dead in trespasses . . . did he quicken together with him ".   Note also συνήγειρεν (Eph. 2. 6) and συνηγέρθητε (Col. 2. 12). Throughout the Ephesians passage, as in Colossians, there is an emphasis upon the action of God, and upon the new moral life which the death and resurrection of Jesus make possible for the believer.

[6] Eph. 2. 8.   Even if this be not regarded as written by St. Paul himself, it must be allowed that here at least the disciple has exactly retained the Pauline emphasis.

[7] Some commentators on Eph. 2. 8 refer the clause " and that not of yourselves : it is the gift of God " not specifically to the word " faith " immediately preceding, but rather to the whole concept of " salvation " under consideration in this verse.   Haupt quotes the comment of Chrysostom, who, like most of the ancient commentators, supports the former exegesis, οὐδὲ ἡ πίστις φησὶν ἐξ ἡμῶν. εἰ γὰρ μὴ ἦλθεν, εἰ γὰρ μὴ ἐκάλεσεν, πῶς ἐδυνάμεθα πιστεῦσαι; ὥστε οὐδὲ τὸ τῆς πίστεως ἡμέτερον, θεοῦ φησι τὸ δῶρον.   To Haupt himself this interpretation is untenable because

Baptism embodies both these two aspects. It is a solemn showing forth, a " re-presentation ", of that act of God which was achieved once for all in the death and resurrection of Jesus. It is at the same time a concrete expression of faith on the part of the believer. In the words of Bernard Manning: " To understand this close and indivisible unity in Christianity of the act of a man and that which lies behind it—something which that man himself did not perform—is to understand something near the centre of our most holy faith ".[1] Because in his most significant statements about baptism St. Paul so intimately and indissolubly unites these two aspects of the rite, his teaching concerning baptism cannot be truly characterized as other than sacramental.

---

the neuter τοῦτο could not take up the feminine πίστις. He accepts the view of modern commentators from Calvin onwards, which substitutes for this way of taking the passage the other exegesis which refers the clause καὶ τοῦτο. . . to the *whole* of the preceding sentence. Armitage Robinson refers to the older explanation, and claims that " the difference of gender is not fatal to such a view ". But he inclines himself to the modern interpretation on the ground that " the context demands the wider reference ". Moffatt's rendering seems to support this latter exegesis, and E. F. Scott in the Moffatt Commentary clearly takes it this way. Similarly W. L. Knox seems to take it thus, op. cit., pp. 187–188, " They must always remember that they are saved by grace through faith; the gift comes from God, not from themselves, lest any man should boast ". But some modern interpreters have returned to the patristic exegesis; cf. Lueken in *Die Schriften des Neuen Testaments* (1908), p. 356, " Denn auch der Glaube ist Gottes Werk "; Dodd in *The Abingdon Bible Commentary* (1929), p. 1229, " ' saving faith ' must not be regarded as a meritorious activity of the human will, but as itself God's gift "; cf. also V. Taylor, *The Atonement in New Testament Teaching* (1940), p. 126 *n.* On a question of this sort the judgement of a Greek commentator like Chrysostom would seem particularly valuable.

[1] B. L. Manning, *Essays in Orthodox Dissent* (1939), pp. 68–69.

7

Baptism in the Johannine Writings

CONSIDERATION has already been given to two of the Johannine references to baptism, those which represent Jesus or his disciples as actually practising the rite during his ministry in Judæa.[1] It is necessary now to examine two other Johannine passages: that occurring in the conversation with Nicodemus, about the man who is " born of water and the Spirit ", and the statement in the First Epistle that Jesus Christ " came by water and blood ".[2]

Jesus answered and said unto him, Verily, verily, I say unto thee, Except a man be born anew, he cannot see the kingdom of God. Nicodemus saith unto him, How can a man be born when he is old? can he enter a second time into his mother's womb, and be born? Jesus answered, Verily, verily, I say unto thee, Except a man be born of water and the Spirit, he cannot enter into the kingdom of God (Jn. 3. 3-5).

The emphasis of this discourse to Nicodemus is on the need for spiritual " birth " as the essential prerequisite of entry into the Kingdom of God. It will be noticed that the thought expressed in verse 5 has an earlier counterpart in verse 3. In this earlier verse it seems probable that the word ἄνωθεν, which is translated in the R.V. " anew ", should rather be rendered " from above " (cf. R.V. mg.).[3] The question of Nicodemus in verse 4 presupposes that ἄνωθεν has been taken to mean " anew ", but the context makes it clear that this involves a misunderstanding. This misunderstanding provides the occasion for the repetition of the saying in a slightly different form. The ambiguous word ἄνωθεν is replaced by the phrase ἐξ ὕδατος καὶ πνεύματος, and the idea of " seeing " the Kingdom of God gives place to that of " entering into " it. For γεννηθῇ almost all the Latin versions read renatus. By some critics this has been taken to point to a Western reading ἀναγεννηθῇ. But the compound verb ἀναγεννάω is not a Johannine word, and Bernard is probably right in regarding the Latin renatus as an interpretation rather than a direct translation.[4] The attempt has been made to discredit the words ὕδατος καὶ as no part of the

---

[1] Cf. supra, pp. 30-31.

[2] The present writer takes the view that the Fourth Gospel and the Johannine Epistles were written by the same author. For a statement of the arguments against this commonly accepted opinion see the article by C. H. Dodd, Bulletin of the John Rylands Library (April 1937), pp. 129-156; and cf. also the references cited in W. F. Howard, The Fourth Gospel in Recent Criticism and Interpretation (1931), p. 257. Those who dispute the common authorship would agree that the First Epistle represents the views of the Johannine " school ".

[3] Cf. Bernard, op. cit., Vol. I, p. 102.

[4] Op. cit., Vol. I, pp. 103-104. It may be noticed that Justin uses the verb ἀναγεννάω in what appears to be a loose citation of this passage (Apol. i, 61), but no conclusion about the original form of the Greek text can be based upon this, since Justin's quotations seldom agree exactly with the text known to us.

true text of verse 5. It is pointed out that some manuscripts (א a b e, etc.) have inserted these words in verse 8 before πνεύματος, and, since it is clear that they form no part of the original text of that verse, it is argued that they may have been wrongly inserted also in verse 5.[1] There is no manuscript evidence, however, for their omission in verse 5,[2] and no patristic citation of the verse mentions " Spirit " without " water ". It seems reasonably certain, therefore, that the words ὕδατος καὶ should be regarded as original.

Most commentators take the word " water " as an obvious reference to Christian baptism. Among recent writers on the Fourth Gospel Dr. H. Odeberg is exceptional in refusing to allow any such allusion. He thinks that the word " water " must be interpreted against the background of Jewish mystical thought, and that it stands for what he describes as a " divine efflux ". He quotes passages from rabbinic sources concerning the " celestial waters " (cf. Gen. 1. 7), in which " water " seems to be regarded as a generative principle, the " seed " of the spiritual life.[3] It is very possible that such speculations were known to the Fourth Evangelist and that they influenced the expression of his thought. It is more difficult to follow Odeberg in his denial of any allusion to baptism; in a Christian work written at the end of the first century A.D. the mention of " water " and the " Spirit " would surely suggest the Christian rite in which water and the Spirit were strikingly associated. Dr. R. H. Strachan in the revised edition of his book on the Fourth Gospel [4] acknowledges the value of Odeberg's suggestions, but claims that the use by the Fourth Evangelist of these rabbinic ideas about water need not preclude a further reference to baptism. Such a *double* use of the symbol would be thoroughly in line with the method of the Fourth Evangelist, who would thus be interpreting a Christian practice in the light of rabbinic speculations which elsewhere are essential for a true understanding of some passages in this Gospel.[5]

But though a reference to Christian baptism is intelligible in a Gospel written at the end of the first century A.D., it is difficult to believe that such an allusion formed part of the teaching of Jesus, just as the Fourth Evangelist records it. Such a reference during our Lord's ministry could hardly have been appreciated by an enquirer like Nicodemus. It would seem far more probable that we have here a striking conception of Jesus restated by the Fourth Evangelist in the light of the Church's faith and

---

[1] Bernard, loc. cit., refers to the treatment of the passage by Kirsopp Lake, *The Influence of Textual Criticism on the Exegesis of the New Testament* (1904), p. 18. Cf. also F. H. Chase in *J. T. S.* Vol. VI (1905), pp. 504–505.

[2] The only textual evidence which might be used to support the view that the reference to " water " in verse 5 is not original is the fact that the Sinaitic Syriac reads " begotten of Spirit and of water ". This variation of order might be held to point to some degree of textual uncertainty. But it would seem inadvisable to press the evidence of a single authority.

[3] Cf. H. Odeberg, *The Fourth Gospel* (1929), pp. 48–71.

[4] R. H. Strachan, *The Fourth Gospel* (third edition, 1941), p. 135.

[5] Cf. C. H. Dodd in *Bulletin of the John Rylands Library* (July 1935), p. 334, where it is shown that light is thrown upon John 8. 56 by the rabbinic interpretation of Gen. 24. 1.

practice in his own day.[1] The use of the preposition ἐκ elsewhere in the phrase ἐκ θεοῦ γεννηθῆναι (cf. e.g. Jn. 1. 13) suggests that the " Spirit " is here regarded as the " Begetter of believers ",[2] and the association of the " water " with the " Spirit " proves how profound must have been the significance of Christian baptism for the Fourth Evangelist. The rite of water-baptism united with the activity of the Spirit is regarded as the means whereby the Christian is " born from above ". Bernard has remarked that " the representation of baptism as a new birth is infrequent in the N.T.".[3] St. Paul regards baptism as a " dying and rising " with Christ, and does not use the imagery of rebirth. We may recall, however, that when he says " if any man is in Christ, there is a new creation ",[4] his thought is not far from that of " birth from above ".[5] It may further be remembered that the connexion between " baptism " and " Spirit " and " sonship " has been traced in the teaching of St. Paul,[6] and that the suggestion has been put forward that the origin of this connexion may be sought in the baptism of Jesus himself. All this makes it likely that the linking of water-baptism with the " birth from above " which is found in Jn. 3. 5 may be no innovation, but rather the developed and more precise expression of a conception which can be carried back at least to St. Paul, and perhaps earlier still. The *phraseology* of this Johannine saying of Jesus may owe something to the religious background of those who lived in the Græco-Roman world at the end of the first century A.D. There is nothing in the *thought* of the passage to preclude for it a far earlier origin. As Dr. Howard has put it : " We are justified then in saying that we have probably here a genuine saying of Jesus which in its Johannine form has a *nuance* and an application to contemporary needs that is the mark of the Evangelist ".[7]

This teaching about the " new creation ", represented in the Johannine idiom as " birth from above ", is not the only Pauline baptismal idea which may be traced in this third chapter of the Fourth Gospel. The presence of another conception with which St. Paul strikingly links baptism may be discovered in the Johannine discourse. At the conclusion [8] of this discourse to Nicodemus about being " born from above " emphasis is laid on the necessity for our Lord's death. " As Moses lifted up the serpent in the wilderness, even so must the Son of man be lifted up: that whosoever believeth may in him have eternal life " (3. 14–15). Now to " believe " is a characteristic of those who in the Fourth Gospel are called

---

[1] Cf. Bernard, op. cit., Vol. I, pp. clxv, 105.   [2] Cf. Bernard, op. cit., Vol. I, p. 105.
[3] Cf. Bernard, op. cit., Vol. I, p. clxiii.   [4] Cf. 2 Cor. 5. 17.
[5] There are passages in the Epistle of Barnabas (probably more or less contemporary with the Fourth Gospel) connecting baptism with the new creation; " we go down into the water full of sins and foulness, and we come up bearing the fruit of fear in our hearts, and having hope on Jesus in the Spirit "; " when we received the remission of sins, and put our hope on the Name, we became new, being created again from the beginning ", *Ep. Barn.*, xi, 11, xvi 8, cited by Howard, op. cit., p. 220.
[6] Cf. *supra*, p. 69.   [7] Howard, op. cit., p. 220.
[8] Bernard argues that the " comment " of the Evangelist begins at verse 16; cf. Bernard, op. cit., Vol. I, p. 117.

G

" children of God " (τέκνα θεοῦ).[1] It may thus be observed that while (as we have seen) for the Fourth Evangelist this " birth from above " is the work of the Spirit in baptism, so the chief possession of those who are thus made " God's children ", namely " eternal life ", is the direct result of the " lifting up " of the Son of man. Thus it may be affirmed that for St. John, no less than for St. Paul, baptism and the death of Jesus belong to the same circle of ideas.

> Who is he that overcometh the world, but he that believeth that Jesus is the Son of God? This is he that came by water and blood, even Jesus Christ; not with the water only, but with the water and with the blood. And it is the Spirit that beareth witness, because the Spirit is the truth. For there are three who bear witness, the Spirit, and the water, and the blood : and the three agree in one (1 Jn. 5. 5–8).

In this passage the writer is clearly controverting certain erroneous views in the community for which he wrote. He affirms the necessity of the Christian belief in Jesus as the Son of God, and goes on to define this belief more exactly in relation to contemporary heresy. It seems most probable that the false teaching was a form of Docetism which denied that the Crucifixion had any part in the purpose of salvation. Christ was truly baptized, but he did not suffer upon the Cross. This accords well with the account of the teaching of Cerinthus given by Irenæus : " After the baptism there descended upon him [i.e. Jesus] in the form of a dove the Christ from that Ruler who is supreme over all things. He then announced the unknown Father and wrought miracles. In the end however the Christ departed again from Jesus, and, while Jesus suffered and rose again, Christ remained impassible continuing to exist as a spiritual being ".[2] The relevance of verse 6 as an answer to teaching of this sort at once becomes apparent. Christ and Jesus, and Baptism and Crucifixion, are not to be sundered. The author asserts that " this is he who came by water and blood ", and adds the double name *Jesus Christ*. To put his meaning beyond all doubt he then denies what Cerinthus affirmed (i.e. that Christ came with the " water " alone) and affirms what Cerinthus denied (i.e. that Christ came with the " water " and with the " blood ").[3] In other words, Christ was as truly present in Jesus at the Crucifixion as at the baptism. " Jesus " and " Christ " are one and cannot be separated. To understand this as the primary meaning of verse 6 seems to provide the most satisfactory interpretation, but the

---

[1] Cf. Jn. 1. 12 " as many as received him, to them gave he the right to become children of God, even to them that believe on his name ".

[2] Iren. *Adv. Haer.* I xxvi 1 : " Et post baptismum descendisse in eum ab ea principalitate quae est super omnia Christum figura columbae, et tunc annuntiasse incognitum patrem et virtutes perfecisse, in fine autem revolasse iterum Christum de Iesu, et Iesum passum esse et resurrexisse, Christum autem impassibilem perseverasse, existentem spiritalem " (καὶ μετὰ τὸ βάπτισμα κατελθεῖν εἰς αὐτὸν τὸν ἀπὸ τῆς ὑπὲρ τὰ ὅλα αὐθεντίας, τὸν Χριστὸν ἐν εἴδει περιστερᾶς καὶ τότε κηρύξαι τὸν ἄγνωστον πατέρα, καὶ δυνάμεις ἐπιτελέσαι, πρὸς δὲ τῷ τέλει ἀποστῆναι τὸν Χριστὸν ἀπὸ τοῦ ᾿Ιησοῦ, καὶ τὸν ᾿Ιησοῦν πεπονθέναι καὶ ἐγηγέρθαι, τὸν δὲ Χριστὸν ἀπαθῆ διαμεμενηκέναι πνευματικὸν ὑπάρχοντα.)

[3] Cf. R. Law, *The Tests of Life* (T. & T. Clark, 1909), p. 97 *n.* 1.

acceptance of this exegesis by no means excludes a subordinate and secondary reference to some of the other ideas which have been discovered in the verse. Thus in the work of a writer for whom symbolism meant so much, it is hard to think that when he wrote this verse he had not at the back of his mind the tradition recorded in Jn. 19. 34 (" one of the soldiers with a spear pierced his side, and straightway there came out blood and water "), though it is to be noticed that the words " water " and " blood " there occur in the reverse order. Again, there is a strong tendency among certain commentators, both ancient and modern, to find in the passage an allusion to the Christian sacraments of baptism and the Eucharist.[1] This sort of " veiled " reference would seem particularly appropriate in a writer who appears to avoid direct mention of the sacraments.[2] It is probable, however, if such a sacramental allusion is present in this passage, that the reference is to one rather than to both of the two sacraments of the Gospel. Commentators call attention to the difficulty that, while " water " could well stand for baptism, the use of " blood " by itself as a symbol for the Eucharist is without parallel in the New Testament, or in early Christian literature outside the canonical writings. The attempt has therefore been made to relate " water " to Christian baptism and " blood " to the death of Jesus. A. E. Brooke has criticized such an interpretation as unsatisfactory,[3] but the criticism seems to lose much of its force if it be established that for the early Church it was natural to link baptism with the death of Jesus. It will be remembered that we have seen reason to believe that this connexion made so much of by St. Paul may go back to the earliest Christian tradition,[4] and possibly has its roots in the teaching of Jesus himself.[5] Thus, without abandoning the exegesis, according to which the primary reference of the words " by water " in verse 6 is not to Christian baptism but rather to the baptism of Jesus,[6] we may nevertheless allow a secondary reference to that rite of Christian baptism which, for each believer, was the counterpart of our Lord's own baptism. How pointed becomes the mention of " water and blood " in a single phrase for those who knew that their own baptism with water had become effectual only because it had been preceded by the blood-baptism of Jesus upon the Cross![7] That this Christian rite of initiation should be connected so intimately with the death of Jesus (in a phrase governed by a single preposition) need cause no difficulty, but

---

[1] Cf. the references cited in W. F. Howard, *Christianity according to St. John* (1943), p. 147.

[2] Thus while Jn. 6 contains profoundly sacramental teaching, the Gospel contains no account of the Institution of the Eucharist.

[3] A. E. Brooke, *The Johannine Epistles I.C.C.* (1912), p. 132.

[4] Cf. Rom. 6. 3; and *supra*, p. 60 *n*. 1.   [5] Cf. Lk. 12. 50.

[6] This seems to be demanded by the tense of the participle ἐλθών; cf. Brooke, op. cit., p. 135.

[7] It is tempting to see in this a reason for the difference of order in which " water " and " blood " are spoken of in the First Epistle and in the Fourth Gosepl. When speaking of Jesus (1 Jn. 5. 6), the author mentions the " water " before the " blood ", because the baptism of Jesus himself preceded his Crucifixion. In the Gospel, however (Jn. 19. 34), where the writer is " witnessing " (verse 35) to the reality and the efficacy of the atoning death, he adopts the order " blood and water " because he knows as part of the Christian faith that it was the death of Christ that gave meaning and potency to Christian baptism. But perhaps this is fanciful!

rather lend powerful support to the conclusion to which our study of the evidence seems to be leading us, namely that the connexion of baptism with the death of Jesus, so far from being a Pauline peculiarity, must be regarded as something which formed part of the faith of the primitive Church, and something, moreover, which may actually rest in the last resort upon a striking word of Jesus himself.

The probability that Christian baptism was in the mind of the writer of the First Epistle becomes greater when full weight is given to what he goes on to say concerning the " threefold witness ".[1] The change from the aorist participle ὁ ἐλθών (verse 6) to the present participles τὸ μαρτυροῦν (verse 6) and οἱ μαρτυροῦντες (verse 7) implies that the *primary* reference is now not to the past events of the life of Jesus but rather to a present experience, an experience which, admittedly, is made possible only because those past events actually took place.   The writer emphasizes that the Spirit is the ultimate source of " witness ", and in this function unites the Spirit with the " water " and the " blood ".   The stress on the Spirit may be due to the fact that in the false teaching, which the Epistle was written to confute, a different function from that of " witness " was assigned to the Spirit.   More probably the reason is that for this writer the Spirit is pre-eminently the " Witness-bearer " (cf. Jn. 15. 26).[2]   It may also be noted that the inclusion of the Spirit makes the witness threefold, thus satisfying the full Jewish requirements for a legally valid attestation.[3]   " These three ", says the writer, " agree in one " (literally, " are for the one thing ", " converge upon the one purpose "), namely that of witnessing that Jesus is the Son of God.   Once again in a baptismal context we observe (besides the link of baptism with the death of Jesus) a pronounced emphasis upon the " Spirit " and upon " Sonship ".

After having considered these references separately, we may now usefully try to combine the teaching they contain.   The " faith " which, as we have seen, is the characteristic of those whom the writer calls " children of God ", consists in the conviction that " Jesus is the Son of God ".   In developing the meaning of that confession, the writer seizes upon two supreme moments in the life of Jesus, his baptism and his death. The passage in the First Epistle might almost be paraphrased : " this is he who received the twofold baptism, the water-baptism in the Jordan and the blood-baptism upon Calvary ".   Just as the baptism of Jesus by John initiated his earthly ministry and marked the bestowal of the Spirit upon Jesus himself, so the Cross inaugurated a yet wider Messianic

---

[1] It is hardly necessary to emphasize that the reading of the Authorized Version in verses 7–8 (" in heaven . . . in earth "), according to which three " heavenly witnesses " are contrasted with three " earthly witnesses ", forms no part of the true text.   This " interesting but unfortunate gloss " seems to have found its way into the Latin Bible (perhaps in Spain) in the fourth century, but it is found in no Greek manuscript earlier than the fourteenth century.   Cf. Brooke, op. cit., pp. 154–165.

[2] Cf. Brooke, op. cit., p. 136.

[3] Cf. Deut. 19. 15.

ministry [1] and marked the release of that fuller activity of the Spirit which became possible for others only when Jesus had been " glorified ".[2] We recall the Synoptic passage in which Jesus speaks of his death as a " baptism " (Lk. 12. 50). It was suggested earlier that in these words our Lord implies that his death is that by which the full powers of the Kingdom are to be released.[3] The counterpart of this Synoptic saying may be found in the Fourth Gospel; " except a grain of wheat fall into the earth and die, it abideth by itself alone; but if it die, it beareth much fruit " (Jn. 12. 24). The " glorification " (i.e. the death) of the Son of Man must precede the harvest of the Kingdom. This conception accords closely with the use of the preposition διά in 1 Jn. 5. 6, where " the idea may be that of the door, so to say, through which Christ entered upon His mission ".[4]

This teaching in the First Epistle so closely linking the baptism and death of Jesus with the " witness " of the Spirit concerning his " Sonship " must be set alongside the saying to Nicodemus which asserts that the birth " from above " as a result of which a man enters the Kingdom of God must be " of water and the Spirit ". It would seem that in Johannine teaching the rite of baptism, whereby a man is " born from above ", " of water and the Spirit ", becomes a " child of God ", and " enters into the Kingdom of God ", is for the Christian regarded as the counterpart of the baptism of Jesus. As Robert Law wrote: " It is evident that for the writer of the Epistle the Baptism (though it is not definitely recorded in the Fourth Gospel) was no mere incident in the life of Jesus, no merely formal inauguration of His Messianic ministry. It was by His Baptism 'with the Holy Ghost and with power ' that Jesus was qualified to be the Saviour of the world. The Holy Ghost by whom His humanity was begotten in the Virgin's womb, who formed and nurtured and trained in Him that sinless manhood which brought back the lost image of God to earth, was then first poured out upon Him ' not by measure ', that from Him it might again proceed in life-giving stream through the world of souls. It was thus that the Divine Life became in Him a perennial and overflowing fountain of regenerative power; and to this as a fact of history, to say nothing more, the Sacrament of Baptism is the abiding witness in the Church. Christian Baptism apart from the Baptism of Christ would be meaningless. Only He who has the fulness of the Spirit can impart the Spirit." [5] Thus we are induced by yet another part of the New Testament evidence to recognize one of the chief antecedents of Christian baptism in the baptism of Jesus himself.[6] Both may be said to inaugurate the Kingdom of God and to mark the descent of the Holy Spirit, the one

---

[1] Cf. Law, op. cit., p. 96, " When . . . it is said that Jesus the Son of God ' came ' by water and by blood, it is signified that first by His Baptism and then by His Death, Jesus entered actively and effectively upon His Messianic ministry ".

[2] Cf. the implication of Jn. 7. 39, " the Spirit was not yet given; because Jesus was not yet glorified ".

[3] Cf. *supra*, p. 32.

[4] Law, op. cit., p. 96 n. 2.

[5] Law, op. cit., pp. 121–122.

[6] Cf. *supra*, pp. 33, 42, 69 n. 2.

for Jesus himself and the other for him who " believes " and has " eternal
life ".   Further, we must give full weight to the fact that, just as in the
First Epistle the baptism of Jesus is linked in a single phrase with his
death, so in the Fourth Gospel the reference to Christian baptism occurs
in a discourse which concludes with a striking saying about the " lifting
up " of the Son of Man.[1]   The truth would seem to be that in Johannine
teaching the antecedents of the Christian sacrament are twofold; the
baptism of Jesus and his death upon the cross.   If this be acknowledged,
there is no difficulty in accounting for the main ideas with which Christian
baptism is associated in the Johannine writings.   To be " born from
above ", to be a " child of God ",[2] is, for the Christian, the counterpart of
that " Sonship " of which Jesus became uniquely conscious at his own
baptism.   Further, it is only to be expected that the Spirit should be
linked with Christian baptism in view of the prominence of the conception
of the Spirit in the stories of the baptism of Jesus.[3]   Again, to " enter the
Kingdom of God " was possible for the baptized convert, because behind
every Christian baptism was the death of Jesus that " opened the Kingdom
of Heaven ", or, to express the same idea in Johannine language, that
" lifting up " of the Son of Man through which it made possible that
everyone who believed should in him have eternal life,[4] or again, that
" glorification " of the Son of Man which released the full powers of the
Spirit for those who believed on him.[5]

Attention has often been called to the fact that, though in the Johannine
writings there is to be found some of the most profoundly sacramental
teaching in the New Testament, nevertheless the references to the sacraments themselves are veiled and indirect.   This marked characteristic
of the Fourth Evangelist is probably to be explained, at least in part, by
the circumstances of the age for which he wrote.   Dr. Howard has
recently pointed out that within half a generation a prominent leader of
the Church was to formulate the sort of sacramental doctrine which is to
be found in the letters of Ignatius.[6]   It seems probable that the Fourth
Evangelist was in sympathy with the attitude which resulted in such
teaching, and yet at the same time was fully aware of the perils to which

---

[1] Jn. 3. 14–15.

[2] For the evidence that in the Johannine idiom these are alternative ways of expressing one
and the same conception, cf. *infra*, pp. 93–94.

[3] The Fourth Evangelist does not narrate the Baptism of Jesus, but alludes unmistakably to
it in 1. 32, and here the emphasis is laid upon the descent of the Spirit and its " abiding " upon
Jesus.   The Johannine reticence concerning the actual Baptism may be due to a desire on the
part of the author to lend no support to those who at the end of the first century A.D. unduly
exalted John the Baptist.   (Cf. also what is said on this page, about the veiled character of the
Johannine sacramental allusions.)   It is noteworthy that in this passage containing the allusion
to the Baptism of Jesus there is also a testimony about the redemptive efficacy of his death,
" Behold the Lamb of God, which taketh away the sin of the world! " (1. 29).   Here again
there is a close link between the baptism and the death of Jesus.

[4] Jn. 3. 14–15.   [5] Jn. 7. 39.

[6] Cf. W. F. Howard, *Christianity according to St. John* (1943), p. 145.   A typical passage from
Ignatius is that in which he speaks of the Bread in the Eucharist as " the medicine of immortality "
(φάρμακον ἀθανασίας), *Ad Eph.*, xx.   For the fuller quotation of this and other references, cf.
Howard, op. cit., pp. 129–130.

such teaching might lead. Thus while he was keenly alive to the truth contained in such sacramental teaching and practice, " deeply responsive to the harmonious appeal of form and spirit ", it is also true that " the perils of such an attitude to sacramental grace were clear to this practical mystic ". He knew the power of a sacramental religion to nourish spiritual life and build up Christian character, yet he knew also the dangers of a false sacramentalism, and perhaps recognized in the world of contemporary religious thought, both Christian and non-Christian, tendencies which, if uncorrected, might result in a form of religion that was little more than superstition. In such a situation it was the part of a wise Christian leader to present his sacramental doctrine in the form of veiled allusions, that while, on the one hand, the discerning might appropriate such teaching and lose none of its benefits, those, on the other hand, who might misunderstand would not thereby be confirmed in a false and unethical sacramentalism.

The question concerning the extent to which the author of the Johannine writings is consciously making use of Hellenistic terms has in recent years been vigorously discussed. Some modern commentators are convinced that the Johannine conception of the New Birth must be linked with the ideas of " regeneration " current in the mystery religions, and the claim is made that the Johannine language cannot be explained save as the result of such Hellenistic influences.[1] It is quite obvious that by the date of the Johannine writings Hellenistic ideas may well have begun to affect the presentation of Christian truth. The preachers of the Gospel could hardly be blind to the existence among those to whom they ministered of religious ideas and terms which were neither Jewish nor Christian in their origin.[2] Thus it is not surprising that close parallels to some of the Johannine expressions are to be found in Hellenistic documents. It may still be questioned, however, whether the Johannine conception of " birth from above " should be included among these parallels. The Johannine conception is not, strictly speaking, one of *regeneration*—the compound verb ἀναγεννάω is never used either in the Gospel or in the Epistle. It is possible that judgement on this question has been unconsciously influenced by the fact that the Latin versions uniformly render the Johannine term by the word *renatus*. But the simple verb γεννάω, when used in the passive, as it is so frequently in the Fourth Gospel and the First Epistle, seems not so much to suggest Hellenistic ideas of " regeneration ", but rather to be a somewhat more vivid way of expressing the idea contained in the phrase τέκνα θεοῦ. A comparison of one or two passages reveals

[1] Cf. e.g. W. Bauer, *Das Johannesevangelium* in *Handbuch zum Neuen Testament* (1923), pp. 48–49, " Diese Anschauung ist auf synkretistischem Boden gewachsen. In den Mysterienkulten bewirkten Weihe und Sakrament die Umwandlung des Menschen zum Sohn der Gottheit. Und das heisst ' Erzeugung ' ".

[2] Cf. Howard, op. cit., p. 200, " It may well be granted that a missionary religion such as Christianity could not do other than avail itself of the popular phraseology which was so widely current in the Hellenistic world ". For a valuable discussion of the whole question see the whole of the note from which this quotation is taken (op. cit., pp. 197–201).

that for statements using the verb γεννάω parallels may be found, often in the immediate context, which employ the noun τέκνα. Thus " children of God " (τέκνα θεοῦ) in Jn. 1. 12 are described in the following verse as " those who were born . . . of God " (οἳ . . . ἐκ θεοῦ ἐγεννήθησαν). Again, in 1 Jn. 2. 29 (the last verse of the chapter) the words " everyone that doeth righteousness has been begotten of him " (πᾶς ὁ ποιῶν τὴν δικαιοσύνην ἐξ αὐτοῦ γεγέννηται) are followed in the opening verse of Chapter 3 by the passage, " Behold what manner of love the Father has given us, that we should be called children of God " (τέκνα θεοῦ κληθῶμεν). Again, in 1 Jn. 3. 9–10 " everyone who has been begotten of God " (πᾶς ὁ γεγεννημένος ἐκ τοῦ θεοῦ) is picked up three lines farther on by the phrase " the children of God " (τὰ τέκνα τοῦ θεοῦ). Similarly, in the opening verses of Chapter 5 the passage " everyone who loves him who begat loves him that has been begotten of him " (. . . ἀγαπᾷ τὸν γεγεννημένον ἐξ αὐτοῦ) is followed immediately by the statement, " Hereby we know that we love the children of God " (. . . ἀγαπῶμεν τὰ τέκνα τοῦ θεοῦ). In view of these passages, it is difficult to believe that the use of the verb γεννάω is dictated by a Hellenistic conception of " regeneration " any more than the use of the phrase τέκνα θεοῦ. If one form of expression conveys any more meaning than the other, we may only say that the use of the _verb_ enables the writer to lay a more explicit emphasis upon the divine initiative. It would seem hardly necessary to seek a Hellenistic source for so characteristically Biblical a conception.[1]

St. John is but underlining and making yet more explicit a conception used by St. Paul and by Jesus himself. St. Paul, as we have seen, spoke about " children of God " (τέκνα θεοῦ),[2] and also about " sons of God " (υἱοὶ θεοῦ).[3] The phrase " sons of God " (υἱοὶ θεοῦ) is found in the teaching of Jesus.[4] We may notice also our Lord's saying, " Except ye turn and become as little children " (ὡς τὰ παιδία).[5] If full weight is given to the significance of these pre-Johannine references to " children of God ", and, further, if due attention is paid to the substantial identity in the Johannine writings between " children of God " and " those who are born of God ", the theory which demands a Hellenistic _origin_ for this strain of Johannine teaching becomes yet more improbable. It is far more likely that the connexion of the " birth from above " with baptism (Jn. 3. 3, 5) and the linking of " sonship " with baptism (Gal. 3. 26–27) are different ways of expressing one essentially Christian experience. Both may go back ultimately, by steps which we cannot fully trace, to the

[1] Cf. E. C. Hoskyns, _The Fourth Gospel_, ed. by F. N. Davey (1940), Vol. I, p. 230, " The Evangelist is . . . not introducing the language of generation in order to accommodate Christianity to the soil of Hellenism, where immortality was supposed to be conferred by sacramental regeneration; . . . he is rather confronting the visible Christian practice and experience of baptism with that invisible and spiritual baptism which is the miracle of God ".
[2] Cf. Rom. 8. 16, 17, 21; 9. 8; Phil. 2. 15; Eph. 5. 1.
[3] Cf. Rom. 8. 14, 19; 9. 26; Gal. 3. 26, 4. 6, 7. It is noticeable that St. John never speaks of Christians as " sons of God " but rather as " children of God ". For him Jesus alone is " Son of God " (cf. Jn. 1. 18, 34, 49 etc.; 1 Jn. 1. 3, 7 etc.).
[4] Matt. 5. 9; cf. Matt. 5. 45 and Lk. 6. 35.   [5] Matt. 18. 3.

teaching of Jesus. No doubt many of the earliest readers of the Fourth Gospel and of the First Epistle interpreted this teaching about being " born of God " in the light of Hellenistic conceptions already familiar to them. But the source out of which this teaching originally sprang was that fact of Divine Sonship experienced uniquely by Jesus at his own baptism, and experienced in a secondary and derivative sense by a succession of early Christian believers who, as they emerged from baptism, knew that they had been " born of water and the Spirit " and were in truth " children of God ".)

The objection may be raised that, had there been this connexion from the beginning between " sonship " and Christian baptism, then Jesus would have made it explicit, and the sayings about " sons of God " in the Synoptists would have been definitely linked with a mention of baptism. To this it may be replied that such references would have been entirely premature and almost unintelligible during our Lord's ministry. That Act of God, the death and resurrection of Jesus, which makes Christian baptism effective, had still to take place. It was only *after* that Act that the rite of Christian baptism could possess its full meaning and potency. Thus we need not feel any surprise that in the Synoptic Gospels there are no passages linking the teaching of Jesus about men as " sons of God " with baptism. This Synoptic silence about baptism [1] is a measure of the faithfulness with which the records of the ministry and the teaching of Jesus have there been presented. If the Synoptic Gospels were simply reflecting the conditions of the Apostolic Age in which they were written (as much of the recent " Form-Criticism " would seem to imply), then it would surely be natural to find a " command to baptize " in the Mission Charges to the Twelve and to the Seventy.[2] No such injunction is to be discovered in either passage. This striking silence about baptism in a part of the Gospels where an insertion might have seemed so obvious (when we remember that the rite was practised from the Day of Pentecost onwards) [3] is a fact that may well be taken into account by those who seek to estimate the trustworthiness of the Synoptic record. But while neither of the two earliest Synoptic sources speaks of Christian baptism, it is to be observed that both in Mark and in Q there is a quite extraordinary emphasis laid upon the Baptism of Jesus himself. In this a rite of water-baptism is conjoined with a descent of the Holy Spirit and with a unique experience of Divine Sonship. The fact that the three things which stand out prominently in the story of our Lord's Baptism are three characteristics of Christian baptism can hardly be accidental.

But if the Synoptists refrain from reading back any reference to Christian baptism into the record of the ministry and teaching of Jesus (with the exception of the passage at the end of Matthew, to be considered later),

---

[1] For a discussion of Matt. 28. 19, cf. *infra*, pp. 105–109.
[2] Mk. 6. 7–13; Matt. 10. 5–14; Lk. 9. 1–6; Lk. 10. 1–11.
[3] It will be remembered that it has been argued in Chapter 4 that the evidence of Acts 2. 38 may be accepted as trustworthy; cf. *supra*, pp. 43–48.

that silence is broken in the Fourth Gospel. It is there, as we might expect, that such a reference would seem to have been inserted into the record of our Lord's teaching. In that Gospel the deeds and the words of Jesus are narrated again in the light of two generations of Christian thought and experience. The author who knows that he and his fellow-Christians have been " born from above " through the Christian baptism of " water and the Spirit " attributes to Jesus a statement which, incomprehensible as it would have been to an enquirer during his earthly life, yet simply expresses a reality of experience for those first-century Christians who through Christ had become God's children, had entered his Kingdom, and in the Son of Man who was " lifted up " had eternal life as a present and abiding possession.

8

Other References in the New Testament and Summary of Teaching concerning Baptism.

THE remaining references to baptism in the Epistles comprise two passages in Hebrews (6. 2, 10. 22),[1] one in 1 Peter (3. 21), and one in Titus (3. 5). These will now be examined in turn, after which consideration must be given to the " command to baptize " attributed to Jesus at the end of the First Gospel (Matt. 28. 19).

Wherefore let us cease to speak of the first principles of Christ, and press on unto perfection; not laying again a foundation of repentance from dead works, and of faith toward God, of the teaching of baptisms, and of laying on of hands, and of resurrection of the dead, and of eternal judgement (Heb. 6. 1-2).

The author bids his readers not to rest content with the rudimentary elements of Christian teaching, but to press on to maturity. He enumerates six of these elementary doctrines, and one of these he describes as " teaching about baptisms ". We note that the word used is not that usually employed to denote Christian baptism.[2] Further, it is used in the plural. The reason for both is probably that the writer wishes to include a reference not only to Christian baptism, but also to certain ceremonial " washings ". The elementary " teaching "[3] spoken of by the writer probably had to do with the difference between these " washings " and Christian baptism. As Dr. Moffatt puts it, " the distinctively Christian uses of water had to be grasped by new adherents ".[4]

The main contribution of this passage to our knowledge of early Christian baptism is to confirm the impression derived from other parts of the New Testament that baptism mattered much for those desirous of becoming Christians, and that instruction about its significance formed part of elementary Christian teaching. In the list of " fundamentals ", among which baptism finds a place, may be noticed several of the conceptions which elsewhere in the New Testament are found in close association with baptism—repentance, faith, resurrection of the dead and eternal judgement. Thus for the author of the Epistle to the Hebrews, as for

[1] The reference of βαπτισμοῖς in Heb. 9. 10 is purely to Jewish " washings " and has nothing to do with Christian baptism.

[2] The word used here is βαπτισμός, not βάπτισμα, as is common elsewhere in the New Testament. The word βαπτισμός occurs as a well-attested variant in Col. 2. 12, and may there be original. Cf. supra, p. 62 n.

[3] It makes no difference to the sense whether we read διδαχήν or διδαχῆς. Dr. Moffatt argues that the former, though supported only by B, the Harklean Syriac and the Old Latin, is probably original; cf. J. Moffatt, Hebrews I. C. C. (1924), pp. 74-75. The witness of Pap. 46 is now to be added to these authorities for διδαχήν; cf. F. W. Beare in Journal of Biblical Literature, Vol. LXIII (Dec. 1944), p. 394.

[4] Moffatt, op. cit., p. 75. Dr. Moffatt thinks that the instruction may have covered not only baptism but also the ablutions required from Christians in connexion with their worship.

other New Testament writers, the *eschatological* connexions of baptism are prominent. The remaining " first principle ", namely teaching about laying on of hands, confirms the impression derived from various references in the Acts of the Apostles, that the laying on of hands was at a quite early period, in some quarters, associated with Christian baptism.[1]

> Having therefore, brethren, boldness to enter into the holy place by the blood of Jesus, by the way which he dedicated for us, a new and living way, through the veil, that is to say, his flesh; and having a great priest over the house of God; let us draw near with a true heart in fulness of faith, having our hearts sprinkled from an evil conscience, and our body washed with pure water (Heb. 10. 19-22).

This passage forms part of a longer section in which the author, having concluded his main argument, goes on to draw various practical applications. Since Jesus, the High Priest " after the order of Melchizedek ", by his sacrificial death has opened up a new [2] way of approach to God, whereby men may come to him with " boldness ", and have unrestricted fellowship with him, the author urges his readers to draw near to God, their heart purified from an evil conscience, and their body washed with pure water. The background of this language is to be found in the Old Testament passages describing the consecration of priests. They needed to be purified from " uncleanness " by being sprinkled with sacrificial blood (cf. Exod. 29. 20–21; Lev. 8. 23, 24, 30), and also to be washed with water (cf. Exod. 30. 19–20, 40. 32; Lev. 16. 4). But the purpose of these illustrations is to bring out the meaning of the Christian " purification ", namely baptism. As in 1 Pet. 3. 21, it is emphasized that the actual bathing of the body in water represents a purification that goes far beyond the physical. The outward washing of the body typifies the inward cleansing of the soul, a cleansing made possible because of the sacrificial death of Christ. Here again we find the teaching that Christian baptism derives its meaning from the death of Christ. The author of Hebrews expresses the relation in a quite different way from that adopted by St. Paul. Whereas St. Paul fixes upon the imagery of immersion, this writer, as we might expect, finds his analogy in the ceremonial of the Tabernacle; but both make this unmistakable connexion between baptism and the death of Christ.

We notice also in this passage that baptism is associated not only with the death of Christ (verses 19 and 22), but also with faith (verse 22) and the new moral life (verse 24); while the reference to hope (verse 23) and to the Day drawing nigh (verse 25) recalls the eschatological atmosphere, which St. Paul in a baptismal context often expresses by mention of

---

[1] Cf. *supra* p. 44 *n*. 1.

[2] The adjective πρόσφατος meant originally *newly slain*, as in Homer *Iliad*, xxiv, 757. Later the meaning of the second part of the compound was forgotten, but in Hebrews a backward glance at the original etymology would be not inappropriate; cf. A. Nairne, *The Epistle of Priesthood* (Second Edition, 1915), p. 381. Moffatt denies any such sacrificial allusion, op. cit., p. 142.

" heirs " (cf. Gal. 3. 29) or " inheritance " (cf. Eph. 1. 14) or " glory " (cf. Rom. 6. 4).

Because Christ also suffered for sins once, the righteous for the unrighteous, that he might bring us to God; being put to death in the flesh, but quickened in the spirit; in which also he went and preached unto the spirits in prison, which aforetime were disobedient, when the long-suffering of God waited in the days of Noah, while the ark was a preparing, wherein few, that is, eight souls, were saved through water: which also after a true likeness doth now save you, even baptism, not the putting away of the filth of the flesh, but the interrogation of a good conscience toward God, through the resurrection of Jesus Christ (1 Pet. 3. 18–21).

The author has been urging his readers to face suffering with Christ's example before them. He was " put to death in the flesh, but made alive in the Spirit ". The fact that verse 21 concludes with the words " through the resurrection of Jesus Christ " suggests that it may have been the mention of the resurrection and the Spirit in verse 18 that reminded the author about baptism, in accordance with what we have come to recognize as a familiar early Christian connexion. Baptism is for this author what Dr. Moffatt describes as " the manifestation of Christ's risen power in the Spirit ".[1] But a further reason for referring to baptism is the reference in this context to the story of the Flood and the " eight souls " who " were saved through water ".[2] This naturally suggests the Christian counterpart of this ancient story. Just as Noah and his family were " saved through water ", so Christians are saved by baptism. The author then passes to an aspect of baptism which has no parallel in the story of the Deluge. Baptism—as it was then, by immersion—clearly removes dirt from the flesh, but that is not its real significance. What matters is the moral and spiritual meaning of the rite, which the author goes on to define by the phrase translated in the R.V., " the interrogation of a good conscience toward God ", or, in Dr. Moffatt's rendering, " the prayer for a clean conscience before God ". The general sense is clear:[3] that baptism is significant according as it means the desire for a new moral life; a new life brought about by the same power of God in which Jesus was raised from the dead.

The passage is noteworthy because of the stress laid on moral requirements from those who offered themselves as candidates for baptism. We have seen that more than once in the Pauline Epistles mention is made of

[1] Cf. J. Moffatt, *The General Epistles, Moffatt N. T. Commentary* (1928), p. 140.

It may be noticed that baptism would be in the author's mind throughout, if the theory of Perdelwitz be accepted that 1. 3—4. 11 were originally an address to the newly baptized, cf. B. H. Streeter, *The Primitive Church* (1929), p. 123.

[2] Cf. Moffatt, op. cit., p. 142, " the water was at once the means of destruction and the agent of salvation ". Cf. also E. G. Selwyn, *The First Epistle of St. Peter* (1946), pp. 202 f.

[3] The precise meaning of ἐπερώτημα is uncertain. The word occurs nowhere else in the New Testament. It may mean " enquiry " or " request " or again " question ". The following genitive may be subjective or objective; εἰς θεόν may = " towards God " or, " in the presence of God ", and may go with συνειδήσεως or with ἐπερώτημα. Cf. the full treatment of the phrase in B. Reicke, *The Disobedient Spirits and Christian Baptism* (1946), pp. 173–187, and cf. also the note in G. W. Blenkin, *I Peter, Cambridge Greek Testament* (1914), pp. 81 f.

" newness of life " in a baptismal context (Rom. 6. 4; cf. also 1 Cor. 6. 9–11 and Col. 2. 13). This ethical connexion of baptism recalls an association of proselyte baptism. It will be remembered that proselytes were instructed in the moral demands that would be expected of them, and some of the major and minor commands of the Law were actually recited during the ceremony of baptism.[1] Again, in John's baptism the emphasis was, as we have seen, on the moral rather than on the ritual side.

Bishop Carrington in a recent book has claimed that behind the ethical teaching of various New Testament writings there is a common framework of moral instruction. He shows in a series of tables how the main elements of this teaching keep reappearing in different books, including this Epistle. His contention is that here we have a glimpse of the catechism that was actually taught to early Christian candidates for baptism, and that this in turn was largely modelled on the traditional Jewish method of instructing and admitting proselytes.[2] Dr. Carrington has adduced a considerable amount of evidence in support of his thesis, and it seems probable that much of the ethical teaching in early Christianity may, so far as concerns its form and a good deal of its content, be modelled closely upon Jewish originals.

But where Christian teaching seems to have gone beyond Judaism is in setting forth not only the moral ideal but also the power by which that ideal could be realized.[3] That is what we find brought out so clearly in a passage like this from 1 Peter. The " prayer for a clean conscience before God "—that longing for " clean hands and a pure heart " without which a man could not " ascend into the hill of the Lord " and " stand in his holy place " [4]—that desire is actually realized by means of a moral renewal, the secret of which is no other than that power of God through which Jesus rose from the dead. What makes it all the more striking is that the " Pauline " [5] teaching that the God who raised Jesus from the dead can enable Christians to walk " in newness of life " is here expressed in quite un-Pauline phraseology. The implication seems to be that this teaching is not peculiarly Pauline at all, but rather forms part of the primitive apostolic tradition. The early Apostles called men to a new way of living, and claimed to be in possession of the secret by which this miracle could be accomplished. So for the author of this Epistle this moral renewal is the very meaning of Christian baptism.[6] It does not come about by human striving, but through the working in men of the same power that was active in Christ's resurrection. " It is on the resurrection

---

[1] Cf. *supra*, p. 7.

[2] P. Carrington, *The Primitive Christian Catechism* (1940).

[3] Cf. the passage quoted from Strack-Billerbeck (cited *supra*, p. 9 *n.* 1), to the effect that rabbinic teaching looked for moral renewal *only in the Age to come*.

[4] Cf. Ps. 24. 3, 4.

[5] Cf. Rom. 6. 4.

[6] It may be recalled how St. Paul confuted the antinomian plea, " let us continue in sin, that grace may abound ", by appealing to the basic Christian experience (cf. ἢ ἀγνοεῖτε . . .; Rom. 6. 3) that *baptism means moral renewal*—hence the very thought of " continuing in sin " is absurd.

of Jesus Christ that Christian baptism depends for its efficacy. . . . Christ can impart the new life because He has entered into it ".[1]

It may further be noticed in this passage how, alongside the references to the resurrection and the new moral life, mention is made also of the Spirit (verse 18), and of the death of Christ (verse 18; cf. also 4. 1). Thus once more in a baptismal context we mark the presence of several of the " associated ideas ".

But when the kindness of God our Saviour, and his love toward man, appeared, not by works done in righteousness, which we did ourselves, but according to his mercy he saved us, through the washing of regeneration and renewing of the Holy Ghost, which he poured out upon us richly, through Jesus Christ our Saviour; that, being justified by his grace, we might be made heirs according to the hope of eternal life (Tit. 3. 4–7).

This reference to baptism forms part of a section in which the writer [2] is describing the sort of conduct characteristic of Christians. Earlier in the Epistle he has stressed the need that Christians shall live good lives, not least in order that they may give no cause for pagan calumnies.[3] But here he finds the chief motive for a good life in the richness and abundance of divine grace imparted to the world when Christ came. He reminds his readers that formerly their life was one of slavery to sin,[4] (and here he identifies himself with them); their lives were stained with the vices of paganism. But what a transformation of character has been brought about through the saving power of God—that kindness (χρηστότης) and " humanity " (φιλανθρωπία) suddenly made manifest to the world in Christ! The change was brought about not as a result of man's striving to fulfil a law of " righteousness ", but simply as something in accordance with God's nature, " whose property is always to have mercy ". The means of this salvation was " through a washing of regeneration and renewing of the Holy Spirit ";[5] the statement that God " poured out " the Spirit recalls the description of Pentecost (Acts 2. 17, 18, 33), where the verb ἐκχέω occurs in a quotation from the prophet Joel. The purpose behind all this saving activity of God was that, being " counted righteous " as a result of his grace, men might become " heirs ", and so live their lives here and now in hope of an eternal life to come.

The whole passage is remarkable for the way in which it combines a number of phrases drawn from earlier Christian teaching (especially that of St. Paul) with other words that seem to strike a new note. Thus the emphasis on the divine initiative in salvation, the reference to the " kindness " (χρηστότης) [6] of God, the rejection of " works ", the link between

[1] J. H. B. Masterman, *The First Epistle of St. Peter* (1900), pp. 135–136.
[2] I assume the conclusions of Dr. P. N. Harrison about the authorship of this Epistle; see his book, *The Problem of the Pastoral Epistles* (1921). There seems no reason to regard these verses as one of the " genuine fragments " attributable to St. Paul himself.
[3] Cf. Tit. 2. 8.   [4] Cf. δουλεύοντες in Tit. 3. 3.
[5] It seems probable that not only παλινγενεσίας but also ἀνακαινώσεως should be regarded as depending grammatically upon the preceding genitive λουτροῦ; so Dibelius, Lock and Moffatt.
[6] Cf. Rom. 2. 4; 11. 22.

baptism and the Holy Spirit,[1] the mention of "justification", and the description of Christians as "heirs" living in hope of a future inheritance, are all reminiscent of St. Paul. (Whether or not we regard the description of baptism by the term λουτρόν as Pauline will depend upon our judgement concerning the authorship of Ephesians.) But the mention of God's "humanity" (φιλανθρωπία),[2] the description of *God* as "Saviour" (σωτήρ),[3] the linking of baptism with "regeneration" (παλινγενεσία), and the description of the Holy Spirit's activity as that of "renewing" (ἀνακαίνωσις)—all these seem fresh, if not in idea, at least in phraseology. The reference to God's "pouring out" of the Spirit, which we have already noticed as reminiscent of Acts and Joel, is not Pauline.[4] Further, it has been pointed out that some of the reminiscences of St. Paul turn out on closer examination to be verbal rather than real. Thus whereas for St. Paul ἔργα meant "works" of the Mosaic Law, the author here uses the term in reference to moral well-doing in a quite general sense. Again, Dr. E. F. Scott has contrasted the Pauline use of "grace" and "justification" with the use made of the terms here. "With Paul these words have reference to something definite which was achieved for men by the death of Christ. Here they apply generally to the deliverance which we owe to God's goodness as displayed in the whole Christian message".[5] It is true that for the thought of this writer the death of Christ is not so central as it was for that of St. Paul, yet it is hardly correct to suggest that in this context the Cross has no place. We notice in a closely adjacent verse (2. 14) a reference to the sacrificial self-giving of Jesus Christ, i.e. his life offered in death. Thus the thought of the death of Christ cannot have been far from the author's mind when he penned the opening verses of Chapter 3, in which this reference to baptism occurs. (This indeed is what we should expect, if our contention is sound, viz., that for early Christian thought baptism was in the closest way linked with the death of Christ, as that which gave the rite its meaning.) [6] Further, in reference to "justification", we may notice that, according to Professor Dodd, one aspect of the Pauline meaning of the term is "vindication".[7] This is not far from the idea of "deliverance". Thus, though the author of the Pastorals places the emphasis somewhat differently from St. Paul, he is very far from contradicting the main lines of the Pauline teaching about salvation.

[1] Cf. 1 Cor. 6. 11, 12. 13; 2 Cor. 1. 22; Eph. 1. 13, 4. 4–5.
[2] The word φιλανθρωπία is used of "humanity" shown in the ransoming of captives, cf. Dem. *De Chersoneso* 107, 15, cited by Lock, *The Pastoral Epistles, I.C.C.* (1924), p. 153.
[3] So far as concerns the New Testament, this application of the term σωτήρ to God is a usage of the Pastoral Epistles, apart from Lk. 1. 47 and Jude 25.
[4] St. Paul uses the verb ἐκχέω only once; it occurs in Rom. 3. 15 in a citation of Isa. 59. 7, "their feet are swift to shed blood".
[5] E. F. Scott, *The Pastoral Epistles*, Moffatt *N. T. Commentary* (1936), p. 176.
[6] Cf. *supra*, pp. 32, 72–73, 89–90, and *infra*, pp. 122–125.
[7] Cf. C. H. Dodd, *Romans*, Moffatt *N. T. Commentary* (1932), pp. 10–12, where it is shown that the background of the Pauline idea of "justification" must be sought in the Old Testament, and particularly in Deutero-Isaiah.

But Dr. E. F. Scott also claims that the attitude towards baptism expressed in this passage is fundamentally different from that of St. Paul. He thinks that to the author of the Pastorals baptism is a " mysterious rite through which the Spirit works for our renewal. . . . Paul had recognized a real value in baptism, but was careful to insist on faith as the indispensable condition, without which baptism was of no avail ". With this author " the dying with Christ, which for Paul was the whole meaning of baptism, falls out of sight, and baptism is little more than a purifying rite." [1] It may freely be granted that in this Epistle, in spite of the echoes of Pauline words and phrases, there is a marked change of tone. We look here in vain for the burning and tumultuous words in which the Apostle sought to describe the new life by faith " in Christ ". We miss the vivid application of the imagery of immersion, such as we find in Rom. 6 or in Col. 2. It must, however, at the same time be observed that in this passage from Titus *faith* is not wholly absent. The emphatic insistence of this author on the free, unmerited grace of God, and the fact that human salvation is unreservedly attributed to God's love for men, both do much to conserve, in a different way and, as it were, at a considerably lower spiritual temperature, the religious truth that St. Paul expressed so much more intensely and personally by his teaching about salvation " in Christ " and by his stress on faith as " the complete abandonment of spirit . . . to One upon whom the soul of man rests for time and eternity ".[2] This note of " abandon ", which we rightly recognize as characteristically Pauline, gives place, in the Pastoral Epistles, to a more sober and restrained " piety ".[3] But there is still in these writings a clear grasp of the fact that salvation comes from God alone, and that any out-ward rite, such as baptism, is effective only because the love of God is using it as a means of grace. We notice, moreover, that when the author goes on, in verse 8, to draw the practical conclusion that follows from his statement of the Christian Gospel, he describes Christians as " those who have set their faith in God " (οἱ πεπιστευκότες θεῷ). The conception of faith is here very differently expressed from that in St. Paul, but faith is not absent from the thought of this writer. His affinity is rather with the *auctor ad Hebræos*, for whom faith is not a personal trust in Christ but rather a conviction concerning the reality of God. Moreover, it may be observed that the representation of baptism as a " purifying rite " is not necessarily un-Pauline. It is found in Eph. 5. 26, and in his commentary on this Epistle Dr. E. F. Scott himself has argued cogently for its Pauline authorship.[4] It would appear, therefore, that to say of this passage in the

---

[1] Scott, op. cit., pp. 176–177.

[2] V. Taylor, *The Atonement in New Testament Teaching* (1940), p. 137.

[3] For εὐσέβεια as one of the leading conceptions of the Pastoral Epistles, see the valuable treatment of the word by Sir Robert Falconer in *The Pastoral Epistles* (1937), pp. 30–39.

[4] Cf. E. F. Scott, *Colossians, Philemon and Ephesians*, Moffatt N. T. *Commentary* (1930), p. 121, where, after speaking of " the inimitably Pauline stamp on all its thinking " (i.e. of Ephesians) Dr. Scott continues, " It may be confidently said that there is nothing in Ephesians which Paul might not have written ". For a consideration of Eph. 5. 26, cf. *supra*, pp. 64–66.

H

Epistle to Titus that " the Church is now on its way towards a magical estimate of baptism ", seems hardly to take due account of the author's reiterated stress on the divine love poured out so richly upon undeserving men. If the essence of magic lies in the belief that by the use of material *media* a man can exert compulsion on the deity to fulfil his desires, then magical ideas are surely absent from this passage. The " washing of regeneration and renewing of the Holy Spirit " is no merely human device: it is rather the instrument of the divine goodness, the means whereby the free unmerited love of God is imparted to men and makes them " heirs to the hope of life eternal ".[1]

The term " regeneration " used to express the meaning of baptism was derived originally from Stoic sources. It denoted the periodic restoration of the world after destruction by fire. In Matt. 19. 28 it is employed in reference to the Messianic renewal to which men looked forward as a striking feature of the future Age. The author of the Pastorals uses the term here, however, not with a " futurist " significance, but rather in a sense that depends upon " realized eschatology ". Dr. L. S. Thornton has suggested that here the word denotes that " rebirth " of the Messianic community which was inaugurated at Pentecost.[2] Thus the term παλινγενεσία expresses much the same idea as the " birth from above " in the Johannine writings. This in turn, as we have seen, is not so very different from what St. Paul teaches about the " new creation " which comes about when a man is " in Christ ".[3] There is nothing in the *idea* of " regeneration " that cannot be fully accounted for from Jewish and Christian sources; " its use in this connexion in Titus 3. 5 is wholly congruous with the teaching of the New Testament as a whole ".[4] It is possible that the particular *word* used here in Titus may represent the beginnings of that influence upon Christian teaching from the Hellenistic side which later proved so powerful.[5] If such a relation between the Hellenistic and the Christian ideas of " regeneration " is to be admitted, it is important that we should also recognize the marked differences that separate the one from the other. Dibelius has drawn attention to the " ecstasy " which was so regular a feature of the process whereby, for

[1] That salvation depends entirely upon the divine initiative is brought out also by the phrase " renewing of the Holy Spirit ", i.e. brought about by the Holy Spirit.

[2] Cf. L. S. Thornton, *The Common Life in the Body of Christ* (1941), pp. 190–191, " The new creation of the messianic community as a whole had its historical inauguration in the event of Pentecost. Through baptism the individual is placed within that event. He is there taken into the eschatological crisis of re-birth, whereby the people of God were once for all renewed. The descent of the Spirit at Pentecost was that event whereby the new life of the risen Christ was precipitated into his community. By sharing the outpoured Spirit they were re-born in Christ. They partook of the new life which is his life; but also that fact constituted a renewal of their nature effected by the Holy Spirit ".

[3] Cf. 2 Cor. 5. 17. It is important to remember that to be " in Christ " is not the result of a purely *individual* relationship between Christ and the believer: it is something *corporate*, mediated to the Christian through his membership in the " New Israel ", of which baptism is the " effective symbol ".

[4] Thornton, op. cit., p. 190.

[5] Dibelius in *Handbuch zum Neuen Testament*, ad loc., quotes, among possible Hellenistic parallels, Apuleius *Met.* xi 21.

example, the Mithraic initiate came under inspiration. Again, it was characteristic of the mystery cults that such a process needed from time to time to be repeated. Further, full initiation in the mysteries was not open to all: it was reserved for a privileged few. Dibelius contrasts with this the experience under consideration in this passage of Titus.[1] This was not a temporary ecstasy, but an enduring renewal of life effected by the agency of the Spirit. Nor was the Christian experience confined to a chosen few: it was something that could be shared by every believer. Thus, though it is possible that there is here, within the New Testament, a passage in which teaching about Christian baptism was being related to the general outlook of contemporary non-Christian religions, and though we are certainly no longer treading the mountain heights of Pauline experience, yet the writer was still in sufficiently close touch with the main stream of Christian life to be able to emphasize what it was that made the Christian outlook distinctive. As in 1 Peter and as in the Pauline Epistles, so for this writer also baptism meant moral renewal.

Once again in a baptismal context we notice a number of the conceptions often associated elsewhere with the mention of the rite: stress on the activity of God (verse 4), the Holy Spirit (verse 5), the new moral life (verse 5 and the whole context), Christians as " heirs " (verse 7), and faith (verse 8). We may further observe that a few verses earlier the author, has invoked the eschatological hope of the " appearing " of Jesus Christ as a motive for good living;[2] in the next verse (as we have seen) he speaks of the self-giving of Christ, the purpose of which was that he might ransom us from all iniquity, and purify for himself a people for his own possession, zealous of good works. Thus the eschatological hope, the death of Christ, " deliverance ", and the New Israel, four of the regular " baptismal ideas " of St. Paul, are clearly not far from the author's mind.

We turn now to the passage at the end of St. Matthew's Gospel.

And Jesus came to them and spake unto them saying, All authority hath been given unto me in heaven and on earth. Go ye therefore, and make disciples of all the nations, baptizing them into the name of the Father and of the Son and of the Holy Ghost: teaching them to observe all things whatsoever I commanded you: and lo, I am with you alway, even unto the end of the world (Matt. 28. 18–20).

This passage, which forms the conclusion of the Matthæan resurrection narrative, provides the chief evidence for the traditional view that Christian baptism was instituted by Jesus.[3] For many centuries the

---

[1] Dibelius, loc. cit.

[2] 2. 12–13. The word used for the future " appearing " of Christ is ἐπιφάνεια. The corresponding verb ἐπιφαίνω is used both in 2. 11 and in 3. 4 of the divine grace revealed in the Incarnation.

[3] The reference to baptism in Mark 16. 16 also occurs in conjunction with a command for the universal proclamation of the Gospel. Since, however, it is generally agreed on textual grounds that this section cannot have formed part of the original text of St. Mark, the passage cannot be taken as first-century evidence. It merely gives additional second-century support for the view that baptism had the approval of Jesus. On the critical question see H. B. Swete, *The Gospel according to St. Mark* (Third Edition, 1920), pp. ciii ff.

passage was accepted without dispute; within recent years, however, the critical study of the New Testament has made it difficult to read the verses as an exact record of actual words of Jesus. A clear statement of the case against the trustworthiness of the passage may be found in an article by Professor Kirsopp Lake in the *Encyclopædia of Religion and Ethics*.[1] He develops a threefold argument depending on textual, literary and historical considerations, and contends that " the cumulative evidence of these three lines of criticism is . . . distinctly against the view that Matt. 28. 19 represents the *ipsissima verba* of Christ in instituting Christian baptism ".

The textual evidence is that while in all extant manuscripts and versions the text is found in the traditional form,[2] yet there is reason to believe that another form of text was known to Eusebius. In twenty-one out of twenty-five citations of the passage Eusebius quotes the verse in a shortened form, " either omitting everything between ἔθνη and διδάσκοντες or in the form πορευθέντες μαθητεύσατε πάντα τὰ ἔθνη ἐν τῷ ὀνόματί μου διδάσκοντες κτλ., the latter form being the more frequent ". It is claimed that the four quotations of the verse in the traditional form occur in later writings of Eusebius, where the Scriptural citations may have undergone assimilation. Professor Lake agrees with F. C. Conybeare[3] that the natural conclusion from this evidence is that Eusebius used a text which did not contain the baptismal formula. Conybeare would also find traces of such a " Eusebian " text in Justin Martyr and Hermas.[4] Lake, however, does not regard these as convincing, and is inclined himself to lay more weight upon Justin's failure to cite the passage in a context about baptismal regeneration.[5] Here the practice of baptism in the Threefold Name is supported only by a quotation from Isaiah and on the ground of apostolic tradition. This suggests that Justin knew Matt. 28. 19 only in a form omitting the reference to baptism in the Threefold Name If the existence of this " Eusebian " text be granted, Lake thinks that such a variant has a strong claim to be regarded as the original, because the overwhelming influence of baptismal practice is quite sufficient to account for the absolute predominance of the reading found in all existing manuscripts and versions.

The argument from " literary " criticism seeks to show, by a comparison with other Gospels, that Matt. 28. 19 is no part of the earliest tradition. With Matt. 28. 18–20 Lake compares three other passages, namely, Mk. 16. 15–18, Lk. 24. 44–49 and Jn. 20. 21–23. Since in the " Marcan " passage the reference to baptism does not include the Threefold Name, it seems more probable that the reference arose out of " contemporary

---

[1] *E. R. E.*, Vol. II, pp. 380–381.
[2] Professor Lake points out that " the best MSS. of the African Old Latin and of the Old Syriac versions are defective at this point ".
[3] *Zeitschrift für die neutestamentliche Wissenschaft* (1905), pp. 250 ff.
[4] Justin, *Dial*, xxxix. 258; liii. 272; Hermas, *Simil.*, IX. xvii. 4.
[5] Justin, *Apol.*, i. 61.

usage " rather than from Matt. 28. 19. In the Lucan and Johannine passages there is no mention of baptism. In the Fourth Gospel this might be due to a desire not to over-emphasize a sacrament,[1] but there is no evidence for such a tendency in Luke. Thus a comparison with other Gospels suggests on the whole that the command to baptize in Matt. 28. 19 was not part of the common tradition.

The strongest evidence against the trustworthiness of the tradition is grouped under the third heading of " historical " criticism. It seems clear from the narrative of Acts that early Christian baptism was not in the Threefold Name, but either " in the name of Jesus Christ " [2] or " into the name of the Lord Jesus ".[3] This agrees with the wording of two Pauline passages where the Apostle speaks of Christians being baptized " into Christ " [4] or " into Christ Jesus ".[5] This particular argument of course does not claim that Jesus could not have instituted baptism in any form, but only that it is unlikely that he enjoined baptism in the Threefold Name. Professor Lake, however, goes on to argue that evidence against any form of the institution of baptism by Jesus is furnished by St. Paul's words in 1 Cor. 1. 17. It is claimed that St. Paul would hardly have said, " Christ sent me not to baptize, but to preach the Gospel ", had he known of so impressive and formal a tradition concerning the institution of baptism as that which lies behind the usual text of Matt. 28. 18–20. In answer to this argument the suggestion may be noticed that though St. Paul certainly counted himself " not a whit behind the very chiefest Apostles ",[6] yet here he may be contrasting an original commission to the Eleven involving baptism, with his own commission as Apostle to the Gentiles, which was a commission to *preach*. On this interpretation St. Paul's statement would support the dominical institution of baptism, and not deny it. It would seem less precarious, however, to follow the exegesis suggested in our earlier discussion of this passage.[7] St. Paul is contrasting himself not with the original Apostles but rather with some of his helpers at Corinth. He prefers, in general, that they, rather than he, should baptize, because their administration of the rite was less liable than his own to have wrong deductions drawn from it. The fact that the Apostle acknowledges having baptized certain Corinthians himself [8] supports the view that his unwillingness to baptize is based, not on any explicit direction of the Lord, but rather on practical considerations.

It may be questioned whether the textual argument against Matt. 28. 19 is so strong as Professor Lake would claim. Thus it was maintained by F. H. Chase that the omission of the command to baptize in so many of the citations of the passage by Eusebius was due, not to the use of a different text of the First Gospel, but rather to the *disciplina arcani* whereby the Christian " mysteries " were safeguarded from vulgar profanation.[9]

---

[1] Cf. *supra*, pp. 92–93.　　　[2] Acts 2. 38; 10. 48.　　　[3] Acts 8. 16; 19. 5.
[4] Gal. 3. 27.　　[5] Rom. 6. 3.　　[6] 2 Cor. 11. 5.　　[7] Cf. *supra*, pp. 53–54.
[8] Cf. 1 Cor. 1. 14, 16.　　　[9] Cf. *J.T.S.*, Vol. VI, (1905), pp. 481 ff.

Though Lake counters this contention by the plea that the works in which this shorter " Eusebian " text is found were not specially intended for outsiders or catechumens, nevertheless, in view of the complete unanimity of all known manuscripts and versions in support of the longer traditional text (containing the command to baptize in the Threefold Name), it is probably wiser not to lay too much stress on this textual argument, though the facts to which Lake has called attention are certainly curious.

The position, however, is very different when we turn to the " historical " argument: the facts which may be grouped under this heading seem fatal to the view that the passage contains *ipsissima verba* of Jesus. If he had uttered the command as it stands written here, could baptism " in the name of the Lord Jesus " ever have been so usual as the references in the Acts and the Pauline Epistles would suggest? It is surely an evasion of the difficulty to maintain, as Leipoldt has done, that this phrase is " a mere abbreviation of the longer formula ".[1] It seems better frankly to admit that the difference in the form of words tells against the precise historicity of Matt. 28. 19. Further, apart from the difficulty about the formula of baptism, there is the marked absence, in the course of the Judaistic controversy, of any appeal to a word of Jesus authorizing the preaching of the Gospel to men of all nations. If there had been current among the early Christians round about A.D. 50 a tradition concerning a command of Jesus so explicit and far-reaching as that recorded here by St. Matthew, it is hard to understand why no one sought to terminate the Judaistic controversy by a citation of this express injunction of the risen Lord that his followers should make disciples of all the Gentiles. We know from 1 Corinthians that St. Paul was accustomed to distinguish courses of action for which he had the explicit guidance of Jesus, from others for which no such " word of the Lord " was available.[2] The conclusion would seem irresistible that, had this tradition been current about the middle of the first century, St. Paul could hardly have failed to invoke a command of Jesus which, addressed as it was to the original disciples, would have provided so conclusive a reply to some followers of those apostles who desired to limit the reception of the Gospel to those who were Jews. These historical objections are so weighty that we cannot with any confidence quote this passage as a verbatim record of the words in which baptism was instituted by Jesus.

It is, however, very important that, in the endeavour to assess justly the weight of evidence against the authenticity of this tradition, we should at the same time take full account of what may be termed the positive testimony of the passage. These verses cannot, without the gravest doubt, be regarded as the literal transcript of actual words uttered by Jesus, but they do provide the clearest evidence from a date certainly not

---

[1] Leipoldt op. cit., p. 33 *n*. 5, referring to " in the name of Jesus Christ " (Acts 2. 38, 10. 48).
[2] Cf. 1 Cor. 7. 10, 12, 25, 9. 14.

later than that of the composition of the Gospel, and possibly earlier,[1] for the conviction that the practice of Christian baptism had the full authority of Jesus behind it.   Though such a precise formulation of this belief is not to be found earlier than this impressive utterance at the end of the First Gospel, yet the practical acceptance of such a belief may well have to be traced back very much earlier in the century.   To this point we shall revert in the final stage of our enquiry, when we discuss the authority behind Christian baptism.[2]   At the moment it may be remarked that by far the most satisfactory explanation of the early and undisputed acceptance of baptism by the early Church would be to acknowledge that *from the first* the followers of Jesus believed, and were justified in their belief, that the practice of baptism rested ultimately on the authority of our Lord himself.

SUMMARY OF NEW TESTAMENT TEACHING CONCERNING CHRISTIAN BAPTISM

The various strands of New Testament teaching about Christian baptism have now been examined in detail.   Before the final part of our discussion is undertaken, a brief summary of the more important elements in this teaching will serve both to bring out its essential unity, and also to raise the question of the authority lying behind it.

ACTS OF THE APOSTLES: The rite of baptism with water in Acts both embodies the *kerygma* in a " symbolic " act and at the same time expresses man's response to that message of salvation.   Those who " repent " and " believe ", who " hear " or " receive the word ", are baptized " into the name of the Lord Jesus ", and thereby are incorporated into the Christian community.   Thus in the earliest days of the Church the rite of baptism derived its meaning from that gospel of salvation through Christ crucified and risen, with the proclamation of which it was so intimately associated. Baptism is twice linked with remission of sins, and there is a frequent connexion of baptism with the gift of the Holy Spirit, which in Acts seems specially to denote the ability to " speak with tongues ".   Sometimes, but not invariably, this endowment is connected also with the " laying on of hands ".

PAULINE EPISTLES: Interpreted against this background, the Pauline statements about baptism are seen to be no innovation but rather the filling out of conceptions already present in primitive Christian teaching. Thus when St. Paul links baptism so intimately with the death and resurrection of Christ, he is bringing out more precisely the relation of baptism to the *kerygma*.   Salvation means such an identification with him who is the subject of the *kerygma* that even his death and resurrection are shared.

---

[1] An estimate of the probable date at which this particular tradition originated depends on our answer to the question whether the passage comes from the final editor of the Gospel or whether it formed part of one of his sources.   The question cannot be answered with certainty, but the first alternative may perhaps be considered the more likely.   Streeter dated the First Gospel A.D. 85; *The Four Gospels* (1924), p. 524.

[2] Cf. *infra*, Chapter 9, and especially pp. 127–129.

This surrender of the whole being to the crucified and risen Christ is what St. Paul means by " faith " (cf. Gal. 2. 20), but it is also for him the meaning of baptism (cf. Rom. 6. 3–4). Elsewhere he describes it as a " putting on " of Christ, issuing in a life of " sonship " (cf. Gal. 3. 26–27; both faith and baptism are emphasized). Again, when St. Paul stresses that baptism means moral renewal, he is interpreting more profoundly that gift of the Spirit which the primitive Church connected with baptism —but now the miracle is one of *agape* rather than of *glossolalia*. Further, when he represents baptism as the means of incorporation into the Body of Christ and as the gateway through which believers enter upon the privileges of the new Israel, he is expressing more fully what the first Christians were content to sum up by the phrase " in the name of the Lord Jesus ". A striking feature of the Pauline baptismal teaching is the way in which in the context of these statements about baptism a number of other " associated ideas " tend to recur. This would seem to suggest that Christian baptism was intimately bound up with many of the things most central in Christian faith. As examples of these " associated ideas " we may note: the activity of God the Father, as exhibited both in the raising of Jesus from the dead and in the " quickening " of the believer to a new moral life (1 Cor. 6. 14; Rom. 6. 4; Col. 2. 12–13; cf. Eph. 4. 6); faith (Gal. 3. 24–26; 1 Cor. 12. 9; Rom. 6. 8; Col. 2. 12; Eph. 1. 13, 4. 5); " in Christ " (Gal. 3. 26; Rom. 6. 11; Col. 2. 10); unity in the Body of Christ (Gal. 3. 28; 1 Cor. 12. 12–13; Eph. 4. 3–6); and the Church as the New Israel (Gal. 3. 29; 1 Cor. 6. 9–10, Col. 2. 11, Eph. 1. 14).

JOHANNINE WRITINGS: In Johannine teaching Christian baptism is the means whereby, through the outward use of water and through the inward agency of the Spirit, a man is " born from above ", and so enabled to enter the Kingdom of God. A passage in 1 John suggests that Christian baptism was viewed as the counterpart for the believer of the baptism of Jesus. This helps to account for the connexion with " sonship " and with the Spirit, found here as also in St. Paul. There is evidence in the Johannine writings that the author realized the importance in this connexion of the death of Jesus, but he expressed it less obviously and less directly than St. Paul. The ultimate source for this link between Christian baptism and the death of Jesus may possibly be found in the saying of our Lord, likening his death to a " baptism " (Lk. 12. 50).

OTHER NEW TESTAMENT REFERENCES: In other Epistles we find the teaching that the outward " washing " of baptism means the inward cleansing from sin which only the sacrificial death of Christ could accomplish (Heb. 10. 22; cf. essentially the same teaching in 1 Pet. 3. 21, but there the connexion is more particularly with the resurrection); and that baptism is the means whereby men are " born again " and experience the " renewing " power of the Holy Spirit (Tit. 3. 5: " sonship " and the " Spirit " prominent in connexion with baptism, as elsewhere in the New

Testament, and as in the baptism of Jesus). All this teaching serves alike to bring out the importance of baptism and the fact that it connoted a moral renewal which could be explained only as the result of an Act of God in Christ. Finally we discover at the end of St. Matthew's Gospel the tradition (echoed also in the conclusion added later to St. Mark) that the rite of Christian baptism was instituted and enjoined upon the early Church, as the characteristic means of entry into the new community, by the authority of the risen Lord himself.

In all these New Testament writings Christian baptism is *a rite with a meaning*. The outward act of water-baptism recalls, and as it were *re-presents*, that act of God done once and for all for man's salvation in the death and resurrection of Jesus Christ. Baptism thus implements that act for each successive believer. It has an outward and an inward aspect which may be separated in thought. The evidence of the New Testament, however, shows that such separation was far less obvious and natural for the early Christians than it is for us.[1] It cannot be without significance that there is no passage in the New Testament which makes any ultimate separation between the outward rite of baptism and the spiritual reality which the rite embodied.[2] Both the act and the meaning of the act mattered—the two formed for the first Christians an indivisible unity.

If this significant rite of water-baptism was practised from the first in the early Church (even though from some words attributed to John the Baptist we should more naturally have expected its abandonment), and if the interpretations by which that significance was expressed were substantially in such close agreement with one another, it is necessary for us to ask what was the authority that established this rite and determined its meaning. We have seen earlier in this chapter that historical considerations make it extremely difficult for us to-day to accept, as it stands, the plain answer which one particular New Testament passage gives to this question. Yet to acknowledge the difficulties of Matt. 28. 18–20 still confronts the student of Christian origins with a problem for which he is bound to seek an answer. Why was water-baptism continued, and how did it come to mean so much to so many in the early Church? It may be observed, in respect of the Matthæan passage, that there is a sense in which, from the historical point of view, the command of the Lord to baptize (without the reference to the Threefold Name) may be held to be more firmly grounded than the command to make disciples of all the Gentiles. It was only after a fierce struggle that all Christians agreed to do the latter. The former, however, they seem to have practised with-

---

[1] Some separation of these aspects is inevitable for us, because the normal practice of most Christian communions to-day is to baptize infants rather than adults.

[2] The passage which comes nearest to doing this (1 Pet. 3. 21, contrasting a purely physical washing with an inward moral cleansing) also goes farthest in the claim it makes for baptism, *as itself the instrument of salvation* (ὃ καὶ ὑμᾶς . . . νῦν σώζει βάπτισμα). The writer sees the meaning of baptism to lie in the inward cleansing, but he can hardly be taken to mean that therefore the outward rite does not matter, when one remembers the illustration of the Flood immediately preceding, and the emphasis on the words διὰ ὕδατος.

out question from the first.   It has been argued earlier [1] that there is no good reason for disputing the evidence of Acts that from the Day of Pentecost onwards baptism was the acknowledged rite of entry into the new community.   A study of St. Paul's teaching has shown that also for him baptism was the normal way by which one became a member of the Church.   It can hardly be too strongly emphasized that the ready acceptance and practice of this rite from the first demand some explanation.   If, for the reasons already stated, we have hesitation in believing that Jesus said precisely what is attributed to him at the end of the First Gospel, we are not thereby absolved from any further consideration of the question whether or not Christian baptism rests upon dominical authority.   The question is obviously of primary importance for any Christian communion which regards baptism as a Christian sacrament. But the problem matters also for the historian of primitive Christianity. As we pass, therefore, to the third and final stage of our enquiry, we observe that our examination of the New Testament evidence about the meaning and practice of Christian baptism has left us with an unsolved problem.   We have to ask what was the nature of the authority behind that belief and practice, and also whether it may still in any sense be maintained that Jesus " instituted " Christian baptism.

[1] Cf. *supra*, pp. 43–48, where the claim is made that, in spite of the arguments of Lake and Johannes Weiss, the statement in Acts 2. 38 is historically sound, and that therefore baptism was practised from the earliest days of the Christian Church.

PART III

THE AUTHORITY BEHIND CHRISTIAN BAPTISM

9

Christian Baptism and the Authority of Jesus

BEFORE an attempt is made to answer the question whether or not early Christian baptism rested upon dominical authority, it may be useful, even at the risk of a little repetition, to be reminded once more of the facts demanding an explanation. From a study of the New Testament evidence we have concluded that baptism was practised from the earliest days of the Christian community. It was accepted without dispute, and there is not a trace of any conflict concerning it during the whole New Testament period. Nor is there the slightest indication that any alternative rite was practised, or even proposed. All the main New Testament writers accept baptism as part of the recognized background of Christian life. Most often they seem to take its meaning for granted, as something not requiring explanation; at times they draw out its implications in a way that presupposes something approaching universal agreement about its fundamental significance.

It is important in this connexion that we should not misrepresent the evidence furnished by the episode of Cornelius.[1] That evidence is complicated, as we have seen, by the fact that the story is told twice, the account in Acts 10 being a plain narrative, while that in Acts 11 is a recapitulation of events by St. Peter, who had overstepped the mark by admitting a Gentile to the Church, and was consequently called to account before the Jerusalem authorities. The plain narrative in Chapter 10 says that Cornelius was baptized.[2] In the recapitulation, however, the clear implication of Acts 11. 16 would seem to be that Cornelius did *not* receive water-baptism. We need to recognize that the experience of Cornelius directly reversed what seems in the early Church to have been the normal sequence of events. As far as we can judge from other passages in Acts, it was customary for a convert to be baptized (generally with the laying on of hands), and *then* for him to show the usual signs of possession by the Spirit, that is, according to Acts, " speaking with tongues ". The reason why the incident of Cornelius excited such notice and caused such perturbation was that here was a man who showed all the usual signs of possessing the Spirit *before he had been baptized at all*. In regard to the difference between Acts 10 and 11, it was acknowledged in our earlier discussion of the passages that the reference to Cornelius' baptism in Chapter 10 may be due to a redactor. It is possible that Cornelius never underwent the rite of water-baptism. But in admitting this possibility it is necessary not to misrepresent the significance of the

---

[1] Acts 10. 44–48, cf. 11. 15–18; *v. supra*, p. 39.   [2] Acts 10. 48.

story. The incident is sometimes quoted as a proof that the actual rite of baptism cannot have mattered essentially in the early Church. Since Cornelius, quite apart from baptism, showed the clearest signs of having received the Holy Spirit, therefore it is claimed the outward rite was something external and unessential. To argue thus is surely to miss the whole point of the incident for those among whom it occurred. The story clearly demonstrates, as we saw earlier, that the grace of God is not bound by the observance of any particular ordinance. Such a reminder was needed in the first century, and is never inappropriate. But we gravely misinterpret the facts if we fail to recognize that the case of Cornelius was exceptional. To base our final judgement concerning the New Testament estimate of baptism mainly on this story would be to give to what was obviously an exception the universal application which rightly belongs only to a typical example. There is no evidence that the episode of Cornelius caused the leaders of the early Church in any way to modify their previous policy about baptism. On the contrary, according to one version of the story, water-baptism was actually administered to Cornelius. It may well be argued that this particular baptism was redundant and unnecessary. It may even be claimed, as we have seen, that it never took place. But that it should be thought appropriate at least testifies to the regard in which the outward rite was held. The truth seems to be that, strange as it may seem to us,[1] New Testament thought could not conceive the idea of any opposition between baptism and faith. The New Testament attitude may be summed up in James Denney's phrase, " baptism and faith are but the outside and the inside of the same thing ".[2] This story stands in the New Testament as a needful warning to those who are apt to be disturbed by any unprecedented activity of divine grace. To such it conveys the reminder that God is not bound by his sacraments. But the incident of Cornelius provides no warrant for setting aside the plain evidence of the rest of the New Testament that, for the overwhelming majority of early Christians, baptism with water, from the Day of Pentecost onwards, was recognized and practised as the accepted mode of admission into the new community.

This conclusion becomes all the more striking when we turn to the Synoptic Gospels. It might have been thought that so characteristic a practice as baptism was among the early Christians would have been foreshadowed in the recorded teaching of Jesus or in some other part of the Synoptic record. We might have expected, for example, something about baptism in the Charge to the Twelve or in that to the Seventy. As we have remarked, there is no such reference in either. Or again, it would

---

[1] It seems strange to us because we so easily forget the full implication of the fact that in New Testament times the typical baptism was the adult baptism of those who had " repented and believed " (cf. the overseas mission-field to-day). It is as unnatural in these conditions to separate baptism from faith, as it is inevitable to make some distinction between them, when the recipient of baptism is, in general, not an adult but an infant; cf. *supra*, p. 82 with *n.* 2 on that page, and for a fuller treatment of the question see Chapter 10.

[2] J. Denney, *The Death of Christ* (1902), p. 185.

be far easier to explain the unhesitating acceptance of baptism in primitive Christianity, if there were in each of the main Synoptic sources a " command to baptize " like that which stands at the end of St. Matthew's Gospel. In fact, as we know, there is no such injunction to be found either in Mark, or in Q, or in the special Lucan material, and the difficulty of accepting as it stands this baptismal command in Matthew simply makes the problem of accounting for the origin of Christian baptism more acute. Again, we could hardly have been surprised if a reference to Christian water-baptism had been read back into the record of John the Baptist's preaching. But actually, as we have seen, the only mention here of a baptism other than John's own is not concerned with a future baptism *with water* at all, but has to do either with a baptism with fire or with a baptism with " holy Spirit ".[1] There is nothing here to explain the continuance of water-baptism in primitive Christianity; what is said here would have accounted more naturally for its abandonment. These facts, it must be repeated, call for some explanation. How was it that, when some six weeks after the death of Jesus his followers came together to live as an organized community, they seem unhesitatingly to have agreed that any fresh adherents to their number must enter by the gateway of baptism? If it is not possible to accept as a literal transcript of words of Jesus the one clear injunction in the Synoptic record about baptism that would of itself sufficiently explain the use of the rite by his followers from the first, it is necessary to ask whether there is any less direct and explicit suggestion in the teaching of our Lord, or any event in his life and ministry, which might make it easier to account for the swift and unhesitating adoption of the rite by his disciples.

Some suggestions have been made in the earlier part of our enquiry which it may now prove useful to gather together.

It is clear that any attempt to identify the immediate antecedents of the Christian rite must give full weight to John's baptism, and that this characteristic activity of John must be interpreted, as we have sought to do in Chapter 2, along the lines of " prophetic symbolism ".[2] We have noted that some of the first disciples of Jesus had previously been followers of the Baptist, and had therefore probably themselves received John's baptism. It is obvious from the references in the Gospels and Acts that this baptizing with water was regarded as the most typical feature of John's activity. The title so frequently accorded to him—ὁ βαπτιστής or ὁ βαπτίζων—is in itself a sign that this rite was thought to embody what was most distinctive in his teaching. The mission and message of John and the rite of water-baptism were inextricably bound up with one

---

[1] Cf. *supra*, p. 19, where it is argued that in the original teaching of John the Baptist baptism *with fire* referred to the impending Judgement, and that the references to the Holy Spirit in the record of John's preaching represent a later Christian interpretation of " fire " which went beyond the Baptist's original intention.

[2] Cf. *supra* pp. 20–22, where the important statements of Dr. Wheeler Robinson on this subject are summarized and applied to the interpretation of John's baptism.

another. But it is also clear from the New Testament that in Christian teaching the activity of John was regarded as that which, as it were, ushered in the ministry of Jesus.[1] The ability to give first-hand testimony about the work of John the Baptist was an indispensable requirement for apostolic witness.[2] It is probable that this is how the opening words of St. Mark's Gospel are to be understood. John's appearance in the wilderness in accordance with ancient prophecy, his baptizing and his proclaiming of this " baptism of repentance unto remission of sin "—all this was itself the " beginning of the gospel of Jesus Christ " (Mark 1. 1). These three facts—John's own prophetic emphasis on the " symbol " of baptism, the known connexion of some of the Twelve with John himself, and the place accorded to John in early Christian apologetic—when taken together with the strongly ethical and eschatological significance with which John invested baptism, go some way towards accounting for the readiness with which the early Church adopted baptism as the distinctive rite of entry into the new community. But there is still left unexplained the difficulty that, whereas in his recorded utterances John seems to have expected that baptism with water would be superseded,[3] in actual fact water-baptism was not superseded, but was taken over into the Christian Church as a permanent part of its practice. Thus, while the influence of John's baptism must undoubtedly be acknowledged, yet it is not sufficient of itself to explain the origin of the Christian ceremony. The influence of some additional factor (or factors) must be recognized, if our account of the emergence of the Christian rite is to be deemed credible.

In this connexion it seems worth while to ask whether " prophetic symbolism " may not have light to throw also upon the activity of Jesus himself. Some of those who have written in recent years about the life and teaching of our Lord have emphasized that he stood in the succession of the Hebrew prophets.[4] In the minds of some there may have been a reluctance to acknowledge the full implication of this fact, from a fear lest any emphasis on this side may cause less than justice to be done to the Christian faith concerning the divinity of Christ. They have felt that to describe Jesus as a " prophet " savours too much of the humanistic approach which was so common a generation ago and is now generally admitted to have been inadequate. But if the word " prophet " be understood not in some reduced modern significance but in its full Biblical connotation, we cannot fail to see meaning in the fact that Jesus impressed

---

[1] Cf. *supra*, p. 13 n. 2.
[2] Cf. Acts 1. 21–22, where a successor to Judas is being sought; an essential qualification is that he must be one " of the men . . . which have companied with us all the time that the Lord Jesus went in and went out among us, *beginning from the baptism of John* ".
[3] Cf. Mk. 1. 8 and parallels.
[4] Cf. C. H. Dodd in *Mysterium Christi*, ed. by G. K. A. Bell and A. Deissmann (1930), pp. 56–66; C. Gore, *The Reconstruction of Belief* (1926), pp. 94–95; F. C. Grant, *The Gospel of the Kingdom* (1940), p. 62; and articles by H. J. Cadbury on " Jesus and the Prophets " in *Journal of Religion*, Vol. V (1925), pp. 607–622, and by P. E. Davies on " Jesus and the Role of the Prophet " in *Journal of Biblical Literature*, Vol. LXIV (1945), pp. 241–254.

his contemporaries as one who stood in the prophetic succession.[1] To acknowledge this to the fullest extent in no way excludes the conviction that this category, like all others, is transcended by Jesus.

If, then, we are entitled, on the basis of the Synoptic record, to see the life and teaching of Jesus as a *prophetic* activity, it is instructive to notice where the emphasis is placed. In one of these passages (Lk. 24. 19) our Lord is described as " Jesus of Nazareth, a prophet mighty in deed and word before God and all the people ". The mention of the " deed " before the " word " is thoroughly in accord with what we saw to be the place of *action* in the ministry of a Hebrew prophet. The emphasis on action is the more striking because the speaker goes on to say " we hoped that it was he which should redeem Israel " (Lk. 24. 21). The suggestion is that the " deliverance " was expected to reveal itself pre-eminently in an act of the prophet, or in a series of acts. Professor Dodd has claimed that some of the actions of Jesus can best be understood in the light of prophetic symbolism. Thus the Triumphal Entry, the Cleansing of the Temple, and especially the giving of Bread and Wine at the Last Supper gain immensely in meaning, if they are regarded as " symbolic " acts.[2] These actions both express the divine reality, the Rule of God, that he came to make known, but they also impart that reality to men and make it actual in their life. Again, we may recall that it is definitely said about the " mighty works ", " if I by the finger of God cast out demons, then is the Kingdom of God come upon you ".[3]

The right approach therefore seems to be, not entirely to dissociate the life of Jesus from all previous prophetic activity on the ground that, if we admit a connexion, we are treating him as a " mere prophet ", but rather to recognize fully the connexion that exists in the earliest records, while at the same time going on to show how incomparably more complete is the expression and realization of the divine will in the significant acts of Jesus than was possible even with the greatest of Old Testament prophets. Even the profoundest utterances or the most significant actions of an Isaiah or a Jeremiah fell far short of a perfect expression or of a completely effective realization of the divine purpose. It is only imperfectly that we may say even of their greatest utterances that they embody the Word of God, it is only in a limited way that their most striking actions can themselves be regarded as helping to make actual the divine will. But it is different when we have to do with the words of one who " spake as never man spake ", and with the activity of him of whom

---

[1] Cf. Mk. 6. 15, " Others said, A prophet, even as one of the prophets " (cf. Lk. 9. 8); Matt. 21. 11, " The multitudes said, This is the prophet, Jesus, from Nazareth "; Matt. 21. 46, " They feared the multitudes, because they took him for a prophet "; Lk. 7. 16, " They glorified God saying, A great prophet has arisen among us; and God has visited his people "; Lk. 24. 19, " Jesus of Nazareth a prophet mighty in deed and word before God and all the people ". See also Mk. 8. 28 = Matt. 16. 14 = Lk. 9. 19, and note the implication of Mk. 6. 4 = Matt. 13. 57 = Lk. 4. 24, and of Acts 3. 22. (For our Lord's own conviction cf. Lk. 13. 33, " it cannot be that a prophet perish out of Jerusalem ".) Cf. also Jn. 4. 19, 6. 14, 7. 40, 9. 17.
[2] Cf. C. H. Dodd in *A Companion to the Bible* (1939), ed. by T. W. Manson, pp. 384–387.
[3] Lk. 11. 20; cf. Matt. 12. 28.

I

it is said in the primitive apostolic record that God had " anointed him with the Holy Spirit and with power ".[1]   If the " symbolic " action of a Hebrew prophet could be so pregnant in meaning as Dr. Wheeler Robinson has shown, how immeasurably more profound must be the significance and the result of an action done by one of whom, though he stood in the prophetic succession, it was yet said by one who had been his intimate follower that " God hath made him both Lord and Christ " ! [2]

Let us now, having observed the bearing of " prophetic symbolism " on the ministry of Jesus, revert to the problem concerning the origin of Christian baptism.   It will be remembered that an answer is being sought to the question why baptism with water was taken over as part of Christian practice, though the recorded teaching of John the Baptist seems to anticipate its abandonment.

It has been suggested more than once in the course of this study that the influence on the Christian rite of the baptism of Jesus needs to be more fully recognized.[3]   That baptism of Jesus by John is seen in a fresh light when we view it as a " symbolical " act, not in our own weakened sense of the adjective but with all the vivid significance belonging to prophetic symbolism in the Old Testament.   The very fact that Jesus, though without personal consciousness of wrongdoing, yet submitted to " a baptism of repentance " indicates that to him in some way the outward act was intensely significant.   In our earlier consideration of the baptism of Jesus we have seen reason to reject the view that would regard the story as a later Christian dramatization of the way in which Jesus became conscious of Messiahship.[4]   The story raised too much difficulty in later Christian apologetic for this to be a likely explanation of its origin.   There seems no good reason for doubting that Jesus was actually baptized by John, and that, in speaking of it later to his disciples, he connected it with an experience of the Holy Spirit and a conviction that he was the Son of God.   Without seeking to probe the mystery of our Lord's Messianic consciousness, we may at least say that Jesus himself underwent baptism at the hands of John, and in so doing set himself alongside those for whom his Messianic office was to be fulfilled.   As Bishop Rawlinson has written in his valuable note on " The Significance of Our Lord's Baptism ", " It was the whole meaning of the Incarnation that God was in Christ identified with sinners, and the self-identification of Christ with a sinful people cannot with any kind of propriety be eradicated from the story of His life ".[5] This aspect of the baptism of Jesus is brought out yet more clearly when, in the light of prophetic symbolism, we see it as the way in which his oneness with those whom he sought to redeem was expressed and effected. He could not separate himself from the sinners whom he would save.[6]

---

[1] Acts 10. 38.   [2] Acts 2. 36.
[3] Cf. *supra*, pp. 32–33, 42 (and *n*. 2), 69 *n*. 2, 91, 95.   [4] Cf. *supra*, p. 28.
[5] A. E. J. Rawlinson, *The Gospel according to St. Mark* (1925), p. 253.
[6] Cf. A. Oepke in *Theol. Wört.*, Vol. I, p. 536; Cf. also J. Denney, *The Christian Doctrine of Reconciliation* (1917), p. 252, " We might have expected that where the work of God was being

We have seen that Jewish thought was realistic enough to believe that the outward act itself made a difference. We have also seen grounds for believing that for Jesus himself this impressive " symbolism " of water-baptism expressed and effected his oneness with the new Israel, and also his consciousness of the Holy Spirit and of being the Son of God. When we regard this act with all the added meaning that is given to our understanding of it by the study of prophetic symbolism, we begin to appreciate more readily why St. Peter and his fellow-Apostles at the Day of Pentecost said to those who had listened to the proclamation of the Gospel and asked what they should do, " Repent ye, and be baptized every one of you in the name of Jesus Christ unto the remission of your sins; and ye shall receive the gift of the Holy Ghost ".[1] It was not simply that they were adapting for their own purposes the rite hitherto employed by John the Baptist; they were rather applying to the use of the new community that particular example of John's baptism which was provided by the baptism of Jesus himself.[2] That the significance of this act had at some time been made clear to the Twelve by our Lord himself both provides the most natural way of accounting for the prominence given to this story in the Synoptic Gospels, and also helps to explain why the Christian rite was a baptism with water. Baptism with water was not superseded, because the outward action, which had possessed such profound meaning for Jesus himself, was found to be expressive of, and also to help in bringing about, that re-direction of personality, that turning to God and acceptance of his rule, which is what the New Testament means by " repentance ".[3] Thus Christian baptism is not so much a direct continuance of the baptism of John; it may far more truly be described as the counterpart in the life of the believer of the baptism of Jesus himself.

It is clear that there were important differences between the baptism of Jesus and the baptism of an early Christian disciple. The " repentance " which the baptism expressed and embodied could not for Jesus be personal: for the Christian disciple it was bound to be. Again, Jesus was possessed by the Spirit, and was Son of God, as one of his followers could never be. But the correspondences between the baptism of Jesus and the Christian rite seem too striking to be accidental. Thus for Jesus his baptism meant that he ranged himself by the side of those to whom he would bring salvation. In this *corporate* sense we may say that even for him baptism expressed repentance. Christian baptism, too, is

---

done, as through the prophetic ministry of John, Jesus would be present; but we should have looked for Him at John's side, confronting the people, assisting the prophet to proclaim the word of God. Yet nothing is more true to the character of Jesus and to the spirit in which He carries through His mission than that He appears not at John's side, but among the people who came to be baptized; His entrance on His work, like the whole work from beginning to end, was an act of loving communion with us in our misery."

[1] Acts 2. 38.

[2] It has actually been suggested that " the baptism of John " in Acts 1. 22 may mean the baptism *of Jesus* by John; cf. Jackson and Lake op. cit., Vol. IV, p. 14.

[3] Cf. what is said *supra*, p. 18 n. 4, about the Hebraic background of the New Testament word μετάνοια.

closely connected with repentance and remission of sins.[1] For Jesus moreover his baptism was associated with the descent of the Holy Spirit. This is also a mark of Christian baptism.[2] Again, for Jesus baptism is linked in the closest way with the consciousness of being Son of God. We have seen that both in St. Paul [3] and in the Johannine writings [4] the Christian experience of being a " son " or " child of God " is connected with baptism.

It would seem to follow that as for Jesus his own baptism was " symbolical ", so correspondingly for those who had faith in him the Christian rite in the New Testament derived much of its meaning from its close reflection of its counterpart in the life of our Lord.[5] If Jesus himself had not come from Nazareth of Galilee to be baptized of John in the Jordan, it may be questioned whether baptism would ever have become a Christian sacrament.

But the baptism of Jesus is not the only fact which has exercised a formative influence upon the Christian rite. In earlier parts of this essay evidence has been adduced, both from Pauline and from Johannine teaching and also from Hebrews and 1 Peter, for linking Christian baptism with the death and resurrection of Jesus.[6] The suggestion has also been made that this link, so far from being a " Pauline " addition to the Gospel, may represent rather the making explicit of a connexion which we have noted as prominent in the teaching set forth in Acts, namely, that between baptism and the *kerygma*.[7] If, for the first Christians, baptism was itself an embodiment of the *kerygma*, we should expect to trace in primitive Christian teaching a growing recognition of the intimate relation between that rite of baptism and the death and resurrection of Jesus, which were the central articles of the apostolic preaching—that, so to say, on which all else in the *kerygma* turned. Thus St. Paul, in relating Christian baptism specifically to the death and resurrection of Christ, was making more clear and unmistakable a connexion which was virtually present in the primitive tradition reflected in the early chapters of Acts. Further, when we asked how in turn the first disciples came to find this outward embodiment of the *kerygma* in the rite of baptism, the claim was made, it will be remembered, that the origin of this association lies in the teaching of Jesus himself.[8] The saying recorded in Luke 12. 50 becomes far more

---

[1] Cf. Acts 2. 38, 22. 16; Col. 2. 12–13.
[2] Cf. Acts 2. 38; 1 Cor. 6. 11, 12. 13; Eph. 4. 4–5; Jn. 3. 5.
[3] Cf. Gal. 3. 26–27.   [4] Cf. Jn. 3. 5.
[5] Cf. B. W. Bacon, *The Story of Jesus and the Beginnings of the Church* (1928), pp. 140 ff. (" . . . primitive Christians rightly conceived of Jesus' baptism as involving all that was involved in their own, and more . . ."). Bacon claimed that there is what he termed " a certain polarity of gospel story ", that is, the whole narrative of the life of Jesus revolves round two centres of interest, baptism and the Lord's supper; cf. op. cit., pp. 147 ff.
[6] For the Pauline evidence cf. *supra* the discussion of Rom. 6. 3–4, pp. 59–60; of Col. 2. 11–12, pp. 61–63. For the Johannine evidence, cf. *supra* the discussion of Jn. 3. 14 (in the same paragraph with Jn. 3. 5), pp. 87–88; of 1 Jn. 5. 6, pp. 88–90. See also the discussion of Heb. 10. 19–22, *supra*, p. 98, and that of 1 Pet. 3. 18–21, *supra*, pp. 99–101.
[7] Cf. *supra*, pp. 49, 73.
[8] Cf. *supra*, p. 72

pointed if the " baptism " for the " accomplishment " of which Jesus waits is not simply a vivid metaphor for the sorrow and pain of the crucifixion, but actually signifies that his death and resurrection will inaugurate that wider ministry to which he looked forward as surely as his baptism in the Jordan was the prelude to his ministry in Palestine.[1] If Jesus thought of his death and resurrection in this sense as a " baptism ", and spoke thus of it to his intimate followers, we may discover in this a further reason why the moment that marked for the believer his appropriation of the salvation wrought for him in Christ should be signalized by an outward baptism with water. St. Paul, in seeing the one as " symbolical " of the other, and representing baptism as a " dying " and " rising with Christ ", is not simply making explicit the connexion between baptism and the *kerygma*, but is actually drawing out the fuller implications of an act of " prophetic symbolism ", the impulse for which ultimately came from Jesus himself. Behind every Christian baptism there lay not only the baptism of Jesus in the River Jordan, but also his other " baptism " upon Calvary.

Because Christian baptism was invested with this tremendous meaning, because behind the water-baptism of the convert there lay the blood-baptism of Jesus, the rite could and did for early Christians prove the gateway into the Kingdom of God. It is not that any rite by itself could effect salvation. That salvation came through the Act of God in Christ which lay behind the rite, but for those who thought in Biblical terms the outward rite itself was very far from redundant. It was an act of " symbolism ", and, as such, itself contributed towards the result that was being brought about. We probably come nearest to the New Testament outlook if we think of baptism as the *kerygma in action*, the means whereby the saving Act of Christ's death and resurrection is made available for successive believers within the Christian fellowship. Only when this " objective " significance of baptism in the New Testament is clearly grasped can the relation between baptism and faith be properly appreciated. It is right and necessary that the fullest emphasis should be laid on faith. There is no opposition in the New Testament between baptism and faith: part of the function of the former, as we have seen, is to express the latter. In Denney's phrase quoted earlier in this chapter, for the thought of the New Testament, " baptism and faith are but the outside and the inside of the same thing ". Once again we see the meaning of what was brought out by a consideration of the references to baptism in Acts. It will be recalled that almost invariably they occur in close conjunction with the mention of " hearing the word " or " believing ".[2] For the believer baptism is the normal and natural way of expressing *faith*. Or again, in Eph. 5. 25–26 it is said that " Christ also loved the church, and gave himself up for it; that he might sanctify it, having cleansed it by the washing of water with the word ". Here there is the

[1] Cf. *supra*, pp. 31–32.	[2] Cf. *supra*, p. 49.

same objective emphasis on the divine *Agape* revealed and imparted to men in the death of Jesus, the linking of this with baptism, and the further stress on the " word ", which here probably means not the Word of the Gospel but the " confession " of a Christian believer in response to that Gospel.   Once again, baptism means *faith*.[1]   But we must beware of any suggestion that it is this human faith that gives baptism its potency. The truth is rather (to use in this connexion a phrase of P. T. Forsyth) baptism can be *subjectively significant* only because, first of all, it is *objectively real*.   Baptism can provide the typical expression of human faith, because, before that, baptism itself embodies the heart of the *kerygma*, the revelation of the divine *Agape* in the death and resurrection of Christ.   Men are able to " believe " only because they have first " heard " or " received the word ".[2]   That " word of the Gospel " is expressed and made visible in baptism.   " The Sacrament of Baptism . . . emphasizes the objective givenness of the Gospel of Redemption.   Christ has redeemed all mankind, and the divinely given sign of this fact is baptism." [3]   St. Paul taught concerning the Lord's Supper that in celebrating it Christians " proclaim the Lord's death ".[4]   We do not misrepresent St. Paul's teaching or that of other New Testament writers, if we claim that these words might be used, with equal truth, to express their conviction that baptism, no less than the Eucharist, is a Sacrament *of the Gospel*.

If this dependence of Christian baptism on the death and resurrection of Jesus be established, it becomes easier to understand why the Synoptists are so silent about baptism.   The lack of reference to it in their record of our Lord's ministry and teaching serves to demonstrate the care with which they have depicted a state of things very different from that which obtained at the time when they wrote.   We might almost say that during the earthly life of our Lord there could be but one example of Christian baptism, and that the baptism of Jesus himself.   There is a real sense in which the Kingdom of God was present among men during the earthly ministry of Jesus, yet he seems sometimes to regard this aspect of the Kingdom almost in the light of something as yet unshared and unrealized —one might almost say unrecognized.   The Kingdom of God could not come among men " with power " until Jesus had transcended the conditions of that earthly life.   As Professor Dodd has put it : [5]

The whole ministry of Jesus . . . is represented as an " eschatological " crisis, in which the Kingdom of God comes.   That crisis takes the form of a

---

[1] Cf. also *supra*, pp. 79–81.

[2] For St. Paul's insistence that " the word " comes before human faith, cf. Rom. 10. 14, 17, " how shall they believe in him whom they have not heard? . . . So belief cometh of hearing, and hearing by the word of Christ ".

[3] J. S. Whale, *Christian Doctrine* (1941), p. 164.   [4] 1 Cor. 11. 26.

[5] C. H. Dodd in *Christian Worship*, ed. by N. Micklem (1936), pp. 73–74.   In this connexion see also what is said *supra*, pp. 73–75.   The degree to which men become sharers in the Kingdom after our Lord's death and resurrection does not preclude a still greater consummation in the future.   The Pauline way of putting it is that here and now believers have a " first instalment " ($\dot{\alpha}\rho\rho\alpha\beta\dot{\omega}\nu$), cf. 2 Cor. 1. 22, Eph. 1. 14, or a " firstfruits " ($\dot{\alpha}\pi\alpha\rho\chi\dot{\eta}$), cf. Rom. 8. 23, of the inheritance still to come.

developing series of events, but the whole series constitutes a single act of God, in which each element is significant. Thus it is not until the process is complete that men can in any full sense be made sharers in all that it means. Jesus alone, until His work is finished (cf. Luke 13. 32), realizes in Himself the Kingdom of God.

It is probably in this light that we are to understand the Johannine passages, " the Spirit was not yet; because Jesus was not yet glorified ", and " I, if I be lifted up from the earth, will draw all men unto myself ".[1] The Act of God in Christ needed to be consummated by the Cross and resurrection.[2] Only when he had overcome the sharpness of death could he open the Kingdom of Heaven to all believers. Thus in the second chapter of Acts the *kerygma* is proclaimed, the cumulative weight of scriptural and historical testimony leading up to the triumphant assertion, " Let all the house of Israel therefore know assuredly that God hath made him both Lord and Christ, this Jesus whom ye crucified " (verse 36). The subsequent call to repentance and the offer of the Holy Spirit (verse 38) are naturally linked with the injunction, " be baptized every one of you in the name of Jesus Christ unto remission of sins ".

Baptism thus not only embodies the *kerygma* and provides the appropriate response to it, but also is the means whereby the new Israel is to be incorporated into Christ. The phrase used here, " in the name of Jesus Christ ",[3] emphasizes this particular aspect of baptism. The " name " (in accordance with Old Testament usage) [4] offers a mark of ownership and implies the gathering of a community consisting of those who belong to Jesus Christ and confess allegiance to him. So, too, this is what St. Paul means by being " baptized into Christ ",[5] or " into Christ Jesus ".[6] His corresponding use of the phrase about the Israelites having been " baptized into Moses " [7] suggests that in order to appreciate his thought we must once more set his words against an Old Testament background. Recent study of the idea of " corporate personality " in the Old Testament has shown how easily Biblical writers could pass from the individual to the community and back again to the individual.[8] " Hebrew thought refers with equal facility to a representative individual or to the group he represents." [9] In describing such conceptions we have to employ terms which involve antithesis, but closer study of Hebrew ways of thought is revealing that the Biblical writers themselves were not conscious of any

---

[1] John 7. 39, 12. 32.

[2] Thus Oepke in *Theol. Wört.*, Vol. I, p. 536, answering the question why Jesus did not himself baptize, says that it was not because he regarded baptism as something " external ", but rather it was owing to the necessity laid upon him that he should look on to and wait for his Messianic expiatory death.

[3] Acts 2. 38, 10. 48 (ἐν τῷ ὀνόματι Ἰησοῦ Χριστοῦ) ; cf. also Acts 8. 16, 19. 5 (εἰς τὸ ὄνομα τοῦ Κυρίου Ἰησοῦ).

[4] Cf. *supra*, p. 45 and *n.* 2.   [5] Gal. 3. 27 (εἰς Χριστόν).

[6] Rom. 6. 3 (εἰς Χριστὸν Ἰησοῦν).   [7] 1 Cor. 10. 2 (εἰς τὸν Μωϋσῆν).

[8] Cf. H. W. Robinson, " The Hebrew Conception of Corporate Personality ", in *Werden und Wesen des alten Testaments*, herausgegeben von P. Volz, F. Stummer und J. Hempel (Berlin 1936), pp. 49 ff.

[9] S. A. Cook in *Cambridge Ancient History*, Vol. III, p. 493, cited by Robinson, op. cit., p. 56.

13

antithesis. Thus when St. Paul says that the Israelites were " baptized
into Moses ", or speaks of Christians as having been " baptized into
Christ ", he is not employing allegory or " personification ", but rather
making use of a realistic category of Biblical thought, according to which
what we have to call the various individuals, the community, and the
" representative individual ", are all indissolubly bound up in one
" corporate personality ".

It is not difficult to see the relevance of this to Pauline teaching about
the Church as the " Body of Christ ". It is much harder to relate the
Biblical ideas concerning " corporate personality " to modern ways of
thinking and present-day terminology.[1] But the attempt to understand
these older conceptions throws light on a number of New Testament
references to baptism. The rite was conceived realistically as the typical
means whereby the believer was incorporated into the Body of Christ.
To be baptized " into Christ ", and to be baptized into that Body of
Christ which was the new Israel, were one and the same experience.

For as the body is one, and hath many members, and all the members of the
body, being many, are one body; so also is Christ. For in one Spirit were we
all baptized into one body, whether Jews or Greeks, whether bond or free; and
were all made to drink of one Spirit (1 Cor. 12. 12–13).

This new existence could be described in terms of faith-union with the
risen Lord, issuing in a new quality of life. It will be recalled in how many
of the baptismal contexts we examined there is this persistent connexion
between baptism and the new moral life.[2] Baptism expressed the depth
and height of this experience—nothing less than a sharing of Christ's
" death to sin " and of his rising again to " newness of life ".

Are ye ignorant that all we who were baptized into Christ Jesus were baptized
into his death? We were buried therefore with him through baptism into
death: that like as Christ was raised from the dead through the glory of the
Father, so we also might walk in newness of life (Rom. 6. 3–4).

But that experience, though intensely personal, was never purely individual. To be " in Christ " was, as we have seen, to be " a member of
the body ", and in him all the distinctions that separate men were rendered
void. So the Apostle could say in another passage:

For ye are all sons of God, through faith, in Christ Jesus. For as many of
you as were baptized into Christ did put on Christ. There can be neither
Jew nor Greek, there can be neither bond nor free, there can be no male and
female: for ye are all one man in Christ Jesus (Gal. 3. 26–28).

or as the same truth is put in yet another place:

There is one body, and one Spirit, even as also ye were called in one hope
of your calling; one Lord, one faith, one baptism, one God and Father of all,

---

[1] For a recent treatment of the Biblical teaching from this angle see C. Ryder Smith, *The
Bible Doctrine of Salvation* (1941). Dr. Ryder Smith, however, prefers, instead of speaking about
" corporate personality ", to use the term " societary " to describe this element in Biblical
thought; cf. especially op. cit., p. 14.
[2] Cf. 1 Cor. 6. 9–11; Rom. 6. 4; Col. 2. 12–13; Heb. 10. 22; 1 Pet. 3. 21; Tit. 3. 5.

who is over all, and through all, and in all . . . unto the building up of the body of Christ: till we all attain unto the unity of the faith, and of the knowledge of the Son of God, unto a fullgrown man, unto the measure of the stature of the fulness of Christ (Eph. 4. 4–6, 12–13).

It is not for nothing that these passages which speak of unity " in Christ " all make express reference to baptism. Baptism in the New Testament was the gateway into the *koinonia*, the means whereby the believer was " grafted into the Body of Christ's Church ".

Our study of Christian baptism reveals that the grounds for alleging a dominical authority behind the New Testament rite depend on, and are confirmed by, far more than the testimony of any single passage, and are therefore comparatively unaffected by critical or historical reservations concerning any particular text. As we probe beneath the surface and work out some of the implications of statements in the New Testament about baptism, we find that the Christian rite becomes intelligible and full of meaning, just in so far as we can trace, though imperfectly, its beginnings back to the life and ministry of Jesus, and in particular to his death and resurrection. To set the activity of Jesus against the background of " prophetic symbolism ", to see the significance of his own baptism by John in the Jordan, to understand his death and resurrection as that which inaugurated the " new age " and was therefore capable of being likened to a " baptism "—all this helps to make intelligible the ready acceptance from the earliest days of baptism with water as the rite of entry into the new community. Baptism gave outward embodiment to the apostolic preaching; it was a concrete " symbol " of the *kerygma*, the good news of salvation through the crucified and risen Lord. Just because baptism thus derived all its meaning from him who died and rose again, it could at the same time express the response of those who " heard " and " believed " that word of salvation. Baptism was the external counterpart of that inward attitude of repentance and faith to which alone the distinctive gifts of the new salvation, forgiveness and the endowment of the Holy Spirit, could be imparted. Baptism " symbolized " that dying and rising with Christ, that crucifying of the old self and that " putting on " of Christ by which the Christian became in every part of his life more and more fully identified with the crucified and risen Lord. Baptism was the means whereby all who thus repented and believed, whether Jew or Gentile, could be made members of the new Israel, incorporated into the Body of Christ.

It is obvious that a rite with this wealth of meaning cannot justly be regarded as merely the result of some process of more or less casual adaptation on the part of a group of early disciples. The absence of controversy about baptism in the New Testament implies that here at any rate was something about which all Christians substantially thought alike. The most convincing explanation of that unanimity is that the authority for

this rite was known in some unmistakable sense to derive from Jesus
himself.

In answer to the objection that, apart from the doubtful passage at the
end of St. Matthew's Gospel, we have no explicit statement in the New
Testament that Jesus instituted baptism, it may be replied that very
much the same thing would be true about the institution of the
Eucharist, if there had not happened to be at Corinth the need for
correcting misunderstandings about this other Christian rite. The words
" do this in remembrance of me " are found in 1 Cor. 11. 24, 25: [1] they
are not found in Mark, and they occur elsewhere only in Luke 22. 19b,
part of a " Western non-interpolation " which most scholars are inclined
to think did not form part of the original text of the Third Gospel.[2]
If some group of early Christians had developed erroneous views about
baptism, and St. Paul or some other Apostle had in consequence written
more explicitly concerning the primary authority for the rite, we might
have known more than we do concerning the immediate origin of Christian
baptism. We are hardly justified, with this example of the Eucharist
before us, in pressing the argument from silence to mean that Jesus did
not institute baptism, seeing that the evidence of the New Testament taken
as a whole seems to demand for the rite some measure of dominical
authority.[3]

In this study we have been endeavouring to weigh probabilities and
discover the most likely explanation for the authority which baptism seems
clearly to have possessed in primitive Christianity. We have concluded
that certain facts in early Christian history are most adequately accounted
for, if Jesus did by some means convey to his disciples his intention that
the entry into the community of his followers should be accomplished
outwardly by the rite of water-baptism. Since for the literal transcript
of such a command to baptize we cannot now look to St. Matthew's
Gospel, it is probable that we shall never recover the exact terms in which
his intention was first made known. But that some such injunction was
in fact given provides by far the most credible explanation for the early
Christian *practice* of the rite. We have also observed, alongside the
practice of baptism, the presence in New Testament writings of a considerable number of references to the *significance* of baptism. When these
are examined in detail and compared with one another, there is seen to be,

---

[1] For a statement of the reasons for believing " that, in recording the sayings which command
the continued observance of the Supper, St. Paul has preserved an original element in the
tradition not mentioned by the Synoptists ", see Vincent Taylor *Jesus and His Sacrifice* (1937),
pp. 206–208, 314. Dr. Taylor thinks that " with some confidence it may be affirmed that the
custom of the primitive Church in breaking bread (cf. Acts 2. 42) is best understood if it rests on
the express word of Jesus ".

[2] For a summary of the textual argument cf. Westcott and Hort *Introduction*, Appendix, pp.
63–64.

[3] Thus one of those who have written most recently on the subject, while recognizing the
historical difficulties in the Matthæan passage, nevertheless concludes that " the existence and
significance of the Apostolate " gives ground for believing that some command of the Risen
Lord was known in the early Church and was interpreted as a command to baptize ; cf. A.
Oepke in *Theol. Wört.*, Vol. I, p. 537.

amid varying methods of expression, an underlying unity of thought. Behind all these references in different writers there would seem to be a fairly consistent and authoritative body of teaching about the meaning of the rite. This underlying unity of thought seems also, if it is to be adequately accounted for, to require the tracing back of its original and creative elements to the teaching of Jesus himself. Both the practice of the rite in early Christianity and the significance belonging to the rite seem alike to look back to Jesus himself and to find in his authority their most convincing explanation.

Thus a critical examination of New Testament belief and practice in relation to baptism, so far from casting doubt on the traditional belief of the Church that baptism was " ordained by Christ himself ", has the effect rather of establishing that belief more firmly on the basis of fuller evidence. The conviction that Jesus " instituted " baptism will rest ultimately not on any single " word of the Lord " ; it will be grounded rather in his whole life and teaching, and especially in that particular divine activity which was manifested in his death and resurrection. It is entirely congruous that one who stood in the succession of the Old Testament prophets should have embodied the divine message of salvation not only in word but also in act. Herein lies part of the meaning of our Lord's own baptism by John. But it is also what we might expect if one, who came not only to announce salvation but also himself to be Saviour, should both himself share in a " symbolic " act and also ordain the repeating of a similar act in the community of his followers, whereby that Act of God for man's salvation, accomplished once for all through his death and resurrection, could be realized and made effective in the life of those who, through faith, desired to receive that salvation and to share in the promised gift of the Holy Spirit.

The conviction that the authority behind Christian baptism has no less weight than this is what we find set forth with such impressive grandeur at the end of St. Matthew's Gospel. The language used there should be read not as that of literal historical record, but rather as that of poetry or drama. Or again, the passage is comparable with the canvas of an old master. With the skill of a great artist, the Evangelist depicts the Risen Lord in his glory, with authority ordaining the means whereby his Church shall be gathered and promising his perpetual presence. It need not surprise us if, as with many an artist, some of the detail of his picture does not belong to the original scene but springs rather out of his own generation and background. Such may be the explanation of the threefold formula. But that the actual command to baptize has an origin other than this seems to be demanded, alike by the belief, as by the practice, of the earliest Christians we know. When we rightly understand these words at the end of the First Gospel, we may continue to see in them a supreme expression of the Christian belief that baptism is no human rite, but rests upon an authority no other than that of Jesus himself.

10

The New Testament Baptismal Teaching in its Relation to the Baptism of Infants

OUR enquiry hitherto has been concerned strictly with the New Testament. We have endeavoured to find out by a detailed examination of all the New Testament evidence what the earliest Christians believed and taught about baptism. Considerable attention has been devoted to the probable antecedents of the rite, and the attempt has been made to determine in what sense Christian baptism rests upon the authority of Jesus. We have seen that the various strands of New Testament evidence show a striking correspondence. There is good reason to believe that this substantial unity of baptismal teaching represents a common tradition of belief and practice, which can be most satisfactorily accounted for on the hypothesis that its main elements derive from Jesus himself.

At this point an enquiry concerning baptism in the New Testament would find its natural conclusion. But since the author of this essay writes not only as an historical student but also as a Christian minister, it may be well to append a concluding chapter in which the attempt will be made to relate this examination of New Testament teaching to the belief and practice of the Christian Church to-day—the belief that baptism is one of the two " sacraments of the Gospel ", and the practice whereby, with certain exceptions, the regular subject of baptism is not an adult but an infant. It is the more necessary to do this, since (as it has been pointed out more than once previously) the practice of infant baptism raises considerations which do not find explicit treatment within the New Testament. It will be argued that the baptism of infants is a thoroughly legitimate development of New Testament teaching, a practice in full accord with the mind of Christ, and, indeed, one that, rightly interpreted, safeguards certain aspects of evangelical teaching even more effectively than the practice whereby baptism is administered only to " believers ". But it is obvious that the most characteristic New Testament baptismal teaching, originally formulated with specific reference to the baptism of adults, must undergo some measure of restatement before it can be applied to a situation in which the typical subject of baptism is an infant.

In this chapter, therefore (which, strictly speaking, is to be regarded by way of an appendix to the main argument of the essay), an endeavour will be made to indicate the grounds on which the common baptismal practice of by far the greater part of the Christian Church may be held to be not inconsistent with, but rather the legitimate working out of, the teaching which is set forth in the New Testament, and with the examination of which we have been occupied in the foregoing pages.

There is no direct evidence in the New Testament for the baptism of infants. Various considerations, however, make it highly probable that some form of infant baptism was known and practised during the period in which the New Testament books were written. Thus the analogy of Jewish proselyte baptism would give some warrant for the usage. If a proselyte on his entry into Judaism had children, it was customary for them to be circumcised and baptized and admitted as proselytes.[1] The fact that the child could not make promises on his own behalf was not regarded as any hindrance. It was argued that such action on behalf of another was permissible so long as it was obviously for his good. This procedure was followed only in respect of children already born to a proselyte before his adherence to Judaism. Any children born subsequently were circumcised but not baptized. The objection, therefore, may be raised that, since proselyte baptism was thus administered only to Gentiles, this analogy could hardly have justified the baptism of children belonging to families already Christian. For this, however, it is probable that another Jewish analogy early proved influential. It will be remembered that St. Paul viewed baptism as the Christian counterpart of circumcision.[2] The fact that this rite was administered to infants born within the Covenant would early encourage Christians to practise infant baptism. Thus baptism was the sign of entry into the New Covenant, just as circumcision was of entry into the Old.[3] All this was in full accord with the Jewish belief in the solidarity of the family, a belief which, of course, was not peculiar to Judaism, but formed part of the general background of ancient thought and life. There is good reason to believe that this conviction was no less powerful in early Christianity. Thus there are several references in the New Testament to the baptism of " households ".[4] It is hardly likely that these households failed to include some young children. The justification for such baptism of households was doubtless that the action of the head of a household, in embracing a new religion, was regarded as carrying with it consequences for all those bound up with him in the corporate unity of that household.

Confirmatory evidence that a number of children had thus received baptism would seem to be provided by two passages in the Pauline Epistles. It is of considerable significance that twice St. Paul addresses children in such a way as to suggest that they are included in the membership of the Church. Both in Colossians and in Ephesians children are instructed

---

[1] Cf. *Bab. Ketuboth*, 11 *a*.

[2] Col. 2. 11–12; J. Jeremias, *Hat die Urkirche die Kindertaufe geübt?* (1949), pp. 40 f., argues that St. Paul, in teaching that baptism for Christians replaced circumcision, opened the way for the baptism of children born to *Christian* parents.

[3] Cf. the passage in which Justin Martyr describes baptism as a " spiritual circumcision ", in contrast with the " circumcision according to the flesh " which was characteristic of the Old Covenant; *Dial. cum Tryph.*, xliii.

[4] Cf. Acts 16. 15 (Lydia), 33 (Philippian jailor), 18. 8 (Crispus), 1 Cor. 1. 16 (Stephanas).

concerning behaviour to parents.[1] This behaviour is " in the Lord ".[2] It is difficult to think that St. Paul would have used this characteristic phrase except of those actually included in the " Body of Christ ". Further, it may be observed that both these Epistles are addressed to " the saints and faithful ",[3] a designation which presumably embraces all the particular groups addressed in subsequent paragraphs. If children could thus be regarded as members of the Church, then it would seem a justifiable inference that they had been baptized, for there is no suggestion in the Pauline epistles that the Apostle knew of any other way of entering the Christian community.

Additional support for the view that infant baptism was practised as early as the first century A.D. is furnished by certain passages in writers of the second and third centuries. Thus Justin Martyr describes as living in his own time " many men and women of sixty and seventy years of age, who became disciples of Christ from their childhood " (οἱ ἐκ παίδων ἐμαθητεύθησαν τῷ Χριστῷ).[4] The verb μαθητεύω, used here by Justin in the passive, is the same verb that is used transitively in the active in the baptismal passage at the end of St. Matthew's Gospel (" make disciples of all the nations, baptizing them . . ." μαθητεύσατε πάντα τὰ ἔθνη, βαπτίζοντες).[5] Further, Justin's use of the verb in the aorist tense suggests that the emphasis here is not upon a continuous period of instruction in the faith, but rather upon a particular moment at which these men and women in their childhood entered the status of " discipleship ". Thus the most natural interpretation of the passage seems to involve the baptism of these people as infants. Sixty or seventy years from the date of the First Apology takes us back to *circa* A.D. 80 or 90. Similarly it is maintained, the words of Polycarp at his martyrdom, " Eighty and six years have I been his slave ",[6] imply that he had been baptized as an infant *circa* A.D. 70. The first clear reference to infant baptism occurs in a passage of Irenaeus (*circa* A.D. 185), where he is describing how Christ saves young and old alike; " for he came to save all through himself; all, that is, who through him are born again unto God, infants, and little ones, and boys, and youths, and old men ".[7] That the words " are born again unto God " (renascuntur in Deum) are here a synonym for " are baptized "seems certain from a comparison with other passages in Irenaeus.[8]

In one of the best-known chapters of his treatise *On Baptism* Tertullian argued strongly against the baptizing of infants, owing to the dangers attendant upon post-baptismal sin, " why does the age of innocence hasten to

---

[1] Col. 3. 20; Eph. 6. 1.   [2] Ἐν κυρίῳ.
[3] Col. 1. 1; Eph. 1. 1.   [4] Justin, *Apol.* i 15.
[5] Matt. 28. 19.
[6] *Martyrium Polycarpi*, ix (Ὀγδοήκοντα καὶ ἐξ ἔτη δουλεύω αὐτῷ).
[7] Iren. *adv. Haer.*, II, xxii, 4, " Omnes enim venit per semetipsum salvare; omnes, inquam, qui per eum renascuntur in Deum, infantes, et parvulos, et pueros, et iuvenes, et seniores ".
[8] Cf. I, xxi, 1, where Irenaeus says that the Gnostics are " instigated by Satan to a denial of that baptism which is regeneration unto God "; and III, xvii, 1, where " the power of regeneration unto God " is clearly a description of the sacrament of baptism; cf. also Justin, *Apol*, i, 61 (ἔπειτα ἀναγεννῶνται).

secure remission of sins?"[1] Yet nowhere did Tertullian produce what would have been a conclusive argument against the practice, namely that infant baptism was not a usage of apostolic days, nor did he anywhere so much as suggest such a possibility. Again, we observe that two centuries later Pelagius (though it would have accorded with his denial of original sin and have strengthened his hand in controversy) seems never to have hinted that infant baptism may not have been a practice from the earliest times. The implication surely is that he knew of no evidence for such a conclusion. Indeed, the followers of Pelagius anathematized those who denied the *necessity* of infant baptism.[2]

When, in the middle of the third century, Cyprian of Carthage replied to Fidus, a country bishop who had sought his advice, we notice that the point at issue was not whether or not infants should be baptized, but rather whether they were to be baptized immediately after birth or (according to the analogy of circumcision), on the eighth day.[3] The whole tone of the letter makes it clear that infant baptism itself was an accepted practice of the Church and one that needed no arguments to be produced in its support. In the absence of any Church pronouncement expressly authorizing the practice, it is reasonable to suppose that its beginnings go back to very early times. In his *Commentary on Romans* Origen went so far as to say that " the Church received a tradition *from the Apostles* to administer baptism even to infants ".[4]

Thus, while the evidence fails to furnish conclusive proof, the available indications seem to point consistently in the direction of the hypothesis that in some parts of the Church infant baptism began to be practised during the first century. Here again it is probably true in regard to infant baptism, as it was of Christian baptism generally, that the determinative influence came from the side of Judaism. It was as natural to regard children as included within the New Covenant as it had been to regard them as included within the Old Covenant. If we give due weight to this analogy, it becomes easier to understand why there seems to have been no early pronouncement on the question. Among those whose religion was grounded in the Bible there was no need for any " authorization " of infant baptism. It may be observed that when, at the beginning of the fifth century, St. Augustine, in his controversy against the Donatists, had occasion to appeal to the practice of infant baptism, he supported its " divine authority " by the plea that, if the practice by the whole Church of what had never been instituted by any council did not guarantee the

[1] Tert., *de Bapt.*, xviii, " cunctatio baptismi utilior est; praecipue tamen circa parvulos . . . Ait quidem Dominus, *Nolite illos prohibere ad me venire*. Veniant ergo dum adolescunt, veniant dum discunt, dum quo veniant docentur; fiant Christiani cum Christum nosse potuerint. Quid festinat innocens aetas ad remissionem peccatorum? "
[2] Cf. the passages quoted by N. P. Williams, *The Ideas of the Fall and of Original Sin* (1927), p. 344 *nn*. 1 and 2.
[3] Cypr., *Ep.* lxiv.
[4] Orig. *Comment. in Epist. ad Rom.*, v. 9, " . . . ecclesia ab apostolis traditionem suscepit, etiam parvulis baptismum dare."

apostolic authority of infant baptism, a true idea of the significance of
the rite might nevertheless be obtained from the analogy of Jewish
circumcision.[1] As we have seen, there is New Testament warrant for
viewing Christian baptism as the counterpart of Jewish circumcision. For
those who once grasped this parallel, the conclusion would swiftly follow
that the one rite, like the other, might be appropriately administered to
infants.[2] The available evidence suggests that such a conclusion may
have been drawn and acted upon in some quarters as early as the latter
half of the first century A.D.

It is not enough, however, to trace the beginnings of infant baptism
back to a date within the New Testament period. If this practice of the
Christian Church throughout the greater part of its history is to be
justified, there is need to show that the administration of the rite to infants
involves no contradiction of the baptismal teaching which we have
observed as present with greater or less explicitness in different parts of the
New Testament.

That there are many Christians to-day for whom the baptizing of
infants offers serious difficulties can hardly be denied. The emphasis
of one of the great Christian communions upon the necessity of " believers'
baptism " carries with it a refusal to administer the rite to infants and the
substitution for the latter of a service of " dedication ". But the reservations about infant baptism are not confined to the Baptist communion.
Many Christians, other than Baptists, view the rite of baptism itself as
little more than such an act of " dedication ", a comely custom whereby
parents may offer their child to God and seek the divine blessing upon
his future upbringing. But that the great New Testament statements
about baptism can have any relevance when the subject of the rite is an
infant would be strongly denied, and often most strongly by some whose
convictions and loyalties set them most definitely within the evangelical
tradition.

At first sight there would seem to be considerable force in this denial.
More than once in our study of the New Testament evidence attention
has been called to the fact that in New Testament times the typical

---

[1] Cf. Aug., *De Bapt. contra Donatistas*, iv, 24, " Si quisquam in hac re auctoritatem divinam
quaerat, quamquam quod universa tenet ecclesia, nec conciliis institutum, sed semper retentum
est, non nisi auctoritate apostolica traditum rectissime creditur, tamen veraciter coniicere
possumus, quid valeat in parvulis baptismi sacramentum, ex circumcisione carnis, quam prior
populus accepit ". The point of the appeal to infant baptism was not that the Donatists had
any objection to the practice, but rather that Augustine sought to prove that baptism at the
hands of ministers whose faith is defective is nevertheless valid, by the argument that baptism
avails for infants, before they can have any faith at all; cf. W. Wall, *The History of Infant Baptism*,
ed. by H. Cotton (1862) Vol. I, p. 161.

[2] The fact that Cyprian in his letter to Fidus urged that baptism should be administered,
not (like circumcision) on the eighth day, but rather as soon as possible after birth, might possibly
be used as an argument against the validity of the parallel between the Jewish and the Christian
rites. To this the reply is that Cyprian's verdict shows only that the parallel did not hold *at
every point*. The terms of the question put to him show that there was felt to be a real analogy, so
much so that by some the statutory time for the one rite was regarded as the appropriate time
also for the other. Though Cyprian recommended that the baptism of infants should not be
delayed till the eighth day, he did not deny that the one rite foreshadowed the other. On the
contrary, he speaks in this letter of baptism as " spiritual circumcision ".

Christian baptism was that of an adult believer. As we saw in the Acts, baptism was the regular response of those who " heard " or " received the word ", who " repented and believed ".[1] How then, it is asked, can teaching originally formulated in respect of this " believers' baptism ", in which faith is paramount, be applied to the baptism of a helpless infant, who can possess no memory of what has been done to him, much less apprehend any spiritual significance in the rite? To such a question the answer must be that New Testament statements about baptism cannot all be used in reference to infant baptism *without modification*. We must frankly recognize that much harm has been done, and a superstitious attitude to baptism too often encouraged, because New Testament language, used originally of believers' baptism, has been applied indiscriminately, as it stands, to the baptism of infants. It was largely in protest against this sort of false and unethical sacramentalism that the Anabaptist sects arose in the sixteenth century; and it is in continuance of such a protest that the modern Baptist communion maintains its witness concerning believers' baptism.

But when these facts have been fully recognized and the historical justification for the Baptist protest freely acknowledged, there is still much to be said on the other side. It is too readily assumed by many who are not Baptists that this important difference between the typical New Testament baptism and the typical baptism to-day in effect empties infant baptism of most of (if not of all) its sacramental significance. It can hardly be denied that many Christians at the present time have an uneasy feeling that all the good arguments really support the Baptist position. Many of those who take this view tend to have rather vague ideas about infant baptism. If these were explicitly drawn out, they would in practice coincide with a drastically reduced estimate of the rite, even though those who think thus are, by their official standards of Church belief, committed to the acceptance of baptism (including infant baptism) as one of the two " sacraments of the Gospel ". There is thus need to-day to bridge this gulf between the working " theology " of so many Christians, for whom infant baptism is no more than a dedicatory rite, and the confessional standards of almost all the great Christian communions, according to which the baptism of infants, no less than that of adults, is a Gospel sacrament. It is impossible, within the limits of this final chapter, to do more than indicate the lines which such a restatement of New Testament teaching might follow.

The sacraments of the Gospel cannot be understood unless they are seen against the background of the Bible as a whole. One fact that is brought out with peculiar distinctness in Biblical teaching is that God's way is to work by the method of particular revelation. The call of Abraham, the history of Israel as a " chosen people ", the concentration upon a godly " remnant " when the people as a whole proved faithless—all this

[1] Cf. *supra*, p. 49.

leads up to, and finds its fitting consummation in, a unique revelation
manifested once for all in the life, death and resurrection of Jesus of
Nazareth. When, in turn, the effects of that unique revelation are being
imparted to the world, we should expect, so long as we think Biblically,
to find the same " particularity " in the means employed for this, as has
marked both the preparation for that revelation and that revelation
itself. Particular means of grace are congruous with the whole
" economy " of the Incarnation.[1]

Thus it is not surprising that the sacraments of the Gospel should
exhibit that which is characteristic of the Gospel itself. May not our
modern unwillingness to take seriously New Testament language about
the sacraments of the Gospel be part and parcel of a deeply rooted aversion
from belief in a genuine Incarnation—a revelation of God at a particular
time and place in a particular human life? This "scandal of particularity " can prove a real stumbling-block even among those who would
claim sincerely to profess the Christian faith. One reason why Christians
need continually to re-test their beliefs by Biblical standards is that thereby
they may be delivered from failure to recognize and to respond to a
divine revelation because its outward form contradicts their own impression of what such a revelation ought to be. Thus to doubt the reality
of God's action in the sacrament of baptism, or to fail in placing the primary
emphasis on that divine action, recalls the attitude of our Lord's own
countrymen concerning whom it was said " he could there do no mighty
work . . . and he marvelled because of their unbelief ".[2] May it not be
that those who make their insistence on the necessity of *faith* a reason for
denying any objective efficacy to infant baptism are themselves betraying
a lack of faith concerning the method of divine revelation and the power
of God to fulfil his own promises? [3]

Christians are less likely to exhibit this " unbelief " if they remember
what is meant by describing the two central Christian observances as
" sacraments of the Gospel ". For Christian faith these are far more than
just illustrative examples of universal spiritual truths. They are, rather
(as their designation implies), the typical means whereby the benefits of
a *particular* divine act are mediated and applied to the lives of men. Thus
the Eucharist is not just the setting forth in picture language of the beauty
and glory of self-sacrifice. It is rather the " proclaiming of the Lord's
death ", and the way whereby, because of that death and all it means,
those who " do this in remembrance " of him are caught up, as it were,

[1] Cf. W. P. Du Bose, *The Soteriology of the New Testament* (1892), p. 377, " Real views of the
sacraments and a real interpretation of their language are necessarily incomprehensible and
absurd to those who have not that conception of the Church, of the Incarnation, and of our
Lord Himself which not only justify, but necessitate them ". The present writer would acknowledge his indebtedness in this chapter to the thought of Du Bose.
[2] Mk. 6. 5–6.
[3] Cf. C. S. Lewis, *Broadcast Talks* (1942), p. 60, and O. Cullman, *Die Tauflehre des Neuen
Testaments* (1948), p. 37; the latter (soon to appear in English) is a reply to Dr. Barth's protest against infant baptism, *Die Kirchliche Lehre von der Taufe* (1943), E. T. by E. A. Payne, *The
Teaching of the Church regarding Baptism* (1948).

into the divine enterprise of salvation. Thus the purpose of God, formerly frustrated by man's sin, may now be fulfilled, both individually and corporately, in the lives of those who, in union with the self-offering of Christ, " offer and present " themselves, both soul and body, a " living sacrifice " unto God. It is not otherwise with the other sacrament of the Gospel. Our study of the New Testament has revealed that Christian baptism, no less than the Eucharist, is a " proclaiming of the Lord's death ". We have seen that when St. Paul linked baptism so emphatically with Christ's death he was stating something that was not just a private belief of his own, but rather something that formed part of the central Christian tradition. One of the positive results of our examination of New Testament teaching has been to lay bare this intimate connexion between baptism and the Gospel. Christian baptism in the New Testament embodied the *kerygma* : it was a " prophetic symbol " expressing, and in some sense re-enacting, what God had done once for all in Christ for man's salvation.

Here surely is something which forms part of the meaning of infant baptism no less than of believers' baptism. The validity of the Gospel does not depend on human faith.[1] The Church's practice of infant baptism witnesses to this " objective givenness " of the Gospel. The primary significance of such a baptism is not that we dedicate the child to God, but that God has done something for the child. This truth could hardly find better expression than in some words of the late Bernard Manning :

" In baptism the main thing is not what men do, but what God has done. It is a sign that Christ claims all men as His own and that He has redeemed them to a new way of life. That is why we baptize children. . . . The water of baptism declares that they are already entitled to all God's mercies to men in the passion of Christ. Your own baptism ought then to mean much to you. It ought to mean all the more because it happened before you knew, or could know, anything about it. Christ redeemed you on the first Good Friday without any thought or action on your part. It is right therefore that as He acted in the first instance, without waiting for any sign of faith from you, so Baptism, the sign of the benefits of His Kingdom, should come to you without waiting for any faith or desire on your part. Every time we baptize a child, we declare to the whole world in the most solemn manner that God does for us what He does without our merits and even without our knowledge. In Baptism, more plainly perhaps than anywhere else, God commends His love toward us in that *while we were yet sinners* Christ died for us." [2]

This passage has been quoted at length not only because it expresses so clearly the way in which infant baptism conveys this " objective givenness " of the Gospel apart from all human effort or desert, but also

[1] Cf. L. Hodgson in *Essays on the Trinity and the Incarnation* (1928), pp. 394–395, " The conscious knowledge of Christ incarnate is the privilege and joy of Christians and their call to service; not the efficient organ of their salvation "; and P. T. Forsyth, *The Church and the Sacraments* (1917), pp. 203, 206–207, " Sacraments are modes of the Gospel (not of our experience) . . . Their standing witness is the priority of grace . . . When we were without strength, Christ died for the ungodly."

[2] B. Manning, *Why Not Abandon the Church ?* (Independent Press, 1939), pp. 47–48.

because it anticipates and answers what many regard as a serious objection to the practice. Many people feel that to lay so great an emphasis upon infant baptism is to encourage in the Church a narrow and exclusive spirit which would confine the divine blessing within a particular channel. Can it be the will of God so to limit the reception of his spiritual gifts to those who are the unconscious subjects of an outward rite? Does the baptized child receive something which it is not God's will that all his children shall possess? In particular, can we believe that the God and Father of our Lord Jesus Christ would allow the omission of baptism to determine a child's destiny for all eternity?

The answer, once again, to these and similar questions is to see baptism as a sacrament *of the Gospel*. We learn from the Bible, as has been said above, that God's way is to impart himself to men through particular revelations; but we have to go on to recognize that, if we may so express it, this particularity is always *representative*, and designed to serve the interests of a wider universalism. God selected a " chosen people ", and at certain stages, no doubt, that divine selection appeared narrow and exclusive; but the ultimate purpose of the concentration upon a single nation was that " many peoples " should " come to seek the Lord of hosts in Jerusalem ", that " ten men " should " take hold of the skirt of him that is a Jew, saying, We will go with you, for we have heard that God is with you ".[1] It is in a similar way, and in accordance with the same method of divine revelation, that infant baptism is a particular application of the universal Gospel. It applies the benefits of Christ's death to an individual life at its very commencement, but that individual application is also representative: it witnesses to the purpose of God that all men shall be saved and come to the knowledge of the truth. Baptism is " a sign that Christ claims all men as his own and that he has redeemed them to a new way of life ". Thus in the baptismal office of the Book of Common Prayer a prominent place is given to the Marcan story of Christ blessing the children.[2] The sacrament of baptism is *verbum visibile*, the Gospel manifest

---

[1] Zech, 8. 22–23; cf. also the teaching of a passage like Gen. 28. 13–14, where " the God of Abraham and of Isaac " promises the land to Jacob and to his " seed "; but not without the further promise, " in thee and in thy seed shall all the families of the earth be blessed ".

[2] Mk. 10. 13–16. The *Marcan* passage seems first to have been used in England, as part of the baptismal office, in the Prayer Book of 1549. Previously, in the " Ordo Baptizandi " according to the " Use of Salisbury ", the corresponding verses in Matthew (19. 13–15) had been read. Cranmer was probably influenced by the Baptismal office, contained in the *Consultatio* of Archbishop Herman of Cologne (1543), in which, similarly, the Gospel follows the Marcan wording. (It is significant that English translations of Herman's *Consultatio* had appeared in 1547 and 1548.) Cf. T. M. Fallow, *The Baptismal Offices Illustrated* (1838), pp. 108–110, where the various baptismal offices are set out in parallel columns.

The change from the Matthæan to the Marcan form of the story was probably due to the far greater vividness and emphasis with which the latter brings out " the good will of our heavenly Father . . . declared by his Son Jesus Christ ". This is especially noticeable in the Greek; cf. the strong word ἠγανάκτησεν (Mk. 10. 14) to express the " indignation " of Jesus with those who would have kept the children from him, and the picturesque word ἐναγκαλισάμενος (Mk. 10. 16) to describe how he " embraced " the children; (ἀγκάλη means the " crook of the arm "). Thus the re-discovery of the *Greek* Testament (cf. the first printed edition, by Erasmus, in 1516) may have been one of the influences helping to shape the Book of Common Prayer.

in action, and pre-eminently so, when the subject of baptism is an infant, The very helplessness of the child, when seen against the whole background of this sacrament of the Gospel, is eloquent of man's universal need for the divine grace, and of the answer God has made to that need in Christ.

It is perfectly true, of course, that this need for God's grace, and the recognition of how that need has been met in Jesus Christ, are not things of which an infant can, at the moment of baptism, himself be conscious. That does not mean, however, that infant baptism has no direct significance for the subject of the rite. In what terms is that significance to be described?

One of the classic answers of Christian orthodoxy has been to base an argument on the New Testament passages which connect baptism with the washing away or remission of sin. In the New Testament this was interpreted of actual sin, but when infant baptism became more and more the universal practice of the Church, some other interpretation had to be found. Since an infant cannot be guilty of actual sin, how was the connexion between baptism and the washing away of sin to be maintained? The common solution was found in the doctrine of original sin. It was claimed that the baptism of infants purified them from the sin of which they were guilty through their membership of the human race. This teaching is supported by a long and impressive tradition, but many Christians to-day find grave difficulty in accepting it. The difficulty is not that the doctrine of original sin is incredible. Whether or not " original sin " is the most appropriate term to describe it, it is obvious to anyone with an eye for moral realities that over all human life, and indeed in some sense over the whole universe, there lies the shadow of an inherited taint of evil. The difficulty lies rather in the assertion that this taint can be removed by infant baptism. As the late Professor Quick wrote, " So far as experience can show, the sinful tendencies or spiritual defects of a baptized and of an unbaptized child are very much the same ".[1] Moreover, this teaching that baptism, in the case of infants, avails for the washing away of *original* sin (while *actual* sin remains as a problem to be dealt with by other means) lacks any firm scriptural foundation, and seems, historically speaking, to have been formulated largely owing to the desire to find some satisfactory explanation for the Church's practice of baptizing infants.[2] We have seen that the practice can find rational justification on other grounds. It would seem more in accord both with the facts of moral experience and with the teaching of the New Testament to describe the relation between baptism and sin by seeing in the rite as

[1] O. C. Quick, *The Christian Sacraments* (fourth edition, 1932), p. 172. Note also the same author's remarks on the answer made by Roman Catholic theologians to this difficulty. They would distinguish between the " guilt " of sin (which is taken away in baptism) and " concupiscence " (which remains though in a weakened form); cf. op. cit., pp. 172–173, *n.* 1.
[2] Cf. N. P. Williams, *The Ideas of the Fall and of Original Sin* (1927), p. 223, " In order of time the practice was prior to, and largely stimulated the growth of, the doctrine, and not *vice versa* ".

administered to infants the divine pledge and promise, for a particular human life, that all sin (whether original sin or actual sin) shall ultimately be overcome, because Christ overcame it once for all in the victory of the Cross.[1]

Another way of describing the significance of infant baptism has been to make use, in connexion with the rite, of New Testament language about regeneration and divine sonship. In the Baptismal Office contained in the Book of Common Prayer the declaration is made that " this child *is regenerate*, and grafted into the body of Christ's Church ". Again, at the beginning of the Catechism there is a prominent reference to " my Baptism, wherein I *was made* a member of Christ, *the child of God*, and an inheritor of the kingdom of heaven ". Here again the use of such language in connexion with the baptism of infants (though once more it is supported by a persistent tradition through the centuries) has proved difficult of acceptance to many Christians. It is noticeable that John Wesley, in several of his published sermons and other writings, subscribed to the teaching of the Church that infants are regenerated in baptism; yet he seems to have dwelt so much on the fact that the gift could be and was frequently lost,[2] and to have become so sure that the " new birth " is a spiritual process by which " our inmost souls are changed, so that of sinners we become saints ",[3] that towards the end of his life he published a revision of the *Sunday Service of the Methodists*, from which almost all references to the baptismal regeneration of infants were expunged.[4] This action of Wesley had a far-reaching influence upon the theology of later Methodism. It has produced the curious result that the Office of Infant Baptism in use among Methodists has been progressively modified, in the direction of excluding that very teaching about the baptismal regeneration of infants which is accepted in some of those *Sermons*, which form part of the doctrinal standards of the Methodist Church. For this inconsistency Wesley himself must largely be held responsible.

It is not possible here to take account of the intricate controversies

---

[1] On the importance of this relation between baptism and " washing from sin ", and the necessity that the Baptismal Office, for infants as well as for adults, should give clear expression to this " objective " aspect of the sacrament, cf. an article by K. Grayston, in *The London Quarterly and Holborn Review* (July 1944), pp. 210–218. Cf. also Selwyn, op. cit., pp. 361 f.

[2] Cf. *Wesley's Standard Sermons*, ed. by E. H. Sugden, Vol. I, p. 296 (Sermon XIV), " Lean no more on the staff of that broken reed, that ye *were* born again in baptism. Who denies that ye were then made children of God, and heirs of the kingdom of heaven? But, notwithstanding this, ye are now children of the devil. Therefore ye must be born again "; and op. cit., Vol. II, p. 238 (Sermon XXXIX), where Wesley denies that the new birth always accompanies baptism, but his denial concerns not *infant* baptism but *adult* baptism! " I do not now speak with regard to infants. It is certain our Church supposes that all who are baptized in their infancy are at the same time born again; and it is allowed that the whole Office for the Baptism of Infants proceeds upon this supposition. Nor is it an objection of any weight against this, that we cannot comprehend how this work can be wrought in infants. For neither can we comprehend how it is wrought in a person of riper years. But whatever be the case with infants, it is sure all of riper years who are baptized are not at the same time born again. ' The tree is known by its fruits '."

[3] *Sermons*, ed. by Sugden, Vol. I, p. 299 (Sermon XV).

[4] Cf. Sugden's note, op. cit., Vol. I, pp. 280–282.

which, in various Christian communions, have gathered round this doctrine. One thing, however, that may be said is that many of the difficulties and misunderstandings seem to have arisen because the protagonists in the various disputes have not been able to agree in their definition of terms. It is arguable that the concept of regeneration has, among many Evangelicals, been given too wide an interpretation, and has been wrongly taken to include spiritual processes, which more properly belong to other stages of the Christian life, and can therefore more appropriately be described by the use of other terms. If this language about " regeneration " and " divine sonship " be understood to refer to the *first beginnings* of the new life (which God alone can implant within the soul), and to the *new status* of those who are received within the Covenant (a status which only God can bestow), then there would seem no good reason why such phrases affirming regeneration should not be used as truly of infant baptism as they were in New Testament times concerning the baptism of adults. Our study of the New Testament has shown that it is in the Johannine writings that this conception of " birth from above " finds most frequent expression. From a comparison of various Johannine passages we concluded that the use of a word meaning " to be born " or " to be begotten " is an alternative way of describing what is often expressed in the same context by the phrase " children of God ", and that this alternative expression, making use of the verb, is employed so as to lay a more pronounced emphasis *on the divine initiative*.[1] The use of the *verb* (rather than a noun) makes it possible for all the stress to be placed upon that act of the divine " begetting ", from which the new life of the Christian takes its origin. If this is the primary significance of the New Testament language which forms the basis for a doctrine of regeneration, then surely such language is not out of place when used in connexion with the baptism of infants. We have seen that the particular and characteristic witness of infant baptism is precisely to this fact of the divine initiative.[2]

Moreover, the analogy of physical birth would suggest a certain appropriateness in the use of this language in reference to the baptism of infants. Just as in the natural order we are " born in another's pain ", so, too, in the spiritual order we have " life by his death "—and each of these antedates our own knowledge and consciousness of the fact. Any teaching about infant baptism which fails to find room for this truth, and indeed to make it explicit, would seem to be less than fully evangelical.

[1] Cf. *supra*, pp. 93–94, where it is shown how, in neighbouring verses, references to " children of God " (τέκνα θεοῦ) are matched by statements employing the verb "to be begotten" (γεννᾶσθαι).

[2] Thus George Herbert wrote in the opening lines of a poem, " Holy Baptisme ":

Since, Lord, to Thee
A narrow way and little gate
Is all the passage, on my infancie
Thou didst lay hold and antedate
My faith in me.

Cf. *The English Works of George Herbert*, ed. by G. H. Palmer (1905), Vol. II, p. 193.

Of the dependence of our " regeneration ", *in this sense of the term*, upon what God did for us in Christ once for all, quite apart from our knowledge and deserving of it, the sacrament of baptism as administered to infants is at once the objective " symbol " and the abiding witness.

This regeneration, this implanting of the new life, is not something magical. It does not work automatically. The new life takes its origin from an act of God, which owes nothing to human initiative, but for the development and growth of that new life the utmost human co-operation is necessary. Far too often that human co-operation is lacking and the new life fails to come to fruition. Such facts bear their own sombre witness to man's sin and to his failure to help his fellows to grow in the Christian life; but such facts no more discredit the reality of the divine gift in baptism than the " great refusal " could be held to prove that the rich young ruler did not receive a true call from our Lord to follow him. The sacrament of baptism, when administered to an infant, represents and embodies the divine purpose for that human soul. It does not bring about any automatic fulfilment of that purpose, but it declares emphatically that the divine purpose for this individual life is that it shall be the life of a child of God, loving the things which he commands, perfectly responsive to his will; and it offers to that life from its earliest days, because of what Christ was and because of what he did, those infinite resources of divine grace without which no fulfilment of that purpose could be looked for. There at the beginning of a human life baptism " symbolizes " the promise and potency of the Christian gospel.

We have seen in our examination of New Testament teaching how rich and varied was the meaning of baptism for the early Christians. They knew that, because of the activity of God the Father in the death and resurrection of Jesus Christ, their sins had been forgiven, the power of evil had been conquered so that Christians " dying " and " rising with Christ " could share his victory and walk " in newness of life ", and the Holy Spirit had been given to them making them sons of God and heirs of his Kingdom. All these conceptions were linked in the closest way with baptism, and clearly possessed a direct and immediate relevance (as often on the overseas mission-field to-day), because the rite was normally administered to believers upon conscious profession of faith. These conceptions do not lose their relevance when the subject of baptism is an infant; but they need to be understood far more by way of prophecy and anticipation than as a description of already realized fact. Even in regard to believers' baptism in New Testament times, there is a sense in which the great affirmations about the significance of the rite were proleptic: they witnessed to a change which had already begun, but there was much that still remained to be realized. Thus St. Paul in 1 Cor. 6. 11 could remind the Corinthians that they had been " washed " in the water of baptism, but the rest of the Epistle makes it clear that the cleansing was still very far from being complete. The Colossians again had been raised together

with Christ, but that did not absolve them from the necessity of continually seeking the things that are above.[1] The manifest difference
between infant baptism and believers' baptism will become much less of
a difficulty when we see the former as offering a far more extreme example
than the latter of the paradox which underlies the whole Christian Gospel,
and constantly confronts us in the pages of the New Testament itself.
Christians have continually to *become* what they *are*. There is a sense in
which they are already " sons of God "; yet, in another sense, they have
" to become God's children ". It has been truly said, " Baptism to St.
Paul symbolized more than it effected, and yet what it left to be effected
afterwards was only the consequence of a reality which it had effectively
symbolized already ".[2]

It may well be that, since (as we must believe) God always sees the
" weight of glory " he destines for each of his children, in his sight the gulf
separating the infant so often crying in the arms of the baptizing minister [3]
from the adult believer accepting baptism upon conscious profession of
faith, is far less vast than it appears to us. The one is starting a little
farther back than the other, but both have a long way to go, and to each
in baptism God offers himself with all the plenitude of his grace for the
fulfilment of the purpose for which he created that human soul. " To
every baptized person Jesus Christ is wholly given in all His death to sin
and in all His life to God." [4]

There is some profound theology in the following stanzas from a
seventeenth-century cradle-song, and if the argument of this chapter is
valid, they are not irrelevant in a consideration of the meaning of infant
baptism :

> Whilst thus thy lullaby I sing,
> For thee great blessings ripening be;
> Thine eldest brother is a King,
> And hath a kingdom bought for thee.
> Sweet baby, then forbear to weep;
> Be still, my babe; sweet baby, sleep.

---

[1] Col. 3. 1.

[2] O. C. Quick, *The Christian Sacraments* (fourth edition, 1932), p. 170. In this valuable book
the late Professor Quick drew a distinction between the *symbolic* and the *instrumental* aspects of a
sacrament. While recognizing the usefulness of this distinction in a study of the philosophy
underlying Christian sacramental practice during nineteen centuries, the present writer has not
borrowed the terms for use in this essay. His use of the term " symbolic " differs from that of
Professor Quick, in that it derives its meaning ultimately from the " prophetic symbolism " of
the Old Testament, and thus combines in a single term those *symbolic* and *instrumental* aspects
which Professor Quick found it convenient to distinguish. Since by far the greater part of
our study has been concerned with baptism *in the New Testament*, it seemed better to avoid terms
which (however useful for later Christian thinking) would involve the drawing of a distinction,
which the Biblical writers themselves appear to have found no occasion to make.

[3] This practical inconvenience of infant baptism was recognized as early as St. Augustine. In
arguing that baptism can avail without faith when the latter is absent " through necessity ",
he instances the baptism of infants. So far from their being able to make any confession of
faith, they can but with their crying and noise disturb the administration of the sacrament. Yet
none doubts the efficacy of their baptism. Cf. Aug., *De Bapt. contra Donatistas*, iv, 23, " Quod
traditum tenet universitas ecclesiae, cum parvuli infantes baptizantur; qui certe nondum
possunt corde credere ad iustitiam, et ore confiteri ad salutem; . . . quin etiam flendo et
vagiendo, cum in eis mysterium celebratur, ipsis mysticis vocibus obstrepunt. Et tamen nullus
Christianorum dixerit eos inaniter baptizari."

[4] Du Bose, op. cit., p. 364.

When God with us was dwelling here,
In little babes He took delight;
Such innocents as thou, my dear!
Are ever precious in His sight.
   Sweet baby, then forbear to weep;
   Be still, my babe; sweet baby, sleep.

A little infant once was He,
And strength in weakness then was laid
Upon His virgin mother's knee,
That power to thee might be convey'd.
   Sweet baby, then forbear to weep;
   Be still, my babe; sweet baby, sleep.

The wants that He did then sustain,
Have purchased wealth, my babe, for thee;
And by His torments and His pain,
Thy rest and ease secured be.
   My baby, then forbear to weep;
   Be still, my babe; sweet baby, sleep.

Thou hast yet more to perfect this,
A promise and an earnest got,
Of gaining everlasting bliss,
Though thou, my babe, perceiv'st it not;
   Sweet baby, then forbear to weep;
   Be still, my babe; sweet baby, sleep.[1]

It is clear that if we would thus view infant baptism as gathering up in a single " sign " all these benefits of Christ's Kingdom, then the rite must, if superstition is to be avoided, never be sundered from its intimate connexion with the worshipping and believing Church, and with the Christian family. The pledge and promise of infant baptism lose the greater part of their meaning unless the rite is set continually in the context of " the whole congregation of Christ's faithful people here on earth ". We have observed in the New Testament that baptism was the acknowledged rite of entry into the community of Christ's followers, which was his " body ". Anything which robs the rite of this " corporate " character gravely impairs its significance, and encourages the growth of false and mechanical ideas concerning its efficacy. It is particularly necessary to stress this aspect of baptismal teaching when the rite is administered to one who will not, for some years to come, himself understand its import. The fact that an infant cannot exercise faith does not mean that in infant baptism there is no place for faith. On the contrary, there is no occasion when faith is more necessary; but the faith is that of the worshipping Church and of Christian parents—the faith of the Church, which knows that it is the Body of Christ, and that it has the power in his name to " receive this child into the congregation of Christ's flock ", and the faith of parents, whose care it is to bring up their children " in the

---

[1] The stanzas are taken from a poem by George Wither (1588–1667), and were first published in his *Hallelujah, or Britain's Second Remembrancer* (1641). A reprint of this rare book was issued in 1857; the quotation is made from this edition, pp. 68–69. Dr. W. R. Inge has included the verses in his anthology, *Freedom, Love and Truth* (1936).

fear and nurture of the Lord and to the praise of his holy name ".[1] If the responsibilities underlying these words were taken more seriously by every minister, every church-member, and every parent, there would be less complaint about the superstitions attending infant baptism, and also less cause for deploring a decline in Church membership.

The recognition by the Church of its responsibility clearly involves the following up of infant baptism by a service of confirmation, or some similar rite. In the Free Churches during recent years it has become customary to assign far more importance than formerly to " Public Reception into Church Membership ", and to take the opportunity thus provided for previous systematic instruction concerning Christian belief and practice. There is still need in many of the Free Churches that the connexion between such a service and the sacrament of baptism should be more openly avowed, and that it should receive more explicit recognition in the actual wording of the service. The intimate relation between the two ought to be as obvious for a Free Churchman as that between baptism and confirmation is for an Anglican.

There is need also for a much more definite emphasis upon the part to be played by the Christian family. We have seen earlier in this chapter that some of the indirect evidence for infant baptism in New Testament times is to be found in St. Paul's teaching about Christian family life, *including that of the children*, as being " in the Lord ". It follows from this that infant baptism is deprived of most of its significance unless it is intimately associated not only with the corporate life of the Church, but also with the continuing influences of a Christian family life in the home. Indeed, there is a sense in which, in order of time, the Christian family comes first. As Matthew Henry wrote in his sermon " On Family Religion ", " When the children of Christian parents are by baptism admitted members of the universal church, as their right to baptism is grounded upon, so their communion with the universal church is during their infancy maintained and kept up chiefly by, their immediate relation to these ' churches in the house ' ".[2] In an age when so many things have combined so seriously to disturb the life of the home, there is the greater call for a renewed stress upon the family as *the* characteristically Christian institution. It has been said that " baptism is essentially the sacrament of the divine Fatherhood, or of man's filial relation to the God of whom all fatherhood in heaven and earth is named ".[3] If these words are true (and we have seen that the whole teaching of the New Testament bears them out), then it may be suggested that one way of securing this needed

---

[1] It may be noticed that when St. Augustine was dealing with this question of faith in connexion with infant baptism, he tended (while not neglecting the faith of Christian parents) to lay the greatest emphasis on the faith of the whole Church, i.e. not just the local church but the whole company of Christian believers; cf. Aug., *Ep.* xcviii, 5, " Offeruntur quippe parvuli ad percipiendam spiritalem gratiam non tam ab eis quorum gestantur manibus (quamvis et ab ipsis si et ipsi boni fideles sunt), quam ab universa societate sanctorum atque fidelium ".

[2] Cited from N. Micklem, *A Book of Personal Religion* (1938), p. 152.

[3] Quick, op. cit., p. 161.

emphasis upon the Christian family lies in a fresh understanding of the meaning of Christian baptism.

Many years of patient teaching and consistent practice will be needed to bring about these results, but it is probable that time and attention given to these objects would do a great deal more to advance the Church's proper work than many of the other activities in which ministers and other church-workers spend themselves so freely.

If the Christian Church at the present time could but train and nurture and retain in its active membership those to whom, as infants, it has administered the sacrament of baptism, the whole Christian situation might, in another generation or two, become very different. It is customary to-day to deplore the prevalent misunderstandings concerning the nature of the Christian Gospel, the confusion of religion with ethics, and the ignorance of what it was Christ came to do and what it means to belong to his Church. The present writer believes that few things could do more to diminish those misunderstandings, that confusion, and that ignorance, than a sincere attempt by practising Christians to think out the meaning and implications of Christian baptism, and especially of baptism as administered to infants. The revolution that this would mean to many of our accepted ideas may be the measure of our need to become as little children before we can enter the Kingdom of Heaven.

Such an attempt in reverent humility to apprehend the meaning of infant baptism, so far from being a betrayal of evangelical principles, is one sure way by which our grasp of the evangelical faith may be delivered from that peril of subjectivism, which necessarily besets any religion laying stress upon " experience ". It was a Protestant Reformer who, when he was tormented by temptations and doubts, was wont to recover his anchorage in the certainties of the Gospel by remembering the words *baptizatus sum.*[1] Martin Luther did not forget his present faith in Christ, but the baptism to which he appealed was not a believer's baptism. Again, it was some of the Puritans who spoke about " making use of " or " improving " their baptism.[2] There at the very beginning of a human life, through this sacrament, God offers himself in Christ with all the benefits of his Kingdom; the chief task during the rest of that life is by the grace of God so to receive and to appropriate and to possess that divine gift, that the work of Christ may not have been in vain.

Infant baptism, so far from being less evangelical than believers' baptism,

[1] Cf. M. Luther, *Werke*, 36 Band (Weimar, 1909), pp. 116–117; and *Tischreden*, 2 Band (Weimar, 1913), Nr. 2631 a, b. I am indebted to Dr. F. Hildebrandt for these references.
[2] Cf. the sermon preached by R. Sibbes in 1640 entitled " The Demand of a Good Conscience ", especially the passage beginning " And let us make use of our baptism upon all occasions . . .", *The Works of Richard Sibbes*, ed. by A. B. Grosart (1864), Vol. VII, pp. 488 ff.; and Matthew Henry's comment on Rom. 6. 3–4, " Thus we must improve our baptism as a bridle of restraint to keep us in from sin, as a spur of constraint to quicken us to duty ", M. Henry, *An Exposition of the Old and New Testament*, ed. by E. Bickersteth (1846), Vol. VI, p. 266.

is in reality more so, because it even more unmistakably embodies the primary truth of the Christian gospel, namely that the grace of God comes before everything else, and that man's only hope of salvation rests upon that Act of God in Jesus Christ, from which (as the chief writers of the New Testament so clearly and so unanimously demonstrate) this sacrament of the gospel draws all its meaning and efficacy.

> Rex tremendae maiestatis,
> Qui salvandos salvas gratis,
> Salva me, fons pietatis.
>
> Quaerens me sedisti lassus;
> Redemisti crucem passus,
> Tantus labor non sit cassus.

APPENDIX

Baptism and Confirmation

During the eighteen months since the typescript of this book was completed there has been considerable discussion concerning the relation between baptism and confirmation.[1] Among many contributions particular mention may be made of two pamphlets by Dr. L. S. Thornton and Dom Gregory Dix, entitled respectively *Confirmation To-day* and *The Theology of Confirmation in Relation to Baptism*.[2] More recently the Bishop of Derby has surveyed the discussion, with a fresh review of the New Testament evidence, in a paper originally read at the first General Meeting of the newly-founded *Studiorum Novi Testamenti Societas*, and later published under the title *Christian Initiation*.[3] Part of the discussion concerns liturgical and historical questions which fall outside the field of this book, but, since appeal has been made also to the evidence of the New Testament, it may perhaps be not inappropriate here to offer one or two comments on the debate.

All who are charged with the cure of souls must be alive to the superstitions and abuses which so often attend the indiscriminate practice of infant baptism. Membership in the Body of Christ far too seldom becomes the living reality which the New Testament plainly declares it to be. There are some who think these conditions can be remedied only by a recovery of the primitive pattern of Christian initiation according to which (so they believe) it is possible to draw a distinction between the blessings which belong to baptism and the gifts which are bestowed only through confirmation. Over half a century ago A. J. Mason argued that, while in baptism there is a gift of forgiveness and regeneration by the action of the Holy Spirit from without, it is only in confirmation that the soul receives the gift of the Holy Spirit's personal indwelling within the life of the believer.[4] A similar position is now being maintained within the Anglican communion by Dr. L. S. Thornton and Dom Gregory Dix, both of whom would recognize confirmation rather than baptism as the predominant element in Christian initiation. Each of these writers has called attention to truths which continually need emphasis. Thus what Dom Gregory Dix says (op. cit., p. 6) about the paradox that a Christian has to *become* what he *is*, accords closely with what we have tried to stress

---

[1] Much of the discussion arose from the document *Confirmation To-day* (a Schedule attached to the Interim Reports of the Joint Committees on Confirmation as presented to the Convocations of Canterbury and York in October 1944).

[2] L. S. Thornton, *Confirmation To-day*, Dacre Press 1946. Dom Gregory Dix, *The Theology of Confirmation in Relation to Baptism*, Dacre Press 1946. Some other contributions to the discussion are cited in the latter pamphlet, pp. 7–8.

[3] A. E. J. Rawlinson, *Christian Initiation*, S.P.C.K., 1947.

[4] A. J. Mason, *The Relation of Confirmation to Baptism*, (1891).

(*supra*, pp. 142–143); or, again, his insistence on the "obstinately Judaic" substance of the Christian liturgical tradition (op. cit., p. 9) may be compared with what is said in the introduction to the present work about the Christian tradition as a whole (*supra*, pp. ix–x). Further, Dr. Thornton's emphasis on the *eschatological* background of Christian initiation (op. cit., p. 10) gives weighty support for one of the outstanding themes of this book. At the same time, however, it is necessary to question the main thesis of these two writers and to ask whether it is, in fact, borne out by the evidence of the New Testament. Admittedly any modern discussion of the relation between baptism and confirmation is complicated by the fact that in the Western Church baptism and confirmation have been separated, whereas in the primitive Church (as the early liturgies show) baptism was closely associated with other rites and it was with these that the gift of the Spirit was often linked.[1] Thus it is possible for those who believe that they have the warrant of the early liturgies for regarding confirmation as more important than baptism, to argue that in the New Testament period water-baptism was connected with some other rite (or rites), and that the gifts which some would associate with the former are more properly to be linked with the latter. The present writer's difficulty lies in the absence of any direct evidence, save in one or two passages, for the existence of any such additional rite (corresponding to confirmation) during the New Testament period.

There is evidence, as we have seen,[2] in the Acts of the Apostles and in the Epistle to the Hebrews for the laying on of hands as a rite associated with, but distinguishable from, the rite of water-baptism. In Acts this laying on of hands is linked with the gift of the Holy Spirit, the clearest witness being afforded by Acts 8. 14–17. But there is scarcely a mention of the rite elsewhere in the New Testament.[3] St. Paul's silence is particularly to be remarked. It *may* be accidental, as has been conceded (*supra*, p. 44, *n*. 1). But it is one thing to fail to refer to the laying on of hands, if it were an additional rite, practised in some quarters of the early Church. It is quite another thing to be utterly silent about it, if it were the rite with which the endowment of the Holy Spirit was pre-eminently and regularly associated. Had the laying on of hands formed the chief element in Christian initiation, it is hard to believe that St. Paul could have failed to mention it. The evidence of the New Testament as a whole seems to justify no more than the conclusion that in *some* parts of the Church from quite early times the gift of the Spirit came to be associated with the laying on of hands.[4] The scantiness of the evidence

---

[1] Cf. Dix, op. cit., pp. 11 ff. [2] Cf. *supra*, pp. 41 ff., 97–98.

[3] It is possible that 2 Tim. 1. 6 may refer to a laying on of hands following baptism, cf. F. H. Chase, *Confirmation in the Apostolic Age*, (1909), pp. 35–41. The other references in the Pastoral Epistles, 1 Tim. 4. 14 and 5. 22, seem clearly to refer to ordination. For the reasons for regarding these passages as not from the hand of St. Paul cf. *supra*, p. 101, *n*. 2.

[4] Cf. Rawlinson, op. cit., p. 19. Dr. Rawlinson points out that the descriptions of the baptismal rite, given in Chapter 7 of the *Didache* and by Justin Martyr, *Apol.* 1. 61 do not include any reference to the laying on of hands as being part of the ceremony, op. cit., p. 16, *n*. 1.

for the laying on of hands has led some to argue that the " matter " of confirmation, in New Testament times, was not constant. Thus Dr. Thornton would find other evidence for confirmation during the New Testament period in the passages which describe Christians as being " anointed " or " sealed " with the Holy Spirit,[1] and would point to these passages as warrant for believing that the rite of unction goes back to the earliest days of the Church. Reference may be made to Bishop Rawlinson's comments on this question, and to his conclusion with regard to the rite of unction that he is " disposed to doubt whether it originated actually within the New Testament period ".[2] The New Testament allusions to " anointing " and " sealing " are so few that there seems no reason for revising the opinion expressed earlier in this book, that these passages are explicable as alternative ways of describing the gifts associated with water-baptism.[3]

Moreover, those who thus stress the connexion of the gift of the Spirit with " anointing " or " sealing " or laying on of hands seem to take insufficient account of New Testament passages which connect the gift of the Holy Spirit directly with baptism. (These passages, it must be emphasized, occur in contexts where baptism seems clearly to possess its ordinary meaning of a rite with water.) Thus Dom Gregory Dix has stated that the Western text of Acts 8. 39 [4] (which most scholars would regard as an interpolation) is " the only piece of New Testament evidence . . . which might suggest that the gift of the Spirit could on occasion be given by water-baptism alone ".[5] But surely such a statement can be accepted only if we fail to understand at least three New Testament passages in their most obvious meaning.

(a) " Repent ye and be baptized every one of you in the name of Jesus Christ unto the remission of your sins; and ye shall receive the gift of the Holy Ghost " (Acts 2. 38). It is hard to see how " be baptized " can mean: submit yourselves to a double rite, the first stage being water-baptism, and the second stage a rite " with matter unspecified ". As we noted earlier (cf. *supra*, p. 43), there is here no mention of the laying on of hands (nor of " anointing " or " sealing "). The condition on which the bestowal of the gift depends is plainly stated. Repentance and baptism in the name of Jesus Christ unto remission of sins will be followed by the reception of the Holy Spirit.

(b) Again, St. Paul wrote: " For in one Spirit were we all baptized into one body, whether Jews or Greeks, whether bond or free; and were all made to drink of one Spirit " (1 Cor. 12. 13). Here too the obvious meaning seems to be that baptism is in the closest way linked with the

[1] 2 Cor. 1. 21–22; Eph. 1. 13, 4. 30; cf. Thornton, op. cit., pp. 7–8.
[2] Cf. Rawlinson, op. cit., pp. 21–25.
[3] Cf. *supra*, pp. 66–68. It is worthy of notice that Hermas, writing towards the middle of the second century A.D., could say " the seal, then, is *the water* ", cf. *Simil*. IX. xvi. 4.
[4] According to this text, " the Holy Spirit fell upon the eunuch ".
[5] Cf. Dix, op. cit., p. 15.

Holy Spirit. Abrahams has shown (as we have seen, cf. *supra*, p. 56, *n*. 2) how common it was in Old Testament and rabbinic usage to employ in connexion with the Spirit verbs appropriate in relation to water. St. Paul's use of ποτίζω (" make to drink ") appears to be a natural extension of such a usage. But surely in this context the word loses much of its aptness, unless the baptism he is speaking about is a rite employing water.

(*c*) Further, there is the evidence afforded by the incident of Cornelius (Acts 10. 44–48). It has been argued earlier (cf. *supra*, pp. 115–116) that this case was exceptional in that here the gift of the Spirit precedes baptism instead of following it, but the story does at least provide the strongest ground for thinking that it was somehow thought appropriate for the gift of the Spirit to be linked with water-baptism. For here, at any rate, baptism cannot be taken in the wider sense which Dom Gregory Dix would give to the term in some other contexts.[1] The " matter " of baptism is here most distinctly specified, and it is not " chrism " but water. " Can any man forbid the water, that these should not be baptized, which have received the Holy Ghost as well as we? " (verse 47). The implication of this story is surely that the endowment of the Spirit was associated by these Christians, not with one of the rites in which it is customary to-day to find an antecedent of confirmation, but, on the contrary, directly with water-baptism. It may be remarked, moreover, that the witness of this story is hardly less strong, even if we think (as some do, on the strength of Acts 11. 16)[2] that Cornelius never received water-baptism. For the editorial insertion, if it be such, at least testifies to a conviction cherished by certain Christians in the latter part of the first century A.D. The story opens a window for us, as it were, into the mind of the early Church, and lets us see what it was with which it was natural for them to link the gift of the Spirit. It is peculiarly instructive to observe that the " omitted rite " with which it was thought proper to regularize the position of a man who had demonstrably " received the Holy Spirit " was not any form of " confirmation " (whether laying on of hands, or anointing, or sealing), but rather the simple act of water-baptism.

As Dr. K. D. Mackenzie has written, " Baptism is a word with a certain etymological meaning ".[3] It would seem precarious, therefore, to discover the principal element of Christian " baptism " in some rite which makes no use of water. We have seen good reason for finding one of the chief antecedents of Christian baptism in the baptism which Jesus underwent at the hands of John. For our Lord in that act water-baptism and the gift of the Holy Spirit were intimately associated. It is not surprising that many early Christians were content to interpret their own experience in the light of what happened to their Master.

It has been freely acknowledged in the course of this work that the

---

[1] Cf. Dix, op. cit., pp. 14–15. [2] Cf. *supra*, pp. 39, 115.
[3] Cf. *Confirmation or the Laying on of Hands*, Vol. I, Historical and Doctrinal, by various writers (1926), p. 294.

Church's practice of infant baptism necessitates a restatement of New
Testament baptismal teaching.   In Chapter 10 we have tried to indicate
the lines along which such a restatement might proceed.   We sought to
show there, moreover, how essential it is that infant baptism shall be
followed up in years of discretion by " confirmation *or some similar rite* ".[1]
In the eyes of some, the admission of the alternative will rob this statement
of most of its value.   The author would claim, however, that such language
is more faithful to the teaching of the New Testament than is the exaltation of confirmation at the expense of baptism.[2]   It has been maintained
earlier that the rite of baptism was practised from the earliest days of the
Church, and, further, that (in spite of the difficulties attending Matt.
28. 19) the rite of baptism possesses dominical sanction.[3]   It is not easy
to make corresponding assertions about the rite of confirmation.   In face
of this we cannot but regard with misgiving any view which would treat
as the supreme sacrament of Christian initiation a rite which our Lord does
not appear to have instituted, and for the universal practice of which by the
earliest Christians the evidence is not forthcoming.   Such primacy, by
reason both of " institution " and of primitive usage, belongs not to any
form of confirmation but rather to the rite of baptism which, with its
antecedents not only in our Lord's own baptism, but also in that other
" baptism " on the Cross, seems (as the argument of this book has sought
to show) alike in the belief, as in the practice, of the early Church to have
provided so striking an embodiment of the Christian Gospel of salvation.

[1] Cf. *supra*, p. 145.
[2] Dr. Thornton's reading of the New Testament compels him to draw the conclusion that
" unconfirmed Christians, it would seem, have not yet entered into the full mercies of the
covenant ", Thornton, op. cit., p. 9.   A Methodist, who has learnt much from Dr. Thornton's
other writings on the New Testament, is grateful also for the words of the Bishop of Derby,
" Our teaching about Confirmation ought not to be of such a kind as in effect to involve as its
corollary the disparagement of the sacrament of Baptism; and we ought not to be in haste to
darw negative inferences with regard to the spiritual state of those who have not been confirmed,
or to relegate those Christian denominations or Churches which at present do not possess Confirmation to the ' uncovenanted ' mercies of God ", Rawlinson, op. cit., p. 32.
[3] Cf. *supra*, especially pp. 43–48, 108–109 and 127–129.

INDEX OF NAMES AND SUBJECTS

153

INDEX OF SCRIPTURE REFERENCES

Old Testament